FOR WHOSE BENE

The everyday realit
welfare reform

Ruth Patrick

P

First published in Great Britain in 2017 by

Policy Press
University of Bristol
1-9 Old Park Hill
Bristol
BS2 8BB
UK
t: +44 (0)117 954 5940
pp-info@bristol.ac.uk
www.policypress.co.uk

North America office:
Policy Press
c/o The University of Chicago Press
1427 East 60th Street
Chicago, IL 60637, USA
t: +1 773 702 7700
f: +1 773-702-9756
sales@press.uchicago.edu
www.press.uchicago.edu

© Policy Press 2017

British Library Cataloguing in Publication Data
A catalogue record for this book is available from the British Library

Library of Congress Cataloging-in-Publication Data
A catalog record for this book has been requested

ISBN 978-1-4473-3348-7 paperback
ISBN 978-1-4473-3346-3 hardcover
ISBN 978-1-4473-3349-4 ePub
ISBN 978-1-4473-3350-0 Mobi
ISBN 978-1-4473-3347-0 ePdf

Cover design by Hayes Design
Front cover image: Dole Animators
Printed and bound in Great Britain by Clays Ltd, St Ives plc
Policy Press uses environmentally responsible print partners

MIX
Paper from
responsible sources
FSC
www.fsc.org
FSC® C013604

This book is dedicated to the memory of
my grandfather,
Richard Sutton (1920–2014).

He was very proud to have been part
of the generation that voted for the
introduction of the welfare state.

Contents

List of tables and figures

Tables

Figures

Glossary

BME	Black and Minority Ethnic
CPAG	Child Poverty Action Group
CRB	Criminal Records Bureau
DLA	Disability Living Allowance
DSS	Department for Social Security
DWP	Department for Work and Pensions
ESA	Employment and Support Allowance
FFW	Fit For Work
IB	Incapacity Benefit
IFS	Institute for Fiscal Studies
ILO	International Labour Organisation
IS	Income Support
JCP	Job Centre Plus
JSA	Jobseeker's Allowance
LwC	living with children
LwP	living with partner
NMW	National Minimum Wage
PIPs	Personal Independence Payments
PWWs	Post-War Welfare Settlement
QLR	qualitative longitudinal research
SDW	Social Division of Welfare
SG	Support Group
SPH	single person household
TA	Teaching Assistant
TUC	Trades Union Congress
UC	Universal Credit
WCA	Work Capability Assessment
WFIs	Work-Focused Interviews
WP	Work Programme
WRAG	Work-Related Activity Group
YTS	Youth Training Scheme

Notes on author

Ruth Patrick is a postdoctoral researcher in the School of Law and Social Justice at the University of Liverpool. Her research interests include poverty, welfare reform, social citizenship, participatory research methodologies and qualitative longitudinal research. Recent publications include 'Living with and responding to the "scrounger" narrative in the UK: exploring everyday strategies of acceptance, resistance and deflection' (*Journal of Poverty and Social Justice*, 2016) and 'Working on welfare: findings from a qualitative longitudinal study into the lived experiences of welfare reform in the UK' (*Journal of Social Policy*, 2014).

Acknowledgements

This book would be nothing without the contributions of the people I interviewed, who let me into their homes and lives with kindness, enthusiasm and a readiness to share their experiences. A very big thanks to each of you for giving up your time, so often on more than one occasion.

Over the five years spent researching and writing this book, I received invaluable advice and guidance from academic colleagues and friends. Special thanks here go to my three PhD supervisors – Nick Ellison, Bren Neale and Simon Prideaux – and to Ruth Lister and Tracy Shildrick for examining my thesis and being encouraging about its potential contribution. I would also like to say thank you to all those who read and commented on draft book chapters: Kim Allen, Kate Brown, Laura Cartwright, Stephen Crossley, John Hudson, Dan Silver, Mark Simpson and Emma Wincup. Further thanks are due to the (very) many family and friends who helped with proof reading, although I take full responsibility for any typos that *still* made it through!

Throughout the book-writing process, I received invaluable feedback from Adrian Sinfield, who painstakingly commented on the whole manuscript. Talking things through with Adrian and Dorothy Sinfield in Edinburgh over lunch or supper helped refine the book's focus and proved a great tonic, and I am very grateful to them both for their continued support and friendship. A particular thanks is also due to Kayleigh Garthwaite, who read *many* chapters *many* times and was always on hand to provide enthusiasm and positivity – much needed at times when my own was waning.

Thanks too to Policy Press (especially Jess Mitchell, Ali Shaw and Laura Vickers) for wanting to publish this book, and for keeping me on track during the submission and publication process.

The final period of writing has coincided with late pregnancy, and I have often worried and joked about which delivery would come first: the baby or the book. In working to get the book submitted before the new arrival (just), I have been a rather impatient, bad-tempered and absent mother and partner. My thanks and apologies in equal measure to Martin, Katie and Liam. It is your love, patience and humour that keeps me going. Thanks also to my parents – Bruce and Hilary – who provide me with a seemingly limitless supply of support. Special mention to the new arrival - Nina - who has been a constant and lovely companion in the final proof reading period.

This book is dedicated to the memory of my grandfather who, shortly before he died, tried to persuade me to take a break from the distant world of academia and instead fight for the future of the welfare state. I didn't listen (sorry Pops), but I hope he would have been pleased with what I have instead produced. I will always fondly remember our political discussions, and he remains an inspiration and role model in all that I do.

Foreword

'Welfare reform' has been a central objective of social policy for successive governments. Many reports and articles have been written about it. But few have explored its implications from the perspective of those most affected. This is what Ruth Patrick's study does – together with the associated 'Dole Animators' film, *All In It Together: Are Benefits Ever a Lifestyle Choice?* – with its emphasis on the lived experience of 'welfare reform'. 'Walking alongside' the participants over a period of time has allowed her to act as a conduit for their voices as they talked about their experiences, anxieties, aspirations and attitudes to the social security system and the cuts and restrictions to which it has been subjected. It also enabled her to understand how the participants coped with the changes over time.

Her findings illustrate how the significance of 'welfare reform' lies not only in its material impact but also in its symbolic/cultural effects – both on those directly affected and on how the social security system and those currently reliant on it are viewed by wider society. From this perspective, the process and political and media representation of 'welfare reform' are as important as the outcome. Take the very way it is framed as 'welfare reform': the use of the stigmatising term 'welfare' in place of social security and the positive term 'reform' in place of cuts and restrictions performs an ideological function, which serves to justify the latter.

First, that neutral term 'reform'. It's true that there have been some genuine elements of reform in the two major pieces of 'welfare reform' legislation introduced by the Coalition and Conservative governments, most notably the replacement of most means-tested benefits by Universal Credit, payable in and out of work. However, genuine reform has been overshadowed – and to some extent undermined – by a series of cuts and the further ratcheting up of conditionality, combined with a more punitive sanctions regime.

The use of the term 'welfare' as a synonym for – and increasingly instead of – social security has been particularly damaging. The original use of the term 'welfare' as applied to the welfare state was intended to convey a positive meaning; one of the state helping its citizens to fare well from cradle to grave. In contrast, its adoption from the US, where it denotes means-tested financial support for people below pension age, was a deliberate attempt to frame social security in a negative way. It conveys a rather miserable, stigmatised, residual form of social assistance for 'them', of no relevance to 'us'. The negative message has been reinforced by the parallel import from the US of the notion of 'welfare dependency' or a 'dependency culture', with its connotations of passivity, addiction and failure, in denial of dependency as a mark of the human condition.

When New Labour in effect abolished the official use of the term 'social security', with the Department for Work and Pensions replacing the Department for Social Security in 2008, the then-Secretary of State, James Purnell (2008b), proclaimed it as 'an ideological break with the past'. He dismissed his predecessors' title of Secretary of State for Social Security:

> 'What a telling name: security as something handed down; welfare as a bureaucratic transfer; people as recipients of funds ... The new title, Secretary of State for Work and Pensions, tells a wholly different story. It tells you that work is the best route to personal welfare and well-being; it tells you that if you work hard and contribute then you deserve your retirement to be free from anxiety about money.' (Purnell, 2008b)

Telling indeed! An alternative reading of the term 'social security' looks behind the 'bureaucratic transfer' in order to understand the end it is attempting to achieve through those two words 'social' and 'security': economic *security* for all, regardless of labour market status, through *social* means. This goal is particularly pertinent at a time of such widespread economic insecurity (Orton, 2015). Language matters; it is therefore crucial that we reframe the debate around 'welfare reform' and restate the case for social security in a way that reminds people that it provides us all with shared protection against a range of risks and contingencies that we each might face during the course of our lives (Lister, 2016). In the words of John Hills, 'there is no "them and us" – just us' (Hills, 2015, p. 266). Social security thus aims not only to relieve poverty but also to prevent it and to provide genuine security. Achieving these aims should be what social security reform is about.

Depressingly, the debate about 'welfare reform' is very much framed in terms of 'them and us'. As Ruth's book shows, the language used to justify it has become increasingly negative in recent years. The nadir was perhaps the division of the population into 'strivers' and 'skivers' or 'shirkers'. 'Strivers' refers to people who do paid work (also known as 'hard-working families'); 'skivers', to people of working age who don't (Davidson et al, 1993, p. 924). A dictionary definition of 'to strive' is 'to make one's way with effort'. As the research of Ruth and others illustrates, generally people living on benefits are trying to make their way with considerable effort. It may be the effort of seeking work, of doing their best by their children or caring for others. Or it may be the effort of simply trying to get by on benefits, which – as research, including Ruth's study, shows – can be hard work.

Moreover, the division of the world into discrete groups of 'strivers' and 'skivers' belies the extent to which at the bottom of today's insecure labour market many people frequently move between paid work and benefits in what has been called the 'low pay–no pay cycle' (Shildrick et al, 2010). It also ignores the growing reliance on benefits or tax credits among those who are in paid work – and not just those on low incomes. An Institute for Fiscal Studies (IFS) analysis shows an element of convergence in income sources for low- and middle-income families: 'the rise in the importance of benefit income for the middle 20% and the rise in the importance of employment income towards the bottom mean that the sources of income between the two groups are much less different now than they used to be' (Belfield et al, 2016, pp. 53-54). In consequence, 'falls in household worklessness are likely to be a less powerful lever in helping the poorest children than was the case in the past' and 'benefit levels have the potential to affect middle-income households with children more than they used to' (Belfield et al., 2016). Indeed, as at July 2016, the IFS estimates that even the total elimination of household worklessness would reduce child income poverty by no more than 5%. The implications for a social security policy that is fixated on reducing household worklessness and creates disincentives for second earners (mainly women) are immense.

A particularly valuable aspect of Ruth's research is its exploration of the impact of dominant discourses about 'welfare' and 'welfare reform' on how benefit claimants see themselves and others, as well as on their identities. Stigmatisation, a sense of shame and the internalisation of negative messages about 'welfare dependency' damaged participants' sense of self and contributed to feelings of exclusion. She throws further light on the phenomenon, observed by others, of what might be called 'defensive othering'. Benefit claimants, identified as 'other' and 'undeserving' by the wider society, can in turn distance themselves from those benefit claimants they identify as less 'deserving' in an attempt to protect their own identities.

The full impact of the current wave of 'welfare reform' is, at the time of writing, yet to be felt. As a result of the Welfare Reform and Work Act 2016, the benefit cap is being reduced, thereby affecting far more households; a new two-child limit is being introduced for tax credits and Universal Credit and the family element/'first child premium' is being abolished; the work–related activity component for Employment and Support Allowance (and its equivalent for Universal Credit) is being abolished and conditionality is being increased for responsible carers of children under the age of five. Less visibly, but potentially no less painfully, most benefit rates are being frozen for four years (DWP, 2016). Given predictions of increases in inflation as a result of Brexit, the consequences may be more damaging than predicted when the Act was going through parliament. Life is likely to get yet harder for people, such as those in Ruth's study, who rely on benefits for some or all of their income. As well as defending them from any further erosion of their social citizenship rights and from continued vilification, Ruth's study is a reminder of the need to make the positive case for a social security system that provides genuine security as part of our common citizenship. In light of the widespread experience of economic insecurity and the partial reliance on benefits and/or tax credits of a significant proportion of the workforce, perhaps the message that social security is for 'us' as well as 'them' will now have greater resonance.

Baroness Ruth Lister of Burtersett
Emeritus Professor of Social Policy, Loughborough University and
Member of the House of Lords
August 2016

Introduction: Beyond *Benefits Street* – exploring experiences and narratives of welfare reform

'The benefits system has created a benefit culture. It doesn't just allow people to act irresponsibly, but often actively encourages them to do so. Sometimes they follow the signals that are sent out ... Other times, they hazily follow them, trapped in a fog of dependency.

We say: we will look after the most vulnerable and needy. We will make the system simple. We'll make work pay. We'll help those who want to work, find work. But in return we expect people to take their responsibilities seriously too. To look for work. To take work. To contribute where they can. It's a vision of a stronger society, a bigger society, a more responsible society and today, the building of that society starts in earnest.' (David Cameron, 2011c)

'My disabilities are not self-inflicted, I didn't choose to become disabled. I'm grateful for benefits but it makes me feel like someone else owns me, like I don't have a future. I disagree that benefits are a "lifestyle choice". Life on benefits breaks your spirit, destroys families, makes folk homeless – who'd want that? You'd have to be a masochist.

Politicians can talk about benefits claimants, they can hold the idea of a "good life" on benefits, as an idea, conceptually, but until they experience it themselves, they have no knowledge of it. It's no easy ride.' ('Cath')

Launching his UK government's 2011 Welfare Reform Bill, the then Prime Minister David Cameron articulated a case for welfare reform that rested upon a need to return responsibility and fairness to the benefits system. For too long, Cameron argued, claimants had been allowed and even encouraged to behave irresponsibly, remaining dependent on out-of-work benefits rather than seeking to 'do the right thing' by securing paid employment. Cameron's analysis assumed firm and static demarcations between responsible workers and those out of work and reliant on social welfare, as well as between 'deserving' and 'undeserving' populations.

'Cath',[1] one of the individuals interviewed for this book, describes her own receipt of benefits and how it feels unchosen and unwanted but – ultimately – necessary. She directs attention towards what she sees as politicians' misunderstanding and ignorance about benefit claimants' lives and challenges the notion of benefits as a lifestyle choice, which so often underpins statements made by Britain's politicians.

Cath and Cameron offer two contrasting accounts of the benefits system, which imply very different problems and thus potential policy solutions. This book unpicks these diverging accounts to explore whether and how far the lived experiences of welfare reform correspond with the dominant political narrative. Drawing on repeat interviews with benefit claimants over a five-year period, it illustrates the ways in which the presumed deficit and irresponsibility of benefit claimants is based upon a simplistic and often groundless depiction that serves to stigmatise and stereotype claimants as 'other'. The research detailed here challenges the argument that recent reforms have the potential to create 'security' for Britain's citizens (Cameron, 2016). It points instead to a 'normalization of social insecurity' (Wacquant, 2009, p. 295) that today characterises both social welfare receipt and paid employment for the millions struggling to hold onto precarious forms of employment. In this chapter, the political and theoretical context is outlined before detailing the methodological approach taken and the book's key messages. First, though, it is important to explain why I wanted to write it and the contribution it seeks to make.

Why is this book needed?

In researching and then writing this book, I have been motivated by a desire to actively listen and engage with the individual lived experiences of those directly affected by welfare reform – experiences that are so often neglected in political discussion and debates about the appropriate direction of changes to our benefits system. This was not conceptualised as a process of giving voice – the individuals I spoke to already had voices, which often demanded to be heard – but rather of providing avenues and opportunities for these voices to be more widely heard. While there is a growing literature on the impact of welfare reform in the UK, which often assesses in quantitative terms the reductions in income and increases in poverty caused (cf. Lansley and Mack, 2015; Lupton et al., 2015; Beatty and Fothergill, 2016), there remains a relative absence of close and detailed interrogations of welfare reform as it is experienced over time. To address this gap in the research evidence, this book provides a dynamic picture of the impact of welfare reform on individual lives. In following a small group of claimants over time, it explores how processes of welfare reform shape individuals' capacity to live in the present, reflect on their past(s) and plan for the future.

This book presents an opportunity to hear from those with a direct, personal insight into poverty and benefits, who are best characterised as 'experts by experience' (AgeUK, 2015). We hear from single parents being moved into a regime of work-search and work-related conditions, from disabled people facing repeat assessments of their eligibility for new disability benefits and from young jobseekers living with the consequences of a tougher approach to promoting welfare-to-work transitions. These individual narratives together create an invaluable evidence base, which details the experiences and impacts of welfare reform. They also generate insight into relationships between benefits receipt and transitions into (and often back out of) employment, as well as into how individuals' identities are affected by the stigmatising narrative around 'welfare'.

The interviews for this book were conducted between 2011 and 2016, meaning the welfare reforms covered are primarily those initiated by the Coalition government led by David Cameron between 2010 and 2015. However, the findings that emerge have a wider relevance. They illustrate the implications of a longstanding context in which social security receipt – being on 'welfare' – is derided, the consequences of an insecure paid labour market and the impact of (often persistent) poverty on individual lives.

This book challenges the popular portrayal of 'welfare' and indicates the human costs of the current policy approach. It reveals a picture much more complicated than the simplistic depiction of distinct groups of 'welfare dependants' and 'hard-working families'. This book makes it possible to grasp these more complex lived realities and to reflect on the implications of the gap it uncovers between the everyday realities of individual lives and the dominant portrayal. My aim in writing it is to share these individual stories and, in so doing, to disrupt aspects of the prevailing narrative.

Researching welfare reform

The interviews that feature in this book took place against a backdrop of significant and potentially far-reaching changes to the social security landscape. Over the past 35 years successive welfare reforms have fundamentally reworked the contract between state and citizen, changing both what is offered to individuals in social security support and what is demanded in return (Dwyer, 2010; Lister, 2011b). In the UK, under Prime Ministers from Margaret Thatcher onwards, the social security offer has been reframed, becoming highly conditional and contingent on participation in state-defined activities. Welfare conditionality (the attachment of behavioural conditions to benefit receipt) has been intensified and extended, with a particular focus on ratcheting up work-related conditions designed to trigger and support transitions from economic inactivity to paid employment (Deacon, 2002; Stanley and Lohde, 2004). At the same time, recent reforms – first under the Conservative-led Coalition government and then the majority Conservative government – have operated to reduce eligibility for, and levels of, social security support. These have included measures such as the Household Benefits Cap, freezes to the uprating of benefits and the abolition of the spare room subsidy (more commonly known as the 'bedroom tax') (McKay and Rowlingson, 2011; DWP, 2012b).

The key political players during the period this book covers were David Cameron, George Osborne and Iain Duncan Smith. As Prime Minister, Chancellor of the Exchequer and Secretary of State for the Department for Work and Pensions (DWP) respectively, these three men shaped the post-2010 welfare reforms. They sought to end benefits as a 'lifestyle choice' and repeatedly articulated an austerity-driven, anti-welfare rhetoric to justify the many changes introduced. While this rhetoric drew on longstanding demarcations between 'deserving' and 'undeserving' populations, it had distinctive elements – particularly its ratcheting up of the negative (Warren, 2005; Hills, 2015), even condemnatory, language reserved for those who rely on benefits for all or most of their income.

Cameron's leadership ended abruptly in the aftermath of the fallout from the UK's referendum vote for Brexit in June 2016; Theresa May replaced him and installed Damian Green at the DWP. On taking office in July 2016, May spoke of her mission to 'make Britain a country that works for everyone', highlighting what she described as the 'burning injustice' that those born into poverty can expect to die on average nine years earlier than others (May, 2016). While May's comments might suggest scope for a reappraisal of the Conservatives' approach to 'welfare' and poverty, so far she has overseen only very modest changes to the overall policy approach (see Chapter Two). Green has promised to continue with the welfare reforms planned by his predecessors, although he has also pledged not to introduce any further reforms or cuts.

In her speech on the steps of No. 10, May went on to say:

> 'If you're from an ordinary working-class family, life is much harder than many people in Westminster realise. You have a job but you don't have any security … If you're one of those families, if you're just about managing, I want to address you directly. I know you're working around the clock, I know you're doing your best, and I know that sometimes life can be a struggle. The government I lead will be driven not by the interests of the privileged few, but by yours.' (May, 2016)

This statement – that partly reads as a rebuke to Cameron et al., who were often characterised as belonging to a privileged and disconnected elite – also focuses upon those in work but struggling, whose cause May commits to championing. Continuing the trend of political leaders coining new terms to describe the populations whose lives they seek to improve (see, for example, Ed Miliband's 'squeezed middle' and Nick Clegg's 'alarm clock Britain'), May has pledged to be there for 'the JAMs': those that are 'just-about-managing' (Sadha, 2016). Within May's rhetorical emphasis on the JAMs, and in her Downing Street speech on becoming Prime Minister, there is, perhaps unsurprisingly, a seeming neglect (if not ignoring) of the needs of those struggling but not in work: not so much those just-about-managing as those not-managing-at-all. It will be interesting to see whether – if at all – May's (2016) pledge to make "Britain a country that works not for a privileged few, but for every one of us" extends to those in receipt of out-of-work benefits.

If May does decide to make an active effort to improve the lives of those on 'welfare', she may find herself going against the tide of public opinion. Over recent years, the overarching direction of welfare reform – and the central arguments posited to defend it – often seem to be supported by the general public (Baumberg, 2014; Taylor-Gooby, 2015). This links to a wider context, which sees political rhetoric, media pronouncements and public opinion all frequently coalescing around an understanding of 'welfare' and those who rely on it as necessarily and inevitably negative and problematic. In recent years, there has been an exponential growth in what some term 'poverty porn': reality TV programmes that purport to show the 'true picture of life on benefits', but in fact provide a highly edited, sensationalised and partial account (Jensen, 2014; Tyler, 2014a). Programmes such as *Benefits Street* reinforce notions of the benefit claimant as an 'other', who the 'hard-working majority' are invited – even encouraged –

to observe and judge. Reinforcing the central moralising messages emanating from 'poverty porn', politicians and the mainstream media often stigmatise, stereotype and (de)moralise benefit claimants. Seemingly compelling caricatures are created, which characterise claimants as inactive, passive and sometimes simply members of a feckless, criminal underclass. The emphasis on passivity was notable in David Cameron's description of claimants "sitting on their sofas waiting for their benefit cheques to arrive" (Cameron, 2010b) and echoed by Iain Duncan Smith's characterisation of those who "have seen their parents, their neighbours and their entire community sit on benefits for life" (Duncan Smith, 2011a). The presumed passivity of benefit claimants is contrasted with the responsible behaviour of the 'hard-working majority', who are assumed to be busy doing the honourable thing by trying to earn a wage and support their own families (cf. Osborne, 2010; BBC Today, 2011; Cameron, 2012b). Dependency is endlessly compared with a supposed independency that is seen to characterise paid employment, with work in the formal labour market valorised and its transformative potential proclaimed (cf. DWP, 2010a; Duncan Smith, 2011b).

While the extent of the censure and critique reserved for benefit claimants in Britain today is certainly marked, it is not new; out-of-work benefit claimants have long been regarded as potentially deviant and all too often 'undeserving' of the support they receive (Golding and Middleton, 1982). Indeed, old divisions between the deserving and undeserving, as well as the traditional folk devils of the 'benefit fraud' and the 'scrounger', are today frequently being recycled and reimagined – most notably in the drawing of dichotomous distinctions between 'skivers' and 'strivers' and between the 'hard-working majority' and 'welfare dependants'. Even in the immediate post-war period, shortly after the foundation of the modern welfare state, there was concern that some of those on benefits were perhaps undeserving of state support (Hudson et al., 2016). What is significant about the present period, however, is the way in which particular groups (most notably disabled people) traditionally incorporated within the 'deserving' poor are today increasingly seen as including many 'undeserving' claimants. These 'undeserving' claimants are typecast as workshy fraudsters who require conditions and repeated medicals to assess their continued eligibility for state support (Briant et al., 2013). The contemporary period is also distinctive in the degree to which there is an overarching consensus on the need to address the 'problem of welfare' and to ensure that all those who can are on a journey from 'welfare' and into 'work' (see Chapter Two). While Jeremy Corbyn was elected leader of the Labour

Party in both 2015 and 2016 on an explicitly pro-social security stance, his opposition has not as yet provided a substantive alternative to the popular portrayal of 'welfare', instead leaving the dominant narrative broadly intact.

Writing about 'welfare'

In its engagement with lived experiences of welfare reform, this book inevitably focuses on the social security system – particularly on what is offered and demanded from individuals in return for the receipt of out-of-work benefits. In recent years, there has been an increasing move to talk not about social security, or even the welfare state, but simply 'welfare': a crude Americanisation employed to focus discussion and critical attention solely on out-of-work benefits (Lister, 2011a; Garrett, 2015). This linguistic sleight of hand serves to suggest that the policy problem requiring redress, especially against a context of state-imposed 'austerity', is out-of-work benefits receipt, with a seemingly deliberate neglect of the various other forms and beneficiaries of social welfare. A narrow focus on 'welfare' can obscure the structural forces that so often drive out-of-work social security receipt – as well as the reality that we are all, in various ways, dependent on the state and our fellow citizens for support.

Nearly 60 years ago, Richard Titmuss – one of the founding scholars of social policy – reminded us of the importance of thinking about the language we use to describe 'welfare' and the 'welfare state' (Titmuss, 1958, 2013). He developed his influential Social Division of Welfare (SDW) thesis to draw attention to the various forms of welfare, which include not only social welfare (the 'welfare state', which itself encompasses heath and education as well as social security benefits and support), but also occupational and fiscal welfare. 'Occupational welfare' refers to welfare available to many in work – employers and the self-employed, as well as employees – such as pensions, salary sacrifice schemes and support with childcare and travel expenses. 'Fiscal welfare' includes forms of tax relief – a particularly expensive but often invisible form of state welfare, which is too often neglected in calculations of the support that government provides to different income groups. There is also a fourth category of welfare – 'informal welfare' – that feminist revisions have incorporated into the SDW (Sinfield, 1978; Rose, 1981; Mann, 2009). Informal welfare includes care for family members and friends, as well as the unpaid and often taken-for-granted forms of support on which so many rely (see Chapter Three). Consistently, over time, social welfare – and specifically working-age social security benefits – has remained the most stigmatised and problematised form of welfare, giving Titmuss' arguments an enduring relevance (Sinfield, 1978). The SDW thesis calls upon both governments and the public to recognise the broad reach of 'welfare' and the complex chains of dependency and interdependency that envelop us all; a call as pertinent today as when Titmuss made it in the 1950s.

Here, the term 'social security' is used to describe social welfare receipt in the form of cash benefits, some of which are available to both those inside and outside of the formal labour market. The term 'out-of-work benefits' is employed to refer explicitly to working-age benefits for those not currently in paid employment. 'The welfare state' is understood as the assemblage of social welfare and allied services, which encompasses what remains of social housing, public healthcare, education, social work, social services and, of course, social security. The term 'welfare' is only employed where it is explicitly used as shorthand by politicians and the participants in the study themselves. Describing the growing consensus on social security as a framing consensus on 'welfare' is done deliberately and provocatively to remind readers that this consensus is tied to a particular, problematic and partial understanding of social welfare and social security (see Chapter Two).

Social citizenship as theoretical lens

As well as detailing the constituent parts of this new framing consensus on welfare, this book explores how benefit changes mesh with processes of citizenship inclusion and exclusion with social citizenship here employed as a theoretical lens. Recent welfare reforms have often been justified as part of an effort to support the social inclusion of benefit claimants by encouraging individuals to become hard-working citizens (Levitas, 1998), creating a particular logic for examining the citizenship consequences of welfare reform for those directly affected. Alongside this, it is also valuable to explore what the social rights of citizenship today provide. These should, at the minimum, guarantee citizens a 'modicum of economic welfare and security' (Marshall, 1950). Whether and to what extent recent welfare reforms have fractured and undermined the social rights of citizenship – and in particular the provision of even a 'modicum' of security – is a central concern of this book.

This book fleshes out dominant citizenship narratives from above (how citizenship is framed and understood by politicians) and contrasts this with citizenship as it is lived and experienced from below. When Cameron talked about responsibility in his speech to launch the 2011

Welfare Reform Bill (see the beginning of this Introduction), he was talking about and developing his understanding of social citizenship – an understanding that showed marked continuity with his New Labour predecessors (see Chapter One). In Cameron's speech and his subsequent policy direction and focus, we can unpick a particular approach to social citizenship from above; one with far-reaching policy consequences. Similarly, in Cath's description of her own life on benefits, we can begin to generate an improved understanding of citizenship as it is lived and experienced from below, noting the significant divergence between political rhetoric and the account of an individual living with the consequences of out-of-work benefits receipt.

The lived experiences of welfare reform study

To develop our understanding of citizenship from below and lived experiences of welfare reform, the research reported here adopted a qualitative longitudinal research design. This methodological choice was driven by a desire to capture a dynamic picture of individual lived experiences rather than only a static snapshot taken at one point in time. Qualitative longitudinal research (QLR) adopts time as both a vehicle and object of study; time is seen as a mechanism for creating a longer and more detailed view of the area being researched, but also as a substantive analytical focus in its own right (Henwood and Shirani, 2012; Neale, 2015). In this case, there is an interest in exploring how experiences of welfare reform and individuals' timeframes and horizons intersect, with later chapters discussing how a climate of ongoing changes to the benefits system can constrain and impede individuals' capacity to actively plan for, and look forward to, their futures.

Time is also employed as a tool for enabling a longer view to emerge of experiences of welfare reform, which details how it is anticipated, experienced and reflected upon, in overlapping processes, which sit alongside other changes in individual lives. The future is a particularly rich terrain, given that it is here that people can imagine the other lives that they would like to lead, as well as explore their hopes and fears of how their unknown future might unfold (Adam and Groves, 2007). Directing attention to the ways in which the welfare state and welfare reform shape the temporal order of individual lives (Walker and Leisering, 1998) reveals particular relationships between out-of-work benefits receipt and people's capacity both to manage in the present and make plans for and think about the future.

By adopting QLR methods, it becomes possible to 'walk alongside' individual participants (Corsaro and Molinari, 2000, cited in Neale and Flowerdew, 2003; Henderson et al., 2006), observing them living with and responding to processes of change. A repertoire develops of reactions and responses to change; responses that, when read against one another, often reveal interesting tensions and dilemmas (McLeod, 2003). This enables the development of a more nuanced and detailed understanding of lives lived through and across time, with particular potential to illuminate the complex interplay of structure and agency in individual lives (Holland et al., 2004).

An interest in social policy's attempts to alter human behaviour – in this case by transforming 'welfare dependants' into 'responsible hardworking citizens' – provided a further logic for researching through and across time. As Corden and Millar (2007, p. 529) note, qualitative longitudinal research's 'focus on change, both how people change and on how people respond to change, is very relevant to the current policy context in which individual behaviour change is seen as key to achieving desired policy goals'. This is particularly pertinent for the welfare reform arena, where political narratives so often imply static and fixed categories of 'welfare dependants' and 'workers' and then seamless transitions out of 'welfare' and into 'work'. By following individuals over time, it has been possible to tease out the much more complex lived realities, as well as to better understand how the policy approach is actually experienced and the responses it engenders.

This research was based in Leeds, a post-industrial city in the North of England, with areas of considerable deprivation that sit alongside pockets of considerable wealth. Leeds contains a higher rate of unemployment than the national average. In Leeds, close to the start date of the study in 2012, the 'worklessness' rate[2] was 12% – comparable to the rate in a number of other major cities (such as Sheffield, Edinburgh and Newcastle), but considerably lower than that of cities such as Liverpool (22%) and Glasgow (21%) (Leeds City Council, 2012). The experience of claiming out-of-work benefits in Leeds may be geographically specific in some ways; this should be borne in mind when considering the research's findings. For example, the worklessness rate may affect experiences of 'welfare-to-work' transitions, while the contracting out of work-related support may mean that the particular experiences of Leeds residents are not mirrored in other regions, where different providers have contracts to deliver initiatives such as the Work Programme. On the other hand, many of the research findings are mirrored by studies exploring similar themes in different locations (Graham et al., 2014; O'Hara, 2014; Roberts and Price, 2014), suggesting that there is also significant commonality in the experiences of benefit claiming across the UK.

With the support of two gatekeeper organisations, 22 individuals were recruited who were all likely to be affected by welfare reform. This sample was purposively constructed to encompass subsamples of single parents being migrated from Income Support onto Jobseeker's Allowance, disabled people being moved from Incapacity Benefit onto Employment and Support Allowance and young jobseekers affected by the tightened conditionality and sanctions regime. It was designed to include men and women, a range of ages and representatives from Black and Minority Ethnic (BME) communities.

Semi-structured interviews were held with each of the 22 participants in 2011. From this sample, a longitudinal sample of 15 was selected on the basis of those most likely to experience welfare reform over the course of the initial research period, which ran from 2011 to 2013. This involved reducing the subsample of disabled people, as some of those interviewed were judged unlikely to have their Incapacity Benefit reassessed during the period of study. Two further waves of interviews were held with these 15 participants approximately six and 18 months after their initial interview in 2011 and 2012/13. Contact was sustained between interview waves through informal mechanisms including telephone, text message, email and social media. This approach to sustaining contact proved successful and contact was lost with only one participant between the second and third interview waves. In 2016, interviews were held with nine participants; and these provided further detail on the ongoing effects and consequences of welfare reform. Rich data was generated from a total of 60 interviews over five years, including transcriptions of the interview discussions as well as exercises completed by the participants, such as timelines and pictures.

Principles of informed consent, anonymity and confidentiality helped create a safe research space for those interviewed and were central to the ethical approach that guided the research. Further, incorporating elements of participatory research practice was seen as an ethical decision, which was linked to the importance of including those interviewed at every stage of the research, including its dissemination. To support this, a research steering group was convened, which included participants and representatives from the gatekeeper organisations. Following a suggestion from one of the participants at a steering group meeting, funding was sought to develop an animated film as one way of disseminating key findings in a more accessible and engaging way that could include the participants themselves. The funding bid was successful; subsequently, seven of the participants were involved in a six-month process to develop and create an animated film, which became known as the 'Dole Animators' project. The participants themselves directed and produced this film and own the film copyright. Through a series of workshops, they made collective decisions about the animation style, substantive content and dissemination of this film, facilitated and supported by three animators and myself (Land and Patrick, 2014). The film – *All In It Together: Are Benefits Ever a Lifestyle Choice?* – was launched in October 2013 with an event at the House of Commons, which the participants attended. It is available to view online at www.doleanimators.org along with a range of resources including information about the participants and the filmmaking process, as well as audio interviews conducted with several of the group members in May 2015.

Structure of the book and key messages

The research produced 'thick' description of experiences of out-of-work benefits receipt during a period of ongoing welfare reform. This book reports upon the research's findings and discusses their implications for understandings of citizenship inclusion and exclusion. Chapter One details the relevance of social citizenship to debates and questions concerning social welfare and welfare reform, as well as introducing the theoretical terrain of liberal and republican theories of citizenship. It also discusses the citizenship thinking evident in recent UK governments: an excavation and exploration of citizenship from above. Chapter Two goes on to explore the UK's welfare reform policy context, detailing the key trends in the reform trajectory on recent years.

The reader is then introduced to those interviewed, with Chapter Three outlining the everyday lives of individual out-of-work benefit claimants and the work that 'getting by' on benefits and coping with day-to-day poverty so often demands. This chapter highlights the various forms of socially valuable contribution in which many were engaged. Chapter Four discusses participants' relationships with paid employment over time, detailing previous relationships with and attitudes to 'work', as well as experiences both in and out of work during the initial research period. Employment journeys included spells in and out of work (characteristic of the low-pay, no-pay cycle (Shildrick et al., 2012b)) and unsuccessful struggles to secure employment. This chapter also discusses the support and help available from Job Centre Plus and the Work Programme and explores individuals' responses to welfare-to-work interventions.

The focus shifts in Chapter Five to the impact of welfare reform itself; there is discussion of how individuals experience and respond to particular reforms, notably benefit sanctions, migration onto Employment and Support Allowance and the exercise of welfare conditionality. This chapter details the pervasive worry and anxiety that characterise experiences of welfare reform and the negative effects this can have on individual health, wellbeing and – ironically – readiness and capacity to make transitions from 'welfare' and into 'work'. Chapter Six explores how benefit claimants see both themselves and others, discussing the reach and consequences of benefits stigma. Drawing on the 2016 interviews, Chapter Seven explores how individual lives changed and evolved over the time of the study, noting the central place of employment, whether as an aspiration or a component of participants' daily lives. The concluding chapter summarises the central findings from the book and discusses their implications for social citizenship.

The central contention of this book is that there is a significant disjuncture between citizenship as it is conceptualised from above and citizenship as it is lived and experienced from below. The mismatch between the policy narrative and approach on the one hand, and the lived experiences of benefit claimants on the other, undermines the overarching welfare reform project and its posited rationale. The dominant citizenship narrative suggests that processes of welfare reform will engender social inclusion by supporting individual claimants to realise transformative change in their own lives, principally by making the transition from 'welfare' and into 'work'. However, in fact, the overarching narrative and associated policy approach more often serves to fracture and undermine the citizenship status of those in receipt of out-of-work benefits. The rhetorical emphasis in recent political accounts on providing 'security' for all is an empty promise when contrasted with the pervasive insecurity that today characterises both out-of-work benefits receipt and low-paid employment for so many of Britain's citizens. If citizenship is to retain its emancipatory potential, the recent subversion of social citizenship as a tool of social control must be challenged and resisted and the 'everyday world' of citizenship (Desforges et al., 2005, cited in Lister, 2007, p. 58) – individual lived realities – given far more prominence in theoretical and political accounts. The disjuncture between citizenship from above and below creates a pressing case for directing our attention to how individuals articulate, live with and respond to the rights and responsibilities of citizenship. It is also vital to explore how individuals' experiences are shaped and so often constrained by narrow, excluding and exclusive characterisations of the expected behaviours of the 'dutiful citizen'. This requires a close engagement with and listening to the experiences of all of Britain's citizens, including those currently marginalised and denied full citizenship status – and it is hoped that this book will here make a useful and timely contribution.

Note

[1]   All participants' names have been changed to protect their anonymity.

[2]   As a proxy for 'worklessness', the DWP suggests the total number claiming Jobseeker's Allowance, Employment Support Allowance, Incapacity Benefit and other income-related working-age benefits (Leeds City Council, 2012).

ONE

Social citizenship
from above

An individual's sense of belonging and inclusion within their wider community and nation state is bound up in and contingent upon their citizenship status and practice; on the rights and responsibilities that come with being, and acting as, a citizen (Lister, 2003). Whether we conceive of citizenship as a status that brings with it a bundle of rights and responsibilities or as a practice that demands the fulfilment of particular duties if one is to be a responsible engaged citizen, citizenship focuses attention on questions of inclusion and exclusion – on who is and who is not included within the citizenry and on what basis (Dwyer, 2010).

Citizenship is of value precisely because there are necessarily and always some that it excludes: advantages and rewards are attached to those, but only those, who are considered citizens (Lister, 2003). The ways in which explicit and implicit decisions are made around who is and who is not included as a citizen are fundamental to the nature of the society in which we live and the basis on which it operates. Close attention to these decisions and the more subtle processes that operate to drive inclusionary and exclusionary forces can illuminate the values and social norms that underpin a society, as well as improving our understanding of the bureaucratic, political and societal domains and how these feed into and affect individuals' everyday politics and lived citizenship realities.

This book adopts social citizenship as a theoretical and analytical lens for better understanding how individuals in receipt of out-of-work benefits experience social welfare and welfare reform. In this chapter, an introduction to ideas of social citizenship is provided, including T. H. Marshall's (1950) classic liberal theory of citizenship. This is followed by a summary of the intersection between citizenship, poverty and participation. The second part of the chapter is concerned with excavating the dominant citizenship narratives evident in the thinking and policy statements of recent UK governments. This analysis focuses on the period from 1997–2016, which includes New Labour as well as the Coalition and Conservative governments led by David Cameron. This exploration highlights the extent to which recent UK governments have drawn upon liberal and civic republican ideas of social citizenship, often in tandem, to construct an argument that positions welfare reform as a tool of social inclusion. Changes to benefits in general and welfare-to-work policies in particular are presented as measures that can support and empower individuals to become included citizens by participating in the formal labour market. By focusing on articulations of citizenship from above, this chapter lays essential groundwork for the later exploration of how social citizenship is lived and experienced from below.

Understanding social citizenship

What is social citizenship?

Citizenship is best understood as denoting membership of a community (Marshall, 1950). In this context, we are most interested in membership of the nation state and the rights and responsibilities attached to that membership. Determining who should be treated as a citizen, what citizens should be entitled to from the state and what should be expected in return demands recourse to normative matters of social justice and fairness (Lewis, 1998; White, 2003). Citizenship is not an absolute and static state; rather, the boundaries between citizen and non-citizen are often fluid and changing (Clarke et al., 2014). There are always people who – although nominally citizens – experience their status as precarious and sometimes find themselves treated as lesser or second-class citizens (Dwyer, 2010). People can and will experience their citizenship status and practices differently at different times, often related to the extent and nature of their engagement in wider society, whether as workers, parents, volunteers or carers. It is not an all-or-nothing status but rather a continuum that people move along depending on the norms, expectations and demands imposed on 'citizens' from above (Lister, 2003). This, of course, gives it a particular relevance to this book's exploration of how individuals experience and respond to changes in their social security entitlement over time – changes that impact upon what it means 'to be a citizen' (Lister, 2003).

Liberal and civic republican theories of citizenship

In exploring theories of citizenship, an important distinction can be made between liberal and civic republican traditions (Plant, 1998), which can also be understood as a distinction between social–contractual and social–solidaristic thinking (Dean and Melrose, 1999).

16

Liberal theories of citizenship focus on the status that social citizenship offers and the rights that come with that status. By contrast, civic republican theories conceive of citizenship as a 'practice' and so are more concerned with the responsibilities and duties of the 'good citizen'. In Plant's (1999, p. 124) words, liberal theories see citizenship as a relatively unconditional status, 'not fundamentally altered by the virtue, or lack of it, of the individual citizen', whereas in republican accounts citizenship is 'an achievement rather than a status'.

Within the liberal tradition (cf. Marshall, 1950; Kymlicka, 1995; Rawls, 1999; White, 2003), theorists conceptualise the individual citizen as the bearer of individual rights and preferences – stressing the importance of upholding the individual's freedom to pursue the life of his or her choosing (Dwyer, 2010). Generally, individual freedom is prioritised over the state dictating the form a 'good' life should take, creating a key dividing line between these thinkers and those within the civic republican tradition. The liberal citizenship tradition has also been described as 'social–contractual' because theorists take as their starting point the idea of a social contract between the individual citizen and the state. Thus, citizenship is most frequently explored as a status to which a bundle of rights and responsibilities – the terms of the contract between the individual and his or her state – is attached.

Social–solidaristic theories of citizenship can be equated with civic republican and communitarian conceptualisations (Dean and Melrose, 1999). Stress is placed on citizenship as a practice and the shared values held by the citizenry as a whole (cf. Walzer, 1983; Taylor, 1990; Sandel, 1998). There is a noted emphasis on the obligations that come with being a citizen, which are often tied to political participation, engagement in paid employment and – in historical accounts – military service. New communitarian thinking is best understood as a particular, often conservative strand of the broader civic republican citizenship tradition. Communitarians focus on the expected behaviour of the 'good' citizen; their policy prescriptions often centre on demanding and instilling individual responsibility and duty (Etzioni, 1995; Willetts, 2008). There is a strong behavioural and moralising dimension to the communitarian perspective, with responsibilities seen as arising prior to, and often irrespective of, rights (Lister, 2003). Today, communitarian thinking remains prominent in both academic and political discourses – a legacy of the long tradition of civic republicanism stretching right back to Ancient Greece and its onus on active participation in the *polis* (Greek city state) (Dwyer, 2010).

Citizenship as engagement

In recent years, there has been an increasing emphasis on citizenship as 'engagement', on the 'acts' of citizenship and upon the constitutive (and often fluid) elements of what being a citizen entails (Ellison, 2000; Isin, 2008). This can perhaps best be understood as a contemporary application of civic republican ideas as part of an effort to illuminate how today's citizens inhabit the 'everyday worlds of citizenship' (Desforges et al., 2005, cited in Lister, 2007, p. 58). Ellison (2000) developed an account of citizenship as 'proactive' and 'defensive' forms of engagement. He argues that citizenship engagement can either be proactive, where individuals assertively seek to secure their citizenship rights (and sometimes acquire new ones), or more defensive, where individuals are only able to reactively attempt to cling onto and reassert their entitlement to existing social citizenship rights (Ellison, 2000). Ellison's analysis is particularly valuable in drawing attention to the ways in which social citizenship can be enacted and engaged with in different ways at different times, as well as reminding us of the extent to which access to resources and other forms of social, cultural and economic capital can affect – and, where absent, constrain – individuals' engagement.

A focus on citizenship as engagement also draws attention to the ways in which it is a dynamic concept (Clarke et al., 2014), evolving over time and in response to changes in both how it is conceptualised from above and how it is experienced and lived from below. Citizenship is best understood as *'imparfaite'* or unfinished; it is constantly being reimagined and reworked, both in theory and practice (Balibar, 2001, cited in Clarke et al., 2014). It is a contested and mobile concept. This gives it particular analytical power, both as a vehicle for tracking changes at the societal level and as a political tool for defending particular policy approaches and agendas. It has been and remains a 'keyword', because it is employed in justifications of very different political programmes and ideas, in which it is utilised as a 'powerful mobilising image for social and political action' (Clarke et al., 2014, p. 84).

Why employ social citizenship as a theoretical lens for examining processes of welfare reform over time?

This book adopts and develops a distinction between citizenship as it is articulated *from above* and citizenship as it is lived and experienced *from below*. It explores how political narratives and policy agendas around welfare reform co-opt and conceptualise social citizenship in their policy defences and discourse (*citizenship from above*). This is contrasted with how individuals directly affected by these processes live with and experience their own citizenship and the degree of their citizenship inclusion or exclusion (*citizenship from below*). This reveals the fluid and evolving nature of social citizenship, as well as the ways in which changes to it from above can cumulatively and gradually transform experiences of it from below.

Later in this and subsequent chapters, the ways in which the social rights of citizenship have been reworked and redrawn by successive governments are explored and their implications discussed for our broader understanding of social citizenship's emancipatory potential, as well as to what social citizenship rights provide to those in receipt of out-of-work benefits. Social citizenship's malleable, contested and unfinished nature gives it particular potential as a theoretical lens for examining changes in social welfare provision and political narratives about what is expected and (increasingly) demanded in return for social welfare. There is particular scope to engage with the declared motivations behind processes of welfare reform, as well as to explore how these processes are actually experienced by those affected by welfare reform. Here, we are able to contrast the promises made in the name of welfare reform – particularly for transformative positive changes for those directly affected – with the ways in which these reforms are lived, experienced and responded to on the ground.

T. H. Marshall: citizenship as 'equality of status'

In exploring welfare reform and social citizenship in tandem, T. H. Marshall's theory of social citizenship is particularly relevant. Marshall developed the classic egalitarian liberal conception of citizenship (Bode, 2008; Dwyer, 2010), emphasising the equality of status of all citizens: 'Citizenship is a status bestowed on those who are full members of a community. All who possess the status are equal with respect to the rights and duties with which the status is endowed' (Marshall, 1950, p.18).

Taking a chronological perspective, Marshall charted the emergence of civil, political and social rights of citizenship in the 18th, 19th and 20th centuries respectively. For our purposes, we are particularly interested in Marshall's conceptualisation of the social rights of citizenship. Unfortunately, however, Marshall did not explicitly detail the nature and extent of the social rights to which a citizen should be entitled, defining them in both minimalist and maximalist terms as: 'the whole range [of social rights] from the right to a modicum of economic welfare and security, to the right to share to the full in the social heritage and to live the civilized life according to the standards prevailing in society' (Marshall, 1950, p. 8). Much debate since has focused on Marshall's interpretation of the extent of social rights and how far these should be provided unconditionally (White, 2003). Importantly, Marshall saw social rights as of intrinsic value, with citizenship having real significance and substance for those living in poverty (Dwyer, 2010). This conceptualisation provides the possibility for citizenship to be used instrumentally when making claims on the state. Marshall's (1950) model can operate as a yardstick against which we can measure and assess how far all citizens in any society obtain the promised 'security' and 'equality of status'.

Further, Marshall's tripartite model illustrates how civil, political and social rights are inevitably intertwined, such that the denial of one category of rights affects and limits an individual's capacity to exercise their other rights – what Twine (1994, p. 97) describes as the 'three legged stool of citizenship'. Further, even in his minimalist definition of social citizenship rights, Marshall emphasised the right to at least a 'modicum' of 'economic welfare and security' (p. 35); notwithstanding the 'modicum' qualifier, this right to an element of security is a relatively challenging benchmark against which to assess current social security provision and reforms.

Marshall's concern with rights has led to criticisms that he neglected individuals' responsibilities (Selbourne, 1994; Etzioni, 1995). Although he did not explicitly codify the duties and obligations that citizens should be expected to fulfil, he did emphasise the importance of paid employment and the duty of citizens to live the life of a 'good citizen' and to put 'one's heart into one's job' (Marshall, 1950, p. 46). Marshall has also been criticised for a faulty chronology and, in particular, a neglect of the reality that women's political rights came much later than his model suggests (Walby, 1994; Delanty, 2000). Combined with a further neglect of issues of disability and gender (Roulstone and Prideaux, 2012; Revi, 2014), this has led some to argue that his model was only ever designed to focus on healthy, white, adult males (Williams, 1992; Dwyer, 2010). While these criticisms are important, Marshall was writing in a particular place, at a particular time and in a particular cultural context. His model was thus inevitably bound up in the emergence of the welfare state during Clement Attlee's post-war government (Bottomore, 1992).

Nonetheless, almost 70 years on, Marshall's tripartite model of social citizenship remains valuable in incorporating social citizenship rights and providing a structure that can be mobilised in defending social welfare. By popularising social citizenship and calling on the state to provide some level of decommodified support to citizens in need, Marshall developed a contractual model that makes comparatively onerous demands of the state. Decommodification is the ability to 'uphold a socially acceptable standard of living independently of market participation' (Esping-Andersen, 1990, p. 37). The provision of decommodified social security support was a key aspect of the post-war welfare settlement and is a central element of Marshall's conceptualisation of social rights.

The ambiguities in Marshall's writing – particularly around his understanding of the nature and extent of social rights – do limit the utility of his ideas. Nonetheless, social citizenship can operate as an ideological discourse (Dean and Melrose, 1999) and Marshall's emphasis on social rights has real resonance when exploring the nature and consequences of welfare reform. Marshall's theory is particularly useful when held up against both the dominant narratives of recent governments and out-of-work benefit claimants' own lived realities.

Social citizenship, poverty and participation

T. H. Marshall's seminal account illustrates the extent to which social citizenship can be of particular value to those living in poverty by granting them entitlement to social rights, while at the same time indicating how experiences of poverty can undermine affected individuals' social citizenship – particularly where individuals experience an inequality of status with their fellow citizens. Living in poverty impinges upon affected individuals' citizenship; all three types of citizenship rights are largely unrealised for those living in poverty (Lister, 1990, 2004; Vincent, 1990). Indeed, Vincent (1991, p. 205) argues that 'properly understood a poor citizen is a contradiction in terms'.

There has been ongoing debate regarding what – if anything – social citizenship offers to the poorest in society, as well as a questioning of what a more egalitarian and socially just social citizenship might entail. In moving towards a post-Marshallian framework for an egalitarian and truly inclusive social citizenship, writers such as Lister (2003, 2004), Fraser (2009), Gaventa (2002), Williams (2012a) and Taylor (1994) have emphasised the importance of looking beyond access to rights and resources towards questions of participation, recognition, respect and voice. While such writers contend that meaningful access to resources is a vital precondition of social citizenship, they also emphasise ensuring that all individuals have the right to be treated with respect and dignity and to have their needs and preferences acknowledged through a politics of recognition. This becomes particularly pertinent for the poorest in society, who often find their voices ignored and even silenced, while their interactions with state bureaucracies and street-level advisers are frequently characterised by an absence of respect (see chapters four and six).

Having the right to give 'voice' to individual experiences and perspectives is closely tied to a right to participate in society. Of course, this right is itself entirely contingent on the right to access those resources to be able to participate fully in society (Gaventa, 2002). Fraser (2003) has written of the importance of seeking to secure 'parity of participation' so that all have equal rights to participate; a demanding objective in current western societies in which the poorest typically find it very difficult to participate, particularly in proactive, positive ways (see Chapter Three). For a right to participate to be meaningful it would need to encompass both familial and community forms of participation, as well as the ability to participate in political decision-making – particularly in those decisions that impact directly upon one's own life. Taken together, then, it is possible to extend Marshall's framework to include not just social, political and civil citizenship rights but also participation rights, incorporating issues of respect, voice and recognition. This represents a demanding framework, and one against which individual lived experiences can be measured and compared.

Having introduced ideas of social citizenship, this chapter now explores the dominant citizenship narratives discernible in the policies and rhetoric of recent governments. This represents an attempt to set out how social citizenship is articulated from above: an essential precursor to later chapters' exploration of how citizenship is lived and experienced from below.

Citizenship from above in the UK: 1997–2016

Sustaining the liberal tradition: the dominance of contractualist rhetoric

When making the case for welfare reform, recent governments have frequently employed contractualist arguments, promoting their new policies as 'fair' measures designed to ensure that people's rights and responsibilities are both upheld (cf. DSS, 1998; DWP, 2008a, 2010c). Contractualist arguments conceive of the relationship between the state and the individual as similar to a contract, with each side expected to claim and be able to fulfil particular rights and responsibilities. There is a neat symmetry to contractualist pronouncements, with a bundle of rights and privileges matched to related duties and responsibilities. Even if this is in fact a mirage, the value of contractualism lies in its apparent appeal to ideas of justice as reciprocity, with the tying of entitlement to contribution. Thus, it is not surprising to find contractualism so readily and repeatedly deployed – a deployment that has a long history. From the Thatcher era's critique of the post-war welfare settlement's surfeit of individual rights and deficit of personal responsibility (Moore, 1988) to Cameron's (2009a) promise to reconfigure the welfare 'bargain', there has been a remarkably consistent focus on defining the appropriate relationship between rights and responsibilities in a functioning welfare state.

Politicians have repeatedly argued that with more support from the state must come more responsibilities for citizens, with the latter most often narrowly construed as taking steps to find and enter paid employment (DSS, 1998; Duncan Smith, 2014b). Blair's government promised to reform the welfare state 'on the basis of a new contract between citizen and state' (DSS, 1998, p. v) to create 'rights and responsibilities on all sides' (p. 24), while the Conservatives (2009, p. 5) pledged that 'everyone who is able to work will be expected to prepare to return to work, and in return we will offer them the support they need to do so'.

Cameron's Conservatives repeatedly borrowed the language and soundbites of their predecessors in government. Thus, 12 years after New Labour's formative Green Paper 'A new contract for welfare' (DSS, 1998), the Conservatives published a pre-election policy paper on welfare-to-work; 'A new welfare contract' (Conservatives, 2010a). Similarly, the idea of a 'something for something' culture where support is explicitly tied to obligations is a rhetorical device that has been employed by both New Labour and the Conservatives (DWP, 2008a; Purnell, 2008a; Cameron, 2014a). While this chapter focuses on the post-1997 period, an emphasis on rights and responsibilities and on seeking to move away from a 'something for nothing' culture was also a marked feature of the Thatcher and Major years (Timmins, 2001).

Recourse to contractualist rhetoric is particularly evident in discussions of the relationship between out-of-work benefit claimants and the state. Indeed, it is in making a contractual case for deepening and extending welfare conditionality that the rights and responsibilities equation most frequently appears. Iain Duncan Smith (2014a) defended the use of benefit sanctions by drawing on contractualist arguments:

'[sanctions] represent a key part of the contract that we
have with people, the contract which says that looking for
a job is your job'.

With welfare-to-work in particular, we see the contractual citizenship
perspective explicitly tied to policy – Labour's New Deal being the
classic example of a populist policy founded on, and justified in
relation to, welfare contractualism. Thus, Gordon Brown defended
the New Deal regime, which included the offer of more support to
unemployed people, alongside the condition to participate or risk
benefit sanctions, on the basis of increasing both rights and obligations
in tandem (DWP, 2008b). Often, the welfare contract is presented in
fairly threatening terms and operates as an instrument of control and
coercion. As Gordon Brown put it:

> those who are fit to work are expected to work. And those
> who cheat the system will not be warned, but punished the
> first time they are caught ... If you won't contribute to our
> society, and fail to play by its rules, then you can't expect
> to be supported by it. (DCLG, 2008, p. 3)

During the 2015 General Election campaign, David Cameron drew
upon contractualist arguments when he introduced proposals to replace
18–21-year-olds' eligibility for Jobseeker's Allowance with a 'youth
allowance', payable in return for participating in community work for
30 hours a week. He explained:

> 'Your first experience of the benefits system should be that
> yes, you can get help – but it isn't something for nothing,
> and you need to put something back into your community
> too.' (cited in BBC News, 2015)

Taking the contractualist rhetoric further, and embedding it in policy
and practice, the Coalition government introduced a 'Claimant
Commitment' to lay down what is expected of each benefits recipient
and the possible sanctions for failure to comply with their side of the
welfare bargain (DWP, 2014). Showing marked continuity with the
Jobseeker's Allowance Agreement introduced by John Major in 1994,
under Universal Credit all claimants are required to sign and comply
with their individual Claimant Commitment as a condition of ongoing
benefits receipt. This extends the Jobseeker's Allowance Agreement
to a broader group of benefit claimants (including, for example, single

parents and disabled people) and is an explicit attempt to create and demand the fulfilment of a 'welfare contract'. David Cameron (2012a) explained the change:

> 'Now you have to sign a contract that says: you do your bit and we'll do ours. It requires you to have a real CV and it makes clear: you have to seek work and take work – or you will lose your benefit'.

Differentiated contractualism

In an interesting development, Iain Duncan Smith, then-Secretary of State for the Department for Work and Pensions (DWP), used his speech at the 2010 Conservative Party Conference to set out his contract with the British people. Extracts from his speech are worth quoting at length, given that they demonstrate how he envisaged the government's contract with three key sectors of the British people, differentiated by their relationship to the labour market:

> 'Today I want to set out the role I see for government in welfare. I want to set out a welfare contract. ...
> We will break down the barriers to work and ensure work pays but in return, we have the right to insist that when work is available you take that work and work hard to keep that job ... We will work with you but you must work with us. That is our contract with the unemployed.
> It is a proud duty to provide financial security to the most vulnerable members of society and this will not change. This is our contract with the most vulnerable.
> Most people in this country don't wake up early in the dark and cold, and head to their job in order for the state to take their money and waste it. They don't slump, exhausted in their chair after work, just to see their taxes spent on people who can work but won't. I want to look every taxpayer in the eye and be able to say that their money is either going to people who are on the path back to independence or ... to people who, without question, deserve society's care. No more spend and waste. This is our contract with British taxpayers.' (Duncan Smith, 2010a)

Tax-paying citizens are judged to be fulfilling their side of the welfare bargain and so are exempt from the conditionality framework – until and unless they need to claim out-of-work benefits. By contrast, those seen as having some capability to work are subject to the full force of welfare conditionality and a regime of conditions and sanctions. A residual category of those judged as 'deserving' and 'vulnerable' is promised protection and security; promises that need to be critically interrogated, given the continued retrenchment in social welfare provision.

Duncan Smith's presentation of these differentiated welfare contracts can be related back to David Cameron's own speech at the same party conference in which he set out his particular conception of fairness, most importantly stating that: "what people deserve depends upon how they behave" (2010b). Essentially, Duncan Smith's contracts were a reworking of Cameron's idea of fairness; both emphasised individual behaviour, responsibilities and duties. Differentiated forms of welfare contractualism are notable in providing a framework that justifies differential treatment of citizens, with a scale of conditionality and interventions depending on distance from, and capability to participate in, the paid labour market. Contracts such as Duncan Smith's take a static, unidimensional perspective on an individual's obligations and rights and neglect to consider how a person's rights and responsibilities might be better thought of as being spread over the life course. With the arrival of in-work conditionality in 2016, those taxpayers in receipt of in-work support are now also subject to conditionality, perhaps complicating Duncan Smith's presentation of these contracts and/or suggesting a new layer of differentiation for those judged to be hard working, but perhaps not hard working *enough*.

The 'contract' between taxpayers and out-of-work claimants

Duncan Smith's (2010a) aforementioned speech detailed the obligation the state owes to taxpayers to ensure their hard-earned wages are not "wasted" on "people who can work but won't". In this way, Duncan Smith created a link between the rights of taxpayers to see their taxes well spent and the obligations of out-of-work claimants to 'work' for their 'welfare' and to demonstrate their deservingness. More recently, delivering fairness for taxpayers was a key argument employed by the DWP in successfully defending the judicial review of the Household Benefits Cap (Larkin, 2016). In both examples there is some evidence of a reworking of the contractual idea, so that we begin to see a particular exploration of the relationship not just between the individual and the state, but also between and among fellow citizens. In particular, there are some undertones of a 'welfare contract' being implicitly drawn between non-working 'welfare dependants' and the responsible taxpayer (Whitworth and Griggs, 2013). This was particularly notable in the speeches of George Osborne who, when Chancellor of the Exchequer, frequently defended reforms to increase the welfare conditionality faced by the economically inactive with recourse to notions of a contractual relationship between out-of-work claimants and taxpayers:

> 'Help to work, incentives to work, and an expectation that people should do everything they can to find work. That's fair for people out of work, and fair for those in work that pay for them.' (Osborne, 2013a)

In a similar vein, Duncan Smith characterised the Claimant Commitment as creating a contract – not between the state and the citizen – but between the out-of-work claimant and the taxpayer:

> 'Under Universal Credit we are … requiring everyone to sign up to a claimant commitment as a condition of entitlement to benefit. Just as those in work have obligations to their employer, much like a contract, this commitment will clearly set out claimants' obligations to the taxpayer.' (Duncan Smith, 2012)

The notion of a contract between taxpayer and 'welfare dependants' is profoundly divisive; it valorises the behaviours of the taxpayer, while suggesting that those on out-of-work benefits require conditions and the threat of compulsion to be made responsible and to fulfil the obligations they owe their fellow citizens. This analysis almost explicitly creates a two-tiered citizenship. It pits citizens against one another, awarding taxpayers an elevated citizenship status as overseers who can make demands on out-of-work benefit claimants by virtue of their working, tax-paying status. By contrast, out-of-work claimants must do what is expected of them or risk tough benefit sanctions, with almost no recognition of their rights under any such 'welfare contract'.

This discussion has demonstrated a sustained reliance by post-1997 governments on a highly contractual, liberal conceptualisation of citizenship, targeted particularly at out-of-work benefit claimants. The language of welfare contractualism is extensively utilised in efforts to detail the *duties* of out-of-work benefit claimants. However, it is very rarely employed to reinforce and uphold the *rights* of these same individuals. A reliance on social–contractual ideas of citizenship that emphasise the responsibilities of out-of-work claimants sits alongside recent governments' articulation of a communitarian citizenship perspective, which places emphasis on the duty of all adults to engage in paid employment in order to fulfil the primary obligation of the good citizen.

Civic republican ideas: the working, dutiful citizen

The civic republican strand of citizenship theorising evident in the thinking of New Labour and Cameron's governments was most marked in relation to their effort to reconstruct the welfare state around the work ethic. Indeed, the equation of 'work' with duty and responsibility is a marked feature of the political approach taken by all governments since at least 1979. Commentators on the New Labour regime consistently observed the single-minded focus on paid work as the primary social obligation that citizens should be expected to fulfil (cf. Dean, 1999; Lister, 2001b; Prideaux, 2010); an observation that can be validly extended to the Conservative-led governments of 2010–16.

Politicians repeatedly describe 'work' in the paid labour market as an unproblematic social good and endow it with transformative properties. Policy documents, political speeches and even tweets inform us of the benefits that come with work, which extend beyond monetary rewards to improved self-respect; dignity; self-esteem; health, wellbeing and family life (cf. DWP, 2006, 2010c; Duncan Smith, 2014c). As Duncan Smith put it:

> 'Work is about more than just money. It is about what shapes us, lifts our families, delivers security, and helps rebuild our communities.' (2014b)

Further, "work is the spine that runs through a stable society." (Duncan Smith, 2015).

Under Blair, Brown and most recently Cameron, work was seen as the ultimate policy panacea – a silver bullet – that can not only end 'welfare dependency' but also deliver people from substance addiction and help Britain's most troubled families back on their feet (HM Government, 2012). At the same time, work becomes both the duty and the reward of the good citizen. Cameron used a high-profile speech on welfare reform to argue:

> 'we've got to recognise that in the end, the only thing that really beats poverty, long-term, is work. We cannot emphasise this enough. Compassion isn't measured in

benefit cheques – it's in the chances you give people ...
the chances to get a job, to get on, to get that sense of
achievement that only comes from doing a hard day's work
for a proper day's pay.' (Cameron, 2012b)

Given the importance attached to paid employment, the benefits system
is tasked with ensuring that those on benefits are being supported to
make the transition from 'welfare' and into 'work'.

Broader civic republican and solidaristic sentiments

Beyond the rhetoric on the duty to 'work', recent governments have
also displayed evidence of broader civic republican thinking on the
potential constituent parts of a 'good' society. In contemporary political
narratives, there is a repeated emphasis on the personal responsibilities of
the good citizen; such pronouncements resonate with aspects of classic
civic republican thinking. Cameron (2009a) repeatedly articulated
the importance of responsibility: "what holds society together is
responsibility ... the good society is a responsible society". Indeed, he
chose his first Conservative Party Conference speech as Prime Minister
to articulate his understanding of citizenship in civic republican terms:

Citizenship isn't a transaction – in which you put your taxes
in and get your services out. It's a relationship – you're part
of something bigger than yourself, and it matters what you
think and you feel and you do. So to get out of the mess
we're in, changing the government is not enough. We need
to change the way we think about ourselves, and our role
in society. Your country needs you. (Cameron, 2010b)

This passage is notable for explicitly challenging a liberal contractual
model of citizenship and calling instead for an approach to citizenship
centred on solidarity and a sense of duty to one's country. The
characterisation of the dutiful citizen that appeared under Cameron's
governments placed increased burdens and expectations on the
individual. The promised 'opportunity' for more control over one's
life (Conservatives, 2010b) can quite easily be recast into an obligation,
with a related duty to eschew reliance on the state wherever possible.

Both New Labour's and Cameron's governments also placed onus
on the community and the family as the units of social action and
drivers for an improved social world, suggesting that their 'good'
society was grounded in fundamentally conservative understandings

of responsibility and cohesion. This was particularly notable during Cameron's time in office. For example, in decrying the 'broken society' they claimed to encounter, Cameron and Duncan Smith emphasised the decline in traditional family forms and marriage and a related preoccupation with the continued rise of single-parent families (Cameron, 2009b, 2011b, 2015b; Duncan Smith, 2010a). Family breakdown was characterised as one of five 'pathways to poverty', with a stable family unit presented as the primary and most important form of welfare and support (Centre for Social Justice, 2009; DWP and DfE, 2011). As Cameron (2016) put it:

> 'Families are the best anti-poverty measure ever invented. They are a welfare, education and counselling system all wrapped up into one. Children in families that break apart are more than twice as likely to experience poverty as those whose families stay together.'

In this way, the 'problem' of family breakdown was characterised as a fundamental driver of child poverty, drawing attention to individual rather than structural causes of poverty, while the 'responsibility' for providing welfare was also increasingly shifted onto the family unit.

The 'big society'

Closely aligned to his emphasis on the importance of the family, Cameron for a time also sought to create a 'big society' (Cameron, 2010a). This was presented as a corrective to the 'big state' and a way of encouraging individuals to better support themselves, their families and their wider communities. While the 'big society' idea gradually disappeared from view, it was prominent in the Conservatives' 2010 General Election manifesto:

> Our alternative to big government is the 'big society', a society with much higher levels of personal, professional, civic and corporate responsibility; a society where people come together to solve problems and improve life for themselves and their communities; a society where the leading force for progress is social responsibility, not state control. (Conservatives, 2010b, p. 37).

In developing the 'big society' thesis, Cameron drew upon a range of philosophical traditions and strands of Conservative thinking, including the 'compassionate conservatism' championed by Blond (2010) and the Centre for Social Justice (2009) as well as the more libertarian and free-market-orientated civic conservatism of David Willetts (2008). What these analyses seemed to share was a reinvigorated focus on personal responsibility, alongside a critique of a disempowering and dependency-generating welfare state. In calling for individuals to become active members of the 'big society', there was recourse to a broader sense of social responsibility in which people work together for the common good (cf. Cameron, 2009b, 2011a). This vision was characterised as an alternative to economic individualism and as a way to create a 'good society' without requiring a 'big state' (Cameron, 2009b). In this analysis, big government was seen as part of the problem and as operating to promote selfishness and individualism, with reform then required to deliver a smaller state (Lister and Bennett, 2010).

This retreat from state intervention and deepening of personal responsibility exhibits elements of civic republican citizenship theorising, wherein the importance of our duty to one another as fellow humans is elevated beyond the rights and expectations we can make of the state through a social contract. The 'big society' critique was also grounded in a broken society rhetoric, describing a status quo characterised by social recession, the decline in civic society and the associated emergence of intergenerational 'welfare dependency' (Social Justice Policy Group, 2006). As Cameron (2011a) explained:

'we do need a social recovery to mend the broken society.
To me, that's what the big society is all about.'

Inevitably, a broken society analysis can serve to devalue and undermine the citizenship status of those characterised as 'broken', while it is not clear how far the characterisation of a big state crowding out civil society actually fits with the lived realities on the ground. Certainly, there are clear parallels between characterisations of a substratum of irresponsible, non-working 'broken Britons' and ideas of an underclass (Prideaux, 2010).

The notion of a 'big society' drew upon ideas of active citizenship, closely intertwined with neoliberalism (Verhoeven and Tonkens, 2013) to suggest a reformulated vision of personal responsibility with an emphasis on the individual's role as an active creator of the 'good' society. Ideas of 'responsible' citizens busily engaged in the 'big society' brought with it the potential to further demarcate those perceived as responsible from the supposedly irresponsible, with these two groups then likely to experience state intervention and 'encouragement' to become active citizens rather differently. Wealthier groups might be encouraged to participate via the odd 'nudge', but those lower down the income spectrum were more likely to experience state intervention as the repeated 'shove' and 'push' (Ellison, 2011).

A study by Verhoeven and Tonkens (2013) explored the different forms of 'feeling rules' implicit in the framing of welfare state reform in England and the Netherlands. They found that 'empowerment talk' was commonly present in discussion around active citizenship in England, whereas 'responsibility talk' predominated in the Netherlands. What this analysis arguably neglects is the ways in which different types of talk may be employed for different types of citizens. This has occurred in the UK in recent years. Those who are already seen as responsible citizens are more likely to be subject to 'empowering talk' that encourages them to do more to engage in society and in their communities. By contrast, those on out-of-work benefits, who are required to take more active steps (steps that are a condition for continued entitlement to out-of-work benefits), are much more likely to experience 'responsibility talk' in which their own shortcomings are emphasised and the need for corrective action stressed (see Chapter Four).

While the 'big society' thesis was found to have little traction with the electorate (Bochel, 2011; Oborne, 2011) and was gradually abandoned by the Conservatives, Cameron's early adoption and emphasis on it remains telling. It can be seen as part of Cameron's wider efforts to detoxify the Conservative brand and create a public imagining and understanding of 'compassionate conservatives'. This attempt followed on from now-Prime Minister Theresa May's 2002 warning that too many saw the Conservatives as the 'nasty party'. Now in charge, it will be interesting to see how May takes forward these citizenship narratives and whether, under her leadership, there is any notable change in the ways in which liberal and civic republican ideas of citizenship are mobilised to make the case for welfare reform. As this book went to press, May chose a high-profile speech to set out her concept of a 'shared society', a successor to Cameron's big society' concept (May, 2017). In a 'shared society', May said:

> 'The shared society is one that doesn't just value our individual rights but focuses rather more on the responsibilities we have to one another. It's a society that respects the bonds that we share as a union of people and nations. The bonds of family, community, citizenship and strong institutions. And it's a society that recognises the

obligations we have as citizens – obligations that make our society work.' (2017)

Whether May's idea of a 'shared society' develops into a more coherent vision and overarching political philosophy will become clearer over time. Nonetheless, it is notable that she has chosen, relatively early on in her time as Prime Minister, to set out a republican citizenship narrative and, like her Conservative and Labour predecessors, place marked emphasis on citizens' responsibilities and obligations.

Promises of inclusion

In recent years, politicians have drawn upon civic republican and liberal theories of citizenships to defend the use of welfare conditionality, benefit sanctions and compulsory engagement in work-related activity. These policy tools are presented as having the potential to assist affected individuals to make the transition into paid employment and so become included within society as responsible, dutiful citizens. For example, in defending plans to remove benefits from young people as part of attempts to ensure all are 'earning or learning', George Osborne (2014) presented the choice politicians faced:

> 'We have a choice between paying our young people for a life on the dole, or giving them the keys to a life of opportunity.'

Here, Osborne argues that reforms that retrench welfare provision and extend welfare conditionality will aid the social inclusion of targeted individuals. Compulsion is thus posited as having the potential to bring young people closer to both the paid labour market and full citizenship. In this way, a narrative of citizenship inclusion has suffused justifications for welfare reform. New Labour equated social exclusion with a lack of employment, drawing upon a social integrationist discourse that emphasises achieving social inclusion by helping people into paid employment (Levitas, 1998; Lister, 2001a). As Tyler (2014c, p. 161) notes, 'New Labour redesigned citizenship under the double axis of inclusion/exclusion and work/worklessness'. This policy analysis and linked emphasis on 'work' was continued and arguably extended by Cameron's governments (see Chapter Two). Questions remain, however, as to whether these policy agendas deliver inclusionary or exclusionary outcomes; questions that later chapters' explorations of the experiences of those at the sharp end of welfare reform should help answer.

Conclusion

This chapter has introduced readers to ideas of social citizenship and argued for its potential value as an analytical and theoretical lens to better understand how welfare reform is experienced over time. It has outlined the scope in exploring citizenship from above and below and introduced the seminal work of T. H. Marshall. It has also explored the recent articulation of citizenship from above, with a particular focus on key messages concerning social welfare entitlement and the central role reserved for paid work in understandings of citizenship duty and responsibility. This exploration illustrates the ways in which civic republican and liberal ideas of citizenship are so often employed in tandem to make a case for continued welfare reform directed at supporting transitions from 'welfare' and into 'work'.

The following chapters explore experiences of and responses to out-of-work benefits receipt and welfare reform, with a focus on the citizenship implications of both policy changes and the dominant citizenship narrative. It is critical to situate this analysis in an understanding of how citizenship is conceptualised from above, recognising the ways in which the accompanying narrative and associated policy regime inevitably impacts upon individuals' citizenship status and ways of 'being' a citizen. By examining 'citizenship from below' in this way, it is possible to better grasp the lived realities of citizenship and begin to consider how best to conceptualise and understand social citizenship in 21st-century Britain. Before looking at citizenship from below in detail, it is first necessary to outline the welfare reform policy context and most recent reform trajectory – the task of the next chapter.

TWO

The emergence of a framing consensus on 'welfare'

Welfare-to-work policies, and indeed social security more generally, are key areas where the relationship between the citizen and the state has been rethought and redefined over recent years (Wright, 2009). This chapter explores the shifting welfare reform policy context in the UK, discussing the ways in which reforms have cumulatively transformed social security provision (Bradshaw, 2015). Over the past 35 years and across diverse nation states and contexts, there has been a sustained emphasis on 'activating' benefit claimants, with a reliance on measures that seek to ensure that all those who can are on a journey from 'dependency' to a fêted independence via engagement in the paid labour market. This is apparent in the US's transformation of its welfare landscape, in Germany's Hartz reforms, in Sweden's active labour market policies and in the UK, where welfare conditionality has been steadily intensified and extended (Finn and Gloster, 2010; Fohrbeck et al., 2014). Following an overview of the dominant framing of the 'welfare' problem in the UK, this chapter outlines the constituent elements of what is best seen as a framing consensus on 'welfare' before summarising the most recent changes. Given this book's exploration of experiences of welfare reform from 2010–16, there is an inevitable focus on the reforms enacted by Cameron's Conservative-led governments from that period. However, this is placed within a context of ongoing welfare reform, under first Margaret Thatcher and then John Major, Tony Blair and Gordon Brown.

What's the problem?

It is helpful firstly to explore how politicians have presented the 'welfare' policy problem and proposed solution over recent years. Bacchi's (1999) work on 'problem representation' reminds us of the roles governments play in the production and representation of policy problems, with these particular, often partial and biased, representations then mobilised to defend a clear policy direction and agenda. This has particular relevance to social security, with successive governments having developed a powerful, and apparently persuasive, narrative concerning the problem of 'welfare'. The dominant problem representation suggests that social security, narrowly equated with 'welfare' (understood as out-of-work benefits for working-age adults), is of itself inevitably problematic. 'Welfare' and those who receive it are problematised, with a focus on cultures of 'welfare dependency' that are supposedly created and encouraged by social security support. There is a repeated emphasis on the notion that 'welfare' 'traps' individuals in 'dependency', with the support provided deterring individuals from taking more active steps to make positive changes in their own lives, principally by moving off 'welfare' and into 'work'.

This problem representation was clearly articulated by David Cameron in his speech following the riots that took place across UK cities in 2011:

> 'For years we've had a system that encourages the worst in people – that incites laziness, that excuses bad behaviour, that erodes self-discipline, that discourages hard work, above all that drains responsibility away from people. We talk about moral hazard in our financial system – where banks think they can act irresponsibly because the state will always bail them out. Well this is moral hazard in our welfare system – people thinking they can act as irresponsibly as they like because the state will always bail them out.' (Cameron, 2011b)

In Cameron's account, 'welfare' is seen as a barrier preventing individuals from supporting themselves which operates to undermine personal responsibility and independence. Most recently, and particularly since the global financial crisis of 2008, there is also a sustained emphasis on the financial unsustainability of what is presented as comparatively generous welfare provision. Social security expenditure is often cited as a major example of the state's long-term profligacy, and thus a reason for state-imposed austerity (Clarke and Newman, 2012).

This dominant framing of the policy 'problem' is also linked to an account of poverty that places emphasis on individual, behavioural causes of poverty and neglects its more structural drivers. Cameron's governments identified five 'pathways to poverty': worklessness; family breakdown; debt, addiction and educational attainment (HM Government, 2014). This represents a one-sided focus on individual, behavioural causes of deprivation and disadvantage. The framing of the policy problems of 'welfare' and 'poverty' consitutes a classic 'individualization of the social' (Ferge, 1997), which directs the corrective lens onto the presumed shortcomings and even deficits of those living in poverty and in receipt of out-of-work benefits. However, this individualising discourse does also emphasise structural issues, with the benefits system judged to be creating and sustaining pernicious cultures of 'welfare dependency' (as seen in Cameron's earlier quote) (Pantazis, 2016). In this way, an individualising discourse is melded with a structural critique of the benefits system in making calls for welfare reform.

What's the solution?

The policy problem posits a very particular policy solution: measures to create a nation of 'hard-working families', all of whom are able to enjoy the transformative rewards said to come with paid employment. As we have already seen, paid employment is endlessly valorised, with contrasts drawn between the dutiful, responsible behaviours of working individuals and the inactivity of those 'languishing' on benefits (see Chapter One). A work-first approach is taken, with welfare-to-work policy firmly focused on assisting out-of-work claimants to make the transition into *any* paid employment (Wright, 2012). There is less emphasis on improving skills and employability than in other countries (what is referred to as a human capital approach, 2012), while there is also a neglect of the reality that not all forms of paid employment deliver transformative rewards (Wright, 2011a, 2012; Patrick, 2014a) (see Chapter Five). This work-first policy solution is positioned as best achieved through activation policies, which set work-related conditions for individual claimants at the same time as providing various forms of (often mandatory) work-related support. Efforts are also directed towards ensuring that financial incentives exist to guide people to make the 'right choices' by increasing the rewards attached to paid employment and/or reducing the financial support available to those on out-of-work benefits.

Over time, this has been accompanied by a shift from a male breadwinner model to an adult worker model, with all working-age adults seen as workers or potential workers (Wright, 2009). An ever smaller residual category consists of those judged not capable of paid work and/or those of whom paid work cannot reasonably be expected, which includes *some* disabled people, *some* single parents and *some* carers. Contrasted with the post-war era, this can be characterised as a shift from a 'welfare society' to an 'active society' (Walters, 1997). Commenting on the US, but with equal relevance to the UK, Wacquant (2009) describes the role of social security changing from 'people processing' to 'people changing'. Today, social security is increasingly seen as a mechanism for triggering behavioural change, judged most successful when it creates the circumstances in which individuals make transitions from 'welfare' and into 'work'. This stance is encapsulated in then-DWP minister Chris Grayling's statement that: 'We want a welfare state which is a ladder up which people climb, not a place in which they live' (cited in DWP, 2011a).

The framing consensus on 'welfare'

The dominant representation of the policy problem and posited solution has wide application and currency; politicians, much of the popular media and public opinion seem to coalesce around a characterisation of 'welfare' as inevitably and necessarily negative. The extent of this agreement, which contrasts particularly with the past, means that today it is appropriate to speak of a framing consensus on 'welfare' that operates to embed a shared understanding of the 'problem' of 'welfare'. This consensus is supported by a 'machine of welfare commonsense' (Jensen, 2014), which pushes forward the dominant framing and creates a climate in which it is very difficult for alternative, resistant narratives to be articulated – let alone heard. Jensen's emphasis on 'commonsense' is important. Commonsense can be understood as a 'form of "everyday thinking" which offers us frameworks of meaning with which to make sense of the world ... Typically it expresses itself in the vernacular, the familiar language of the street, the home, the pub, the workplace, and the terraces' (Hall and O'Shea, 2015, cited in Garrett, 2015, p. 398). The fact that the dominant representation of the 'welfare' problem is regarded as 'commonsense' indicates the extent to which it has become an accepted and mainstreamed aspect of everyday thinking to view 'welfare' as a policy problem that requires correction (Garrett, 2015).

A central tenet of this framing consensus is the emphasis on welfare conditionality as *the* tool to enable individuals to become responsible citizens and to ensure that 'welfare' is effectively and justly targeted at those who not only *need*, but also – and apparently even more critically – *deserve*, state support. There have always been conditions attached to benefits receipt (Griggs and Bennett, 2009; Hills, 2015), but what is marked about the contemporary era is the extent to which conditionality dominates in terms of both political rhetoric and proposed policy responses to deal with each new supposed 'policy problem'. Welfare conditionality directs analytical attention to the steps individuals need to take to become job-ready, employable, working citizens – and so neglects and obscures the structural factors and barriers that can make movements into paid employment difficult, unsustainable and even inappropriate for some individuals (Dwyer, 2010; Patrick, 2011). It frames the 'problem' of non-work and unemployment as an individual issue that requires change and reform at the individual level. Over recent years, the reach and application of welfare conditionality has been steadily extended and intensified so that today it is possible to speak of 'ubiquitous conditionality' (Dwyer and Wright, 2014). Benefit sanctions and strict work-related conditions increasingly dominate the social security landscape, with far-reaching consequences for affected individuals (see Chapter Five).

In delivering social security, particularly via welfare-to-work programmes, there is a sustained reliance on the private and third sectors, which are increasingly paid by results in supporting individuals into employment. The private sector is awarded lucrative, multi-million pound contracts to assess benefit claimants' eligibility for the disability benefits Employment and Support Allowance and Personal Independence Payments. Recent years have also seen a growth in charitable forms of social welfare provision, most notable in the considerable rise in food banks, which today are an everyday feature – whether via a supermarket's invitation to donate as part of a weekly shop, a food bank on the high street or a collection at a harvest festival for the nearest food bank (Garthwaite, 2016). This shifting welfare mix represents a significant change in the way in which 'welfare' is provided.

The framing consensus on 'welfare' is buffered and reinforced by a seemingly endless recourse to dichotomous divisions between deserving and undeserving populations; between 'hard-working families' and 'welfare dependants'. Such distinctions have a long history (Clark, 2014; Hills, 2015), stretching back far further than the birth of the UK welfare state to the 19th-century Poor Laws and beyond. What is particularly notable about the current period is the regularity with which the terms are used and reused and the impassioned language that politicians sometimes employ in their adoption of these stereotypical (and stereotyping) archetypes. The dominant divisions drawn between workers and non-workers – today recast as between 'strivers' and 'skivers' or between 'workers' and 'shirkers' – problematise the behaviour of non-workers just as it valorises and proclaims the behaviours of those in work. In recent elections, politicians have clamoured to be seen as the party to support the 'hard-working' majority, with the implicit (and sometimes explicit) suggestion that they are not in the business of supporting those who rely on benefits for all or most of their income (Gentleman, 2015; Marsh, 2015). Prefacing almost every policy statement with a commitment to support those who 'work hard' directs our attention to those who it is assumed do not, with the suggestion that these individuals are failing themselves, failing their fellow citizens and ultimately failing wider society. The articulation and replication of these simplistic categories creates an environment in which we are all invited to think in terms of 'us' and 'them' – and ultimately to side with the 'hard-working' majority over 'welfare dependants'.

The stability of the framing consensus on welfare – at least among mainstream politicians – might, in time, be challenged by the arrival of Jeremy Corbyn as Leader of the Labour Party in 2015. Elected on an explicitly pro social security stance, and vowing to defend those in receipt of benefits from bigotry and the worst effects of spending cuts, Corbyn and his Shadow Secretary for the Department of Work and Pensions, Debbie Abrahams, have introduced policy proposals that include an end to benefit sanctions and the abolition of the WCA regime (Murphy, 2016). Speaking at the 2016 Labour Party Conference, Abrahams made clear that Labour does want to change how people think and talk about the benefits system:

> 'I want to change the culture of our social security system and how the public see it. I believe that, like the NHS, it is based on principles of inclusion, support and security for all, assuring us of our dignity and the basics of life were we to fall on hard times or become incapacitated, giving us a hand up, not a hand out.' (Abrahams, 2016)

Under Corbyn's leadership, Labour's rhetoric and policy approach mean that the opposition is voicing a challenge to the popular positioning of welfare as inherently 'problematic' and are instead placing more emphasis on the potential for 'social security' to do good, and provide much-needed support. However, his lack of traction with the general public and unstable position within the Labour Party itself arguably reduces the likelihood of his providing a mainstream alternative to the dominant narrative on 'welfare'.

Supporting the framing consensus: the role of 'poverty porn' and the media

In the dissemination of the framing consensus, politicians are supported by the popular media, which recycles and recirculates negative characterisations of claimants. Whether it be tabloid headlines castigating fraudulent claimants, broadsheets investigating 'broken

Britain' or a new television show purporting to show the reality of life on benefits, the media is an active participant in reproducing and reinforcing the dominant consensus. The media has always played a role in the stereotyping, even the demonisation, of benefit claimants (Golding and Middleton, 1982; Briant et al., 2013). However, its interest in claimants – and their behaviours – ebbs and flows over time and is mediated by political pronouncements and shifts in public opinion. For example, there was a sustained attack on the benefits 'scrounger' in the 1970s (Golding and Middleton, 1982) and again today there is a renewed focus on the 'folk devil' of the 'welfare dependant'.

The recent explosion in 'poverty porn' – reality television shows that promise to shed light on the lives of Britain's benefit claimants and those living in poverty – is another important ingredient in the machine of welfare commonsense (Jensen, 2014). Television shows such as *Benefits Street*, *Skint*, *On Benefits and Proud*, even *The Great Big Benefits Wedding* and *Benefits: Too Fat to Work* invite the viewer into benefit claimants' homes and day-to-day lives to watch how 'they' live. The observation of 'them' by 'us' immediately sets up and works with the existing divisions between the 'strivers' and the 'shirkers'. As the 'hard-working majority' watch these very popular shows, they are able to see for themselves the lives and choices made by 'welfare dependants'; the 'other'; the 'shirkers'. While television executives defend their shows as providing a realistic account of life on benefits in Britain today (Plunkett, 2015), they are actually highly edited and sensationalised accounts that mobilise stereotypical 'images of welfare'. This is perhaps best characterised by the opening captions for the first series of *Benefits Street*, which featured sofas on the pavement, men on streets drinking cans of lager and women smoking cigarettes on their doorsteps. This imagery neatly fits with a narrative that seeks to 'other' and problematise those who receive out-of-work benefits – but it is not necessarily aligned with the day-to-day realities of many claimants' lives, as later chapters will illustrate. With the seemingly endless growth of 'poverty porn', the behaviours and lives of some of Britain's poorest are being very successfully and profitably repackaged into light entertainment.

Having introduced the framing consensus on 'welfare' and the machine of welfare commonsense by which it is bolstered, this chapter now explores recent welfare reform enacted by UK governments, focusing particularly on Cameron's governments from 2010 to 2016. Given the scale of continuity between Thatcher, New Labour and the Conservatives, it is important to briefly detail key policy reforms implemented under these earlier administrations, looking first at the Conservative governments from 1979 to 1997.

1979–97: the Thatcher and Major years

During 18 years of Conservative government, the social security offer to unemployed people changed. As part of a sustained attack on 'welfare dependency', entitlement to unemployment benefits was made increasingly conditional on efforts to find work (Page, 2010). Those most affected by the changes introduced were young people and unemployed adults, with both groups' social rights to benefits reduced (Atkinson and Micklewright, 1989). The introduction of Restart interviews in 1986 symbolised the start of a formalised conditional welfare regime in Britain and a critical first step along the path towards activation (Jones, 2012). All those who had been unemployed for a year – soon revised to six months – were required to attend a Restart interview; with sanctions for non-attendance (Digby, 1989). Changes made to the Social Security Act 1989 introduced the 'actively seeking work' test to unemployment benefit receipt (Timmins, 2001); with this effectively a reintroduction of the punitive 'genuinely seeking work' test of the 1920s (Deacon, 1991). Benefit disallowances were threatened to those whose level of work-seeking activity was deemed inadequate, creating a clear link between benefit entitlement and demonstrable efforts to find work.

The Major government continued this extension of conditionality, replacing unemployment benefit with the stricter Jobseeker's Allowance (JSA), and halving the maximum duration for those claiming the benefit based on their previous contributions (rather than on an income basis) (Scott and Brien, 2007). JSA claimants have to demonstrate that they are actively seeking work as a condition of benefit receipt and must sign a Jobseeker's Agreement, which sets out the steps they will take in their effort to secure employment (Dwyer and Ellison, 2009). The JSA regime remains in place today.

Young people were affected by the 1983 introduction of the Youth Training Scheme (YTS), which provided training and work experience for those aged 16 and 17 and not in employment or education. Those participating in the scheme received a training allowance (Riddell, 1989). Changes to the benefit rules in 1988 meant that those who refused an offer of a YTS place would not receive any benefits, except in exceptional circumstances – a reform that ended benefit entitlement for this age group, with exemptions only made for particular sub-groups of young people, such as single parents (Digby, 1989). These reforms had the effect of compelling those young people who wanted support from the state to participate in YTS, which was often criticised as involving menial work for private employers (Loney, 1986) and even derided as 'slave labour' (Walford, 1988). Similar criticisms have been made of New Labour's New Deals and Cameron's various programmes of mandatory work placements and experience (Prideaux, 2001; Daguerre and Etherington, 2014).

Overall, the Thatcher and Major years saw a considerable intensification of the conditionality applied to young people and unemployed adults, as well as a sustained rhetorical attack on what was characterised as a welfare dependency culture. Policies introduced, such as YTS and JSA, signalled a growing utilisation of work-related welfare conditionality – a trend that was continued and extended under New Labour.

1997–2010: enter New Labour

In opposition during the 1980s, Labour had vehemently opposed the Conservative reforms. Indeed, the Labour Party National Executive had signed a 'Charter against Workfare', which stated that all initiatives to encourage people back to work should be voluntary with compulsion derided as a 'recipe for lower standards, resentment and discrimination' (1998, cited in King and Wickham-Jones, 1999, p. 257). Fewer than ten years later – in a radical break with this past that represented a pivotal feature of their 'third way' approach – New Labour announced plans for a programme of New Deals to ensure that benefit entitlement was made conditional on efforts to find and secure work (Timmins, 2001). The totemic New Deals provided training and work experience for those outside the labour market. Those who refused to engage in compulsory New Deals for young people and the long-term unemployed faced benefit sanctions (King and Wickham-Jones, 1999).

In fact, New Labour went further than the Conservatives, drawing single parents and disabled people into welfare-to-work. Neither of these groups had traditionally been expected to participate in paid work as a condition of benefits receipt (Jones, 2012). New Labour transformed the benefits regime for them, first by introducing voluntary measures to support them back to work and subsequently escalating conditionality. Of critical importance was the 2008 introduction of a new benefit for disabled people: Employment and Support Allowance (ESA). The ESA regime remains in place today, with applicants facing a Work Capability Assessment (WCA) to determine their benefit eligibility. Following a Work Capability Assessment (WCA), claimants are placed in one of three groups depending on their judged capability to participate in paid employment (DWP, 2012a). Those with the most severe impairments are placed in the Support Group (SG), in which they receive ESA without any conditions. Those judged to have some limited capability to work are placed in the Work-Related Activity Group (WRAG), in which they receive a slightly lower level of ESA and are expected to participate in work-related activity or risk benefit sanctions. A third group consists of those judged Fit For Work (FFW). This group are refused ESA and invited instead to apply for JSA, for which they will need to comply with the significantly more stringent conditionality regime (DWP, 2012a).

While overseeing a radical extension of work-related conditionality, New Labour also sought to make work pay and to provide support to reduce the barriers faced by people seeking to enter or return to paid work (Page, 2001; Driver, 2009). Policies here have included the introduction of a National Minimum Wage (NMW), tax credits to improve the financial rewards of paid work, extended childcare provision and, for disabled people, anti-discrimination legislation and some financial support for workplace adjustments (Puttick, 2007). Efforts around making work pay included some of the most progressive and socially democratic policies of the New Labour administrations, with tax credits and the minimum wage particularly noteworthy in this respect (Deacon and Patrick, 2011). While New Labour's efforts to make work pay were important, so too was their considerable extension of work-related conditionality, with its application to many disabled people and single parents a central element in the shift to an 'active society' (Walters, 1997).

2010 onwards: a new politics? Cameron's Conservatives

Entering office in 2010 as part of a coalition with the Liberal Democrats, David Cameron promised a new way of doing things, vowing to tear up New Labour's supposedly failed attempts to tackle worklessness. In fact, Cameron's governments showed marked continuity with their New Labour and Conservative predecessors, particularly in their sustained emphasis on welfare-to-work and welfare conditionality. At the same time, however, the policy direction was extended and accelerated in what Lister and Bennett (2010) describe as a process of 'policy leapfrog'. As Prime Minister, Cameron oversaw a rapid extension and intensification of the operation of conditionality, which has sat alongside repeated promises to make work pay, and to ensure that support is provided to enable those who can to move into paid employment. This section summarises these reforms, focusing particularly on those changes that affected the individuals interviewed for this book.

Intensifying and extending welfare conditionality

While New Labour – and Major and Thatcher before them – had expanded the operation of welfare conditionality within the benefits system, the most recent Conservative-led governments have sharpened and deepened the application of conditionality in a process of both intensification (making the conditions tougher and the consequences of non-compliance more severe) and extension (rolling out conditionality to ever more of the working-age benefit-claiming population) (McKay and Rowlingson, 2011). The Welfare Reform Act 2012 ushered in a tough new regime of benefit sanctions and conditions, which now includes the ultimate sanction of three years without benefits for those who fail three times to comply with particular work-related demands. These sanctions can be applied to those in the WRAG of ESA, who have been judged not to be capable of work at the present time, as well as to jobseekers.

The Conservative governments also intensified the work-related conditions made of jobseekers, arguing that looking for work should be a full-time job in itself and in some cases mandating jobseekers to attend Job Centres for 35 hours per week (Watts et al., 2014). They introduced an expectation for people to accept jobs up to a 90-minute journey from their home, with many obligated to participate in welfare-to-work support via the Work Programme, various forms of work placement and/or skills-based training and education to make them more employable. There have also been reports of a changing culture in Job Centre Plus (JCP), with advisers being encouraged to sanction claimants and even given targets for the rate at which they should do so (Domokos, 2011). Rates of sanctioning grew rapidly in the Coalition years, but levelled off and then declined significantly more recently, partly as a result of reductions in the number of people claiming JSA.

As well as increasing the severity of sanctions, the Conservatives rapidly extended the reach of welfare conditionality. The Coalition continued with New Labour's ESA reforms, migrating all Incapacity Benefit claimants onto ESA while also reforming aspects of the latter. Most important here were the decisions to time-limit entitlement to contributory ESA for those in the WRAG to just one year and to extend possible sanctions for non-compliance with the conditionality regime. Previously only threatened with the loss of an element of their benefit, those in the WRAG can now have their benefits completely removed if they are deemed to not be taking part in the work-related activity demanded of them. Despite much criticism from pressure groups, the political opposition and the disabled people's movement, in 2015 the government also legislated to reduce the level of ESA for those in the WRAG by £30 a week to make it equivalent to the rate of JSA.

Cameron's governments also extended the conditionality operable on single parents, who were previously moved from Income Support onto JSA when their youngest child reached the age of seven. The Conservatives changed this requirement so that single parents were moved onto JSA when their youngest child turned five. The Welfare Reform and Work Act 2016 reduced this further, so that from April 2017 parents whose youngest child is three became subject to the full work-related conditionality regime. Young people have also been targeted by the Conservatives' extension of welfare conditionality. During the 2015 General Election, the Conservatives made a manifesto commitment to end 'automatic' eligibility to benefits for those aged 18 to 21, creating an 'earn or learn' system. The Conservatives pledged that, from April 2017, claimants would receive a training allowance equivalent to the youth rate of JSA if – but only if – they are engaged in programmes of education or training.[1]

Universal Credit

One of the most ambitious of the recent welfare reforms has been the introduction of Universal Credit (UC), which was first piloted in April 2013. With the twin goals of simplifying the benefits system and sharpening incentives to work, UC replaces six benefits (JSA, ESA, Income Support, Housing Benefit, Child Tax Credit and Working Tax Credit) and merges in- and out-of-work benefits support. Payments are made monthly to promote 'working habits' and are routinely paid to one individual in the household. Whilst the reforms were sold on the basis of ensuring that 'work always pays', cuts made to the UC budget and issues with the benefit's design mean that incentives to work are not particularly strong for certain groups (most notably single parents and second earners in a household) and there may, in fact, be incentives to work fewer hours than under the current system (Finch, 2016; Millar and Bennett, 2016). Indeed, on balance, UC is 'less generous than the tax credit system for working families' (Finch, 2016, p. 7). Perhaps in response to concerns that changes to the design of UC will impact negatively on working families, and linked to May's rhetorical focus on supporting families that are 'just-about-managing' (JAMs), the Government announced in November 2016 that they would reduce the rate at which UC is withdrawn as people move into work. While this represents a welcome change, it will not offset the retrenchment in UC expenditure also being implemented via reductions to the work allowances, which is part of George Osborne's legacy as a Conservative Chancellor.

There are also gendered implications with the ways in which UC is designed, with the issues around work incentives most likely to affect female claimants (Bennett, 2012). Since its launch, UC has been dogged with delays and difficulties in its implementation; successive targets for its roll out have been repeatedly missed and extended (National Audit Office, 2014b). As of April 2016, single jobseekers were able to claim UC in every JCP in the country, with it gradually being rolled out to other groups. At the time of writing, the government claims that it will now be fully operational by 2021 – some four years later than originally planned.

The gradual roll out of UC also heralds the introduction of in-work conditionality, with the expectation that almost all of those in receipt of the benefit and in work should be seeking to earn the equivalent of the NMW for 35 hours a week. Those earning less will be expected to take steps to increase their hours and/or find additional employment. Failure to do so could result in benefit sanctions to in-work support. These measures potentially extend welfare conditionality's reach to one million working claimants, with JCP charged with developing new methods and ways of working with an employed 'customer' group. The introduction of in-work conditionality interrupts and potentially disrupts the neat dichotomies repeatedly drawn between 'strivers' and 'skivers' (Butler, 2016). As boundaries between 'welfare dependants' and the 'hard-working majority' are blurred and remade, it is possible that low-paid workers reliant on in-work support and claimants of out-of-work benefits will recognise what they share, rather than thinking of their rights and duties in more oppositional terms. Of course, there is also the potential for the 'welfare dependent' badge to simply be handed out to ever more of the population, with all those who receive UC tagged as 'dependent' and the 'hard-working' cohort narrowed to include only those who are completely 'independent' from the most visible forms of state support.

What is clear from the preceding discussion is the extent to which conditionality has been intensified and extended since 2010, in ways that make Dwyer and Wright's (2014) description of 'ubiquitous conditionality' only more prescient. As we saw in Chapter One, the application of conditionality is frequently defended in contractualist terms with the argument that with more support must come more demands. It is to a brief summary of the provision of such 'support' that this chapter now turns.

More support?

On entering office, Cameron's Coalition government pledged more help to ensure that people were supported to make the transition from 'welfare' into 'work'. The Work Programme – a flagship new welfare-to-work programme – was launched, with support delivered by third- and private-sector organisations on the basis of payment by results. While government ministers hailed the newness of the programme, it in fact showed marked similarities with the Flexible New Deal, which was being rolled out just as New Labour left office. After a disappointing start, the Work Programme has performed better against targets, although there has been ongoing concern that it has failed to support those facing the most significant challenges to moving into employment, particularly some disabled people. On average, Work Programme providers refer twice as many people for a sanction as they support into employment, suggesting that the 'support' provided is quite heavily weighted towards compulsion and conditions (Etherington and Daguerre, 2015).

To strengthen the conditionality regime, the Coalition also introduced a range of programmes of work experience and obligatory training, which have been derided by critics as forms of workfare. Following prominent legal challenges, some of these schemes have been altered and the 2015 incoming government announced that the Mandatory Work Activity and Community Work Placement schemes would be phased out. At the same time, however, versions of workfare continue to feature and will be a central aspect of the new 'earn or learn' offer for young people.

In 2015, Cameron's government announced the replacement of the Work Programme with a new Work and Health Programme. As part of the Work and Health Programme, payments to providers will be reduced, which critics warn will reduce and undermine the level of support provided (Neville and O'Connor, 2016). It is anticipated that, under the new programme, funding will be cut by 75% leading to thousands of job losses in the welfare-to-work industry (Butler, 2017). Taken together, these various forms of employment 'support' are a critical element of the contractual 'offer'; one that is also heavily rooted in a promise to 'make work pay'.

Making work pay?

The Conservatives have continued New Labour's emphasis on seeking to shore up the rewards attached to paid employment. There are two ways in which a government can seek to make work pay: they can increase the rewards attached to paid employment or they can reduce those attached to benefits (Stanley, 2010). Both increase the gap between what is received on benefits and what is received in work, thereby sharpening work incentives. Since 2010, we have seen both approaches pursued in tandem, although arguably there has been more emphasis (both rhetorically and in policy terms) on reducing rates of benefits. This is often defended with recourse to nominal notions of justice and 'fairness' in ensuring that people in paid employment are not unfairly paying for those 'on benefits' to receive more than they do in wages. Policies justified in this way have included the household benefit cap, initially set at £26,000 but reduced to £23,000 in London and £20,000 in other areas from autumn 2016. The Coalition also legislated for reductions in the levels of Housing Benefit and Local Housing Allowance, as well as tightening eligibility conditions and removing the Spare Room Subsidy (more commonly known as the 'bedroom tax').

At the same time, both the Coalition and the majority Conservative governments altered the processes for uprating working-age benefits; seemingly technical changes, which mean that benefit rates fall behind inflation and cost of living increases. Benefit uprating refers to the process whereby benefit levels are altered year-on-year to take into account changes (most often increases) in the cost of living. First, the Coalition government moved from using the Retail Price Index to determine rates of benefit uprating to the less generous Consumer Price Index, and then reduced annual increases to a set 1%. Most recently, the majority Conservative government has frozen working-age benefit increases for four years. These changes to uprating rules are profoundly regressive, hitting hardest those in the bottom-income deciles (Hood et al., 2013). They also contrast markedly with the approach taken to support older people, who have been protected by a 'triple lock' that increases the state pension each year by either inflation, the increase in average earnings or 2.5% – whichever is the highest.

In seeking to increase the rewards attached to work – and in a political flourish in his first budget as chancellor of a majority Conservative government – George Osborne announced a 'National Living Wage' in 2015. He promised that this would help the UK to move from a 'low wage, high welfare' economy to a 'high wage, low welfare' economy (Osborne, 2015). The National Living Wage was introduced in April 2016 and provides all those over the age of 24 with an hourly minimum wage of £7.20. While this figure represents an increase on the NMW, it is lower than the living wage rate set by the Living Wage Foundation, which was £9.40 for London and £8.25 for the rest of the UK in 2016 (Living Wage Foundation, 2016).

Wider welfare state residualisation and retrenchment

This brief review of key welfare reforms under Cameron's Conservatives would be incomplete without mention of some of the broader measures of reform, which are perhaps best described as representing welfare state residualisation and retrenchment. Chief among these are disability benefit reforms and changes to eligibility rules governing support for children. Regarding disability, the Coalition announced the replacement of Disability Living Allowance (DLA) with Personal Independence Payments (PIPs), with a 20% reduction in total expenditure on PIPs. DLA is a non-means-tested benefit paid in recognition of the extra costs of impairments. It is sometimes awarded for long periods when it is recognised that people's impairments are longstanding and unlikely to change over time. Under PIPs, all existing claimants of DLA have to be reassessed, following a not dissimilar process to the much-troubled WCA.

As part of their pledge to return 'fairness' to the benefits system, the Conservatives also legislated to limit eligibility for child-dependent benefit payments to two children, with this implemented from April 2017 for new claimants. This was justified by the then Chancellor of the Exchequer, George Osborne, on the basis that working families have to make choices about whether they can afford to have more children and it not being 'right' or 'fair' that those on benefits do not have to do the same thing (Osborne, 2015). The reform is significant in marking a decisive break in the 'welfare settlement'. It severs the link between need and entitlement, a link which has already been undermined with the introduction of the Benefits Cap.

At the same time, reforms to social security need to be set alongside broader cuts to local authority budgets and social services, which have seen significant reductions in local services and support. Local authorities in England lost 27% of their spending power in real terms between 2010/11 and 2015/16 (Hastings et al., 2016). High-profile casualties of these cuts have included Sure Start centres, which were introduced by New Labour to provide early-year interventions, childcare and family support. There were 3,633 Sure Start centres operating across England in 2010; by the end of 2015, there were 2,605, a reduction of 39%. Adding to the ways in which austerity has hit the poorest hardest, the most deprived local authorities have seen the biggest cuts to their funding – cuts of £220 per head compared to £40 per head in the least deprived areas (Hastings et al., 2016).

A note on devolution

Measures of welfare retrenchment include reforms to the Social Fund and Council Tax Support, which have also entailed significant devolution of elements of social security support and funding. Social Fund reform has seen the replacement of Crisis Loans and Community Care Grants with a devolved system of Local Welfare Assistance, with each local authority responsible for administering and setting the funding for its own scheme. This has led to significant differences in provision in different parts of the country. Council Tax Support has also been devolved, with a 10% reduction in funding in England and the expectation that the majority of those who previously had no council tax liability should now make at least some contribution. Since then, there have been significant increases in Council Tax arrears in local authorities across the country, with magistrates' courts seeing an unprecedented number of cases of authorities seeking to recover Council Tax arrears (Spurr, 2016).

Particular contrasts can be drawn between how welfare reform is experienced in England and how it is experienced in the devolved administrations of Scotland, Wales and Northern Ireland. Scotland and Wales have both been able to introduce grants-based replacements to the Social Fund, meaning that residents in these countries can receive emergency non-repayable grants for periods of crisis – something often not available to residents of England. Further, both Northern Ireland and Scotland have used funding to protect their residents from the bedroom tax, again creating geographically differentiated experiences of welfare reform. The scope for Scotland, in particular, to create a different social security landscape is particularly marked – especially following the Scotland Act 2015, which further devolved elements of social security policy to the Scottish parliament. At the time of writing, the Scottish government is consulting on its forthcoming Social Security Bill, which will see the government make use of its new powers with a particular focus on seeking to build principles of respect and dignity for all into the legislative framework. There is a need for further research and exploration of how welfare reform is experienced differently in different places and the roles that devolved administrations and local authorities can play in mediating and shaping (and sometimes protecting individuals from) experiences of welfare reform.

'Welfare' policy under May

It will also be critical to closely monitor the ongoing evolution of 'welfare' policy and roll out of further welfare reform under the Conservative government now led by Theresa May. At the time of writing, and just four months into May's premiership, there have been some small but potentially significant changes on 'welfare' policy. In the November 2016 Autumn Statement, Chancellor of the Exchequer, Philip Hammond, reduced the rate at which Universal Credit will be withdrawn as individuals move into work (what is known as the taper). This step is a positive one, but will only slightly reduce the scale of the cuts to UC with which the government is still proceeding. These cuts – announced by George Osborne and retained by May's government – will adversely affect low-income families, and so undermine May's repeated pledge to help those who are 'just-about-managing': the *JAMs*. The government has also announced that it will end the practice whereby those with chronic and life-limiting conditions face repeated Work Capability Assessments, although the detail of who this will affect, and how, is as yet unclear. May's administration will no longer roll out 'Pay to Stay', a policy under which it was proposed that those living in social housing earning above a certain threshold would be charged market rents. Taken together, these modifications to the 'welfare' policy programme of the Conservatives do not appear to amount to an overarching change in direction, and both May and Green have made clear that they will press ahead with the remaining welfare reforms already timetabled by Cameron and Osborne. However, it is as yet too early to tell whether the policy focus on Brexit, and the rhetorical emphasis on supporting the JAMs, will lead to more substantive changes to the political approach taken in the future. May's government may face sustained pressure to alter their policy agenda here, especially as further evidence emerges of the impact of welfare reforms on those groups that May claims to be most wanting to help and support.

Policy impact

As the preceding discussion illustrates, the post–2010 governments presided over a large and ambitious programme of welfare reform, benefit changes and cuts. A central task of this book is to explore the consequences of some of these changes for a small group of benefit claimants living in Leeds. Later chapters highlight the insecurity, anxiety and worry caused by a climate of change and large-scale reworking of benefit entitlement and conditions. They illustrate how those interviewed lived with and responded to changes in their benefits, as well as how individual consequences so often clash with policy makers' narratives and reported policy intent.

These lived experiences can be situated in the wider and growing evidence base about the macro impact of welfare reform, particularly the statistical information available about the contemporary landscape of poverty and insecurity – a landscape in part shaped by changes to our social security system. A small number of headline statistics here are both telling and damning. First, the scale of the cuts to the social security budget. By 2020, Beatty and Fothergill (2016) estimate that the cumulative loss from the welfare reforms from 2010 onwards will be equivalent to £27 billion a year, or £690 per annum for every adult of working age. Second, there has been an exponential rise in food-bank use over recent years. Between April 2015 and March 2016, the Trussell Trust's network of 424 food banks provided 1,109,309 three-day emergency food supplies to people in crisis (Trussell Trust, 2016). This compares with just 25,899 provided in 2008–9, representing a 4,183% increase in just seven years. Conservative politicians repeatedly refuse to accept this rise is linked to benefit reforms and increased use of sanctions. Countering this, researchers and food-bank providers claim they are very clearly linked (Garthwaite, 2016). Third, it has been estimated that 1,252,000 people in the UK are currently destitute, including 312,000 children (Fitzpatrick et al., 2016). Here, destitution is defined as those who cannot afford to buy the essentials to eat, stay warm and dry and keep clean.

Contemporary Britain sees food bank use spiralling, a large number of people living in destitution and a significantly reduced social security budget. These trends point to the extent to which 'austerity' and successive welfare reforms have altered the society in which we all live. The statistical evidence base on the financial impact of welfare reform is still emerging, particularly as many of the reforms are only gradually being implemented and felt. Those analysing welfare reform's impact, such as the Institute for Fiscal Studies and the Child Poverty Action Group (CPAG), repeatedly note the ways in which reforms are regressive, hitting the poorest hardest and pushing up levels of both relative and absolute poverty (CPAG, 2013; Browne and Elming, 2015).

The impact of welfare reform is disproportionately felt, with certain groups – most notably women and disabled people – hardest hit. The Women's Budget Group's gender impact assessment following the 2016 budget found that, cumulatively, 86% of savings in the period from 2010–20 will have come from women's pockets (Women's Budget Group, 2016). Single parents are particularly adversely affected by the cumulative impact of tightening conditionality, withdrawal and reductions in available support and the introduction of UC, which may actually reduce their incentives to work or increase their hours of employment (Gingerbread, 2010b; Millar and Bennett, 2016). Disabled people have also borne the brunt of successive waves of welfare reform, often being simultaneously hit by changes to out-of-work benefit provision, reductions in local authority social care and associated budgets, as well as being affected by broader reforms such as those to Housing Benefit entitlement and the rules governing the social housing sector. Starting with the 2008 ESA reforms and gathering momentum ever since, it has often seemed as if disabled people are 'fair game' as politicians seek to trim the 'welfare' budget and make social security more efficient and better targeted towards those who need it most: the 'genuinely vulnerable'. In this effort, we have seen a significant redrawing of the boundaries between deserving and undeserving populations and the tacit suggestion that many disabled people are perhaps not *really* disabled – or at the very least could be doing more to transition off benefits and into paid employment.

Conclusion

This chapter has provided an overview of the welfare reform policy context, summarising the reforms undertaken by Cameron's governments from 2010 onwards. Emphasis has been placed on the extent of continuity between Cameron and his predecessors, with a clear legacy not only from Thatcher and Major but also from New Labour under Blair and Brown. In examining the contemporary climate – and despite the arrival of Jeremy Corbyn as Leader of the Labour Party – it feels most appropriate to talk of a framing consensus on 'welfare', given the dominance of a 'commonsense' view of 'welfare' and those who rely upon it as necessarily and inevitably problematic. Politicians play a key role in circulating this view, employing stereotypical and demeaning portrayals of claimants in the process. Successive waves of welfare reform are framed as necessary as part of efforts to secure the rewards of paid employment to ever more of the population. These same reforms have cumulatively radically reshaped the social security landscape and extent and nature of benefit entitlement, particularly for working-age adults (Taylor-Gooby, 2012).

Indeed, it is possible to draw a fairly stark contrast between what existed in the 1950s and 1960s as part of any Post-War Welfare Settlement (PWWS) and the considerably more fractured and piecemeal provision that is in place today. Bradshaw (2015) describes a gradual unravelling of the social security safety net, which is now in 'tatters'. Starting with Thatcher and continuing apace, Britain's social security provision has been fundamentally reworked in ways that also rewrite and re-interpret the rights and responsibilities of social citizenship. Under the PWWS, social welfare and the provision of a (comparatively generous) safety net were seen as positive elements of a 'good society' that offered necessary protection to all those who needed it (Timmins, 2001). By contrast, today 'welfare' is increasingly characterised as an obstacle to individuals fulfilling their personal responsibilities as working citizens. The implications of this shift from a 'welfare' to an 'active society' (Walters, 1997) are a central focus of this book. In exploring how this shift has been experienced by those directly affected by welfare reform, it is first important to introduce the individuals interviewed for this book and to explore the ways in which they sought to 'get by' on benefits; the purpose of the next chapter.

Note
[1] This policy was still being rolled out at the time of writing.

THREE

The everyday realities of out-of-work benefits receipt

'I'm 27 years old and live in a one bedroom flat. I am currently receiving Jobseeker's Allowance. I am looking for a full-time job as a means to pay my bills and support myself but my long-term goal is to undergo full training to become a housing support worker.

I have a seven-year-old daughter who comes and stays with me alternate weekends. I don't receive any money for my daughter so most times I find myself going without a meal so she can eat when she's in my care. I find it extremely hard living on benefits and have found myself in some desperate situations, especially since having to pay towards Council Tax.

I don't believe anyone would choose to live on benefits: why would anyone want to suffer and struggle like me? In the future, I look forward to supporting myself and maybe one day being able to go to bed with a full tummy, no stress or worry about money / debt and a smile on my face.' ('James')

As part of this research, some of the participants worked with an animator and myself to create a film about their experiences of welfare reform. This became known as the 'Dole Animators' project. A website was developed to accompany the project (www.doleanimators.org), for which each participant wrote a brief biography that captured their experiences of benefits and hopes for the future.

In his account, reprinted above, James mentions many of the themes explored in this book. He highlights the ways in which being on benefits carries negative associations and requires him to make difficult choices and sacrifices. His narrative explicitly challenges the notion popularised in political accounts of benefits as a lifestyle choice and hints at some of the hardship that welfare reform is causing. He powerfully illustrates the challenges of surviving on benefits while simultaneously hoping for a better future.

Individuals such as James were interviewed on three (sometimes four) occasions, enabling their experiences of out-of-work benefits to be tracked over time and the dynamic interactions between benefits receipt, relationships with paid employment and experiences of welfare reform to be captured. Popular notions of claimants 'languishing on welfare' (Duncan Smith, 2014a) and trapped in a 'cycle of dependency' (Cameron, 2014b) were critically examined and the extent of the (mis)match between these dominant representations and lived realities explored.

This chapter introduces the individuals interviewed: their past lives, everyday realities and imagined futures. The reasons for individuals' out-of-work benefits receipt are discussed first; before a detailed exploration of the day-to-day work that 'getting by' on benefits demands. This is followed by an outline of the various forms of socially valuable contribution in which many were engaged. Finally, the aspirations and orientations to the future of those interviewed are summarised. This chapter begins the work of detailing the 'everyday worlds of citizenship' (Desforges et al., 2005, cited in Lister, 2007, p. 58) of those experiencing out-of-work benefits receipt and welfare reform. A central finding from this chapter is that, for most of those interviewed, their receipt of benefits was unchosen and associated with hard and intensive work – work that characterises the struggle to manage on a low income.

The out-of-work benefit claimants interviewed

Twenty-two people receiving out-of-work benefits were initially interviewed in Leeds in 2011. All were expected to experience welfare reform during the initial research period, which ran from 2011 to 2013. The sample was selected to include single parents, young jobseekers (aged 18–24) and disabled people. From the initial sample, a smaller longitudinal sample of 15 was chosen to follow over time on the basis of those most likely to experience further welfare reform during the period of research. Table 3.1 outlines key characteristics of the sample, which included a diverse range of ages and two minority ethnic participants. The sample included men and women and a range of household types.

Triggers for current benefits receipt

Popular accounts of out-of-work benefits receipt commonly depict a fairly homogenous claimant population by suggesting that individuals

The everyday realities of out-of-work benefits receipt

Table 3.1: Research participants

Pseudonym	Gender	Ethnicity	Age group (at first interview)	Benefit-claiming category	Household composition
Adrian	M	White British	18–24	Young jobseeker	Single person household (SPH)
Amy*	F	White British	25–34	Disability benefit(s) recipient	Living with partner (LwP)
Beckie	F	White British	55–64	Disability benefit(s) recipient	SPH
Cath	F	White British	55–64	Disability benefit(s) recipient	SPH
Chloe	F	White British	25–34	Single parent	Living with children (LwC); two children
Dan	M	Caribbean	35–44	Disability benefit(s) recipient	SPH
Isobella	F	White British	55–64	Disability benefit(s) recipient	SPH
James	M	White British	18–24	Young jobseeker	SPH (with shared custody of child)
JD	M	White British	45–54	Disability benefit(s) recipient	SPH
Jim	M	White British	25–34	Disability benefit(s) recipient	LwP
Jessica	F	White British	35–44	Disability benefit(s) recipient	SPH
Josh	M	White British	18–24	Young jobseeker	SPH
Kane	M	White British	25–34	Disability benefit(s) recipient	SPH
Karen	F	White British	25–34	Single parent	LwC; one child
Robert	M	White British	18–24	Young jobseeker	SPH
Rosie	F	White British	25–34	Single parent	LwC; one child
Sam	F	White British	18–24	Young jobseeker	SPH
Sharon	F	White British	18–24	Disability benefit(s) recipient	LwC; one child
Sophie	F	White British	35–44	Single parent	LwC; three children
Susan	F	African	45–54	Single parent	LwC; one child
Terri	F	White British	35–44	Disability benefit(s) recipient	SPH
Tessa	F	White British	35–44	Disability benefit(s) recipient	LwP

*Those in italics were only interviewed once

'choose' benefits over alternative, more responsible 'choices' – principally engagement in the formal labour market (cf. Osborne, 2010; Cameron, 2015a). The structural reasons why people might make a benefit claim are underplayed in this analysis. Undermining such accounts, the individuals interviewed described their receipt of benefits as unchosen and unwelcome, but inevitable and necessary. 'Isobella' had been enjoying paid work when she suddenly became ill:

> 'Six months after I had retrained and got myself a small business running [as an aromatherapist] ... and I was really looking forward and enjoying what I was doing, when I started having a lot of problems with hands and feet, and I was diagnosed with rheumatoid arthritis which was a bugger because it meant that everything had to stop. (W1[1])

For those receiving benefits as a result of the sudden onset or worsening of illness, their ill health had been a 'turning point' (George, 2009) that had multiple – mainly negative – repercussions on their lives.

Of the five single parents, only one described the birth of their most recent child as the trigger for their current benefits receipt. Three of the single parents were claiming benefits due to losing a job and one due to relationship breakdown following domestic violence. Of the five jobseekers within the sample, three claimed benefits after losing a job, while two had never been in employment. Many described their benefits receipt as an aspect of not only their current lives but also their longer life histories, with ten of the sample having been on out-of-work benefits for more than five years. Of those who had been on benefits for more than three years, a significant majority (11 of 17) were on disability-related benefits.

Individuals' past biographies often featured difficult histories and traumatic life events, many of which continued to impact upon their current lives and imagined futures. Such experiences included homelessness, living in care, alcohol and substance abuse, sex work, domestic and sexual abuse, prison/crime and having children adopted. Difficult pasts affected individuals' abilities to live in the present, and impacted negatively upon their mental health. Cath had experienced physical and sexual abuse in childhood:

> 'They tell you it's post-traumatic stress ... I'm thinking, isn't it amazing how you can go through your life, you know it's happened to you 'cause you were there, but you don't feel anything and then when you're 50, it comes up, kicks you up the bum, and renders you a shrivelled-up mess.' (W1)

Experiences of homelessness and of multiple temporary addresses were very common and often caused particular distress. 'Sophie', a single parent with three young children, had just moved into a stable home having previously lived at 33 addresses in three years. James had recently experienced street homelessness:

> '[I was] living on the streets, staying at friends' houses, going to [hostels] just here, there and everywhere. Completely unstable. It were horrible.' (W1)

Overall, many of the participants' past lives could be characterised as difficult and complex, with these histories shaping and constraining their present lives and their capacity to manage and cope on a day-to-day basis.

Applying for and claiming benefits

All of those interviewed were receiving either Income Support (IS), Jobseeker's Allowance (JSA), Employment and Support Allowance (ESA) or Incapacity Benefit (IB) at the time of their first interview. The rates of these benefits in 2011 are shown in Table 3.2. Of course, many individuals also received Housing Benefit, Child Benefit, Child Tax Credits and Working Tax Credits, while some received Disability Living Allowance (DLA) and/or Carers Allowance.

As Table 3.2 shows, young people received particularly low rates of benefits; the young jobseekers interviewed detailed their struggle to manage on just £53.45 a week. Many actually received less due to having deductions taken from their benefits for Social Fund loans, rent arrears, utility debts and/or criminal fines.

To claim JSA, IS or ESA, individuals first had to either telephone Job Centre Plus (JCP) or apply online. It was not routinely possible to make a claim by simply walking into a local JCP. Individuals recounted difficulties in making initial claims, as well as in getting through to the

Table 3.2: Benefit rates

Benefit	Weekly rate (2011/12)
JSA and IS (under 25)	£53.45
JSA and IS (25+)	£67.50
ESA (Work-Related Activity Group)	£94.25
ESA (Support Group)	£99.85
IB	From £71.10 to c.£100.00, depending on whether claiming short or long term and high or low rate

appropriate departments by telephone and obtaining advice that was accessible and relevant:

> 'I don't know if I'm coming or going sometimes 'cause you phone this number then they want you to phone this number. Then phone this number … they do make it a lot harder. Before, you used to go down [to the Job Centre] if you had a problem, 'owt like that, go down to the office. Now you've got to phone up, sit on the phone all day and wait for appointments to go down.' (Sophie, W1)

Those on JSA had regular signing-in appointments at their local JCP – most often fortnightly – while those on ESA, IS and IB had much less frequent in-person contact. Indeed, some spoke of never having to go into a JCP; this was particularly common for those on IB and single parents who had not yet been migrated from IS and onto JSA (see Chapter Four). Individuals did not find the JCP to be a welcoming environment (see Chapter Six) and often felt that benefit officials were reluctant to help them navigate what they experienced as a complicated and confusing system:

Ruth: 'How easy do you find the benefits system to understand?'
Cath: 'Hard, they don't make it easy. They ask you lots of questions, the same questions but in different ways … And when you tell them that you don't understand, they're not really that helpful. They're like "I understand it so why shouldn't you". They're ignorant, they don't care.' (W1)

Benefits and poverty

Many of those interviewed were both relatively and absolutely poor. Measuring absolute poverty involves setting a rate of income that is required to purchase a basic package of goods and services, and below which an individual can be said to be in absolute poverty. The absolute poverty line changes with inflation as people will need less or more to buy the same basic basket of items, but it does not change as society becomes more or less prosperous. By contrast, relative poverty instead focuses attention on people's standard of living *relative* to society as a whole. As Peter Townsend, who pioneered a relative approach, put it, an individual is in relative poverty when their 'resources are so seriously below those commanded by the average individual or family that they are, in effect, excluded from ordinary living patterns, customs and activities' (1979, p. 31). Over recent years, there has been much debate about the best way of measuring poverty, with the Conservatives traditionally reluctant to accept relative measures of poverty. Indeed, a key element of David Cameron's supposed shift towards a more compassionate conservatism was his acceptance in 2006 of the need to measure and act on relative poverty (Cameron, 2006).

Poverty is best conceptualised as a dynamic state (Walker and Leisering, 1998); people move in and out of poverty, often repeatedly, variously experiencing persistent, transient or recurrent poverty (Smith and Middleton, 2007). Of those interviewed, the majority (14 of the 22) were living in 'persistent poverty' (Smith and Middleton, 2007) and could be described as either 'recurrently poor' or 'permanently poor' (Shildrick, 2012). Even those who did leave benefits and found employment in the course of the study were unable to escape poverty (see Chapter Four). Following people over time illustrated the debilitating cumulative effects of experiencing persistent poverty, as well as the ways in which poverty continued even where people did manage to secure employment (see chapters four and seven) (Alcock, 2006). In noting the 'democratisation' and 'temporalisation' of poverty, Beck (1992) argues that poverty is a phase in someone's life rather than a permanent state or something affecting a separate class of people. Yet for those interviewed, poverty had the characteristics of a semi-permanent state, albeit one they still hoped to escape in the future. Those who had experienced persistent poverty repeatedly highlighted the bleak reality they faced:

> 'You only get so much money a month just to live on and once you've paid for your bills and your food and bus fares and stuff you haven't got much money to live on. I don't ever go out ... I just stay at home on my own.' ('Karen', W1)

> 'Disgusting. I hate it. Scrimping and saving. It's horrible.' (Sophie, W2)

Most explained how the receipt of out-of-work benefits demanded creative efforts to manage with very limited financial resources. It is critical to explore what this managing involves and requires of individuals, as well as to consider how far this fits with dominant narratives of out-of-work claimants passively 'sitting on their sofas waiting for their benefit cheques to arrive' (Cameron, 2010b).

A note on agency

When we direct analytical attention to how individuals live with and respond to their benefits receipt, we are inevitably grappling with questions of agency and subjectivity – and how this agency is itself shaped and constrained by broader structural forces and pressures. Of particular relevance here is Lister's (2004, 2015) work on the agency of those living in poverty. Lister develops a typology that shows the everyday and strategic agency of those living in poverty. She draws a distinction between what she describes as the 'everyday' activities that managing in poverty entail and those that are more 'strategic' (such as deciding whether to accept an offer of paid employment). Everyday activities include 'getting by' in poverty (seeking to manage and cope on a limited income) and 'getting (back) at' poverty. The latter can include everyday forms of resistance such as engagement in informal work and other methods of resisting and challenging dominant portrayals of poverty and benefits receipt. More strategic expressions of individual agency include 'getting out' of poverty (commonly, though not exclusively, through engagement in paid employment) and 'getting organised' (taking collective action to challenge the position of those living in poverty). Through this typology, Lister also distinguishes between personal expressions of agency and more political expressions that hint at a form of citizenship engagement, such as organising to challenge the circumstances of living in poverty (Lister, 2004). While focused on poverty in general, Lister's typology can be applied to the experiences of out-of-work benefits receipt in particular; a change in focus that does not necessitate any change to the four quadrants (see Figure 3.1).

Figure 3.1: Lister's (2004) typology of agency, applied to out-of-work benefit claimants

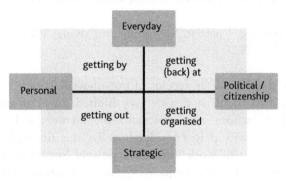

'Getting by' on benefits

A dominant theme for those interviewed was the work and efforts involved in 'coping' with the conditions of poverty (Leisering and Leibfried, 1999) – what Lister (2004) describes as 'getting by'. Managing on benefits frequently entailed hard choices, as available money was insufficient to purchase everything an individual and/or their household required. Cath had to take a break from paying her gas and electricity bills for a fortnight when she needed new underwear (W2), while James explained:

> 'It's scary because obviously there's so much to do and you haven't got a right lot of money to do it with, so you've got to prioritise what comes first. Then sometimes it can be them shoes on her feet can last another weekend but that food in the kitchen won't, so the food comes before the shoes, you know what I mean?' (W1)

Hard choices were linked to what Karen called "constantly juggling" (W2): a never-ending battle to stretch limited funds to meet basic needs and having to choose between competing necessities. Closely connected to this was simply doing without, particularly so that children could have what they needed. Two of the single mothers spoke of foregoing meals so that their children would have enough to eat while others described having to do without basic items such as a washing machine or proper heating:

> 'I go without my meals sometimes. I have to save meals for me kids. So I'll have, like a slice of toast and they'll have a full meal. And if they don't eat something, if they haven't picked at it, I'll eat theirs.' ('Chloe', W3)

> '[When my money runs out] I have tea with sour milk and I do eat bread that's mouldy. But it's only like for two days before I get paid so I'm all right.' (Cath, W1)

Having to make hard, even unhealthy, choices and budgetary sacrifices – or simply going without – are recurrent themes both in this research and in other studies of people living in poverty (Lister, 2004; Shildrick and MacDonald, 2013; Hickman et al., 2014; Lister et al., 2014; Pemberton et al., 2014; Hill et al., 2016).

Food poverty was a common issue; several participants had relied on food banks in the past, a finding that chimes with research showing the growing reliance on food banks across Britain (Garthwaite, 2016). Fuel poverty was also frequently evident, with individuals trying to keep their fuel bills as low as possible:

> 'I had swine flu over Christmas and New Year so I was on the sofa under the blankets. I didn't have the heating on most of the time. I just couldn't. I was scared.' (Cath, W1).

There was a clear relationship between the struggle to get by (and the difficult choices that entailed) and a resultant exclusion, whereby individuals felt unable or unwilling to participate in everyday social activities due to their poverty and relative lack of income. As the Child Poverty Action Group (CPAG) argues: 'at its heart, poverty is about exclusion from social participation' (2001, p. 29). Chloe (W2) felt unable to answer her landline telephone because she was fearful that any phone call would be a demand for a debt that she was unable to settle. Cath (W2) had stopped going on daytrips organised by her housing association as she had to bring a packed lunch to save money and this left her feeling excluded, given that the other tenants ate in cafes. She also chose not to attend various support groups as she found the cost of a coffee in the cafes and museums where they met prohibitive:

> 'I know I bang on about money but, with meeting in a place where a cup of tea's £1.75, I want a hundred tea bags and 2 pints of milk for that.' (W1)

Evidence of the exclusion of people living in poverty from many of the day-to-day activities and practices that most of the population takes for granted illustrates how those in poverty experience citizenship exclusion (Lister, 2004; Dwyer, 2010).

While all of those interviewed described getting by on benefits as a struggle, those who were on disability benefits – particularly those who received DLA – were the most likely to say that they could just about manage. 'Jim' explained how "lucky" he felt to receive ESA, DLA and Carers' Allowance:

> 'I think I get enough [on benefits] to do the things I need to do to maintain wellness. That's why it's a problem when there's any question on my benefits.' (W1)

The extra income from DLA often gave individuals a (very small but sometimes vital) financial cushion, particularly when contrasted with the efforts of those trying to get by on JSA, IS or ESA alone. This finding is pertinent, given the ongoing migration of DLA claimants onto Personal Independence Payments (PIPs), with an allied goal of cutting expenditure on PIPs by 20%. This reform could have particularly adverse consequences for those who have previously received DLA but are judged ineligible for PIPs and so see their income fall.

Given the difficulty that so many faced to afford even necessities, it is unsurprising that they routinely recounted going without what they described as "luxuries". This ranged from the aspiration of many to one day go on holiday to more modest "luxuries", such as being able to buy the food they wanted or take their children swimming:

> 'You're not able to buy a loaf of Warburtons. You've got to get a cheap loaf of bread. You can't afford to get 'owt nice or luxury – you haven't got a choice.' (James, W1)

> 'I can't ever go and do a nice [supermarket] shop where I feel comfortable putting stuff in the trolley – I'm always watching what I'm putting in, do you know counting it up in my head. I wish I could just go and do a nice shop.' ('Rosie', W1).

> 'My kids have never had a holiday. Never.' (Sophie, W1)

Individuals frequently mentioned being unable to afford to go on holiday. The absence of holidays is a signifier of what living in financial hardship entails and how it impacts upon and constrains family life (Shildrick and MacDonald, 2013). Having to go without – and not being able to give children the things they wanted, expected and often needed – were causes of guilt for the parents interviewed, reinforcing the findings of other research into the experiences of parents living in poverty (Ridge, 2009).

There is a wide literature on the gendered experiences of poverty (Ridge, 2009; Bennett and Daly, 2014), which details how women are both more vulnerable to persistent poverty and most likely to have to take the lead in managing household expenses. Women living in poverty are at particular risk from the stress and worry this financial management can entail, as well as being disproportionately affected by the adverse consequences of going without when putting their children's needs first. These processes were notable among the single mothers in the study. They were also marked in James' narrative – the only man to be interviewed who had parental responsibilities. In his biographical account that opened this chapter, we have already seen how James described "going without" so that his daughter could have what she needed. He also explained how he tried to protect his daughter from the consequences of his poverty:

'I like to have £10 or something … so if we're going to the park or whatever and she says: "Dad, can I get an ice cream?", I can say: "yes, you can love". … Just nice little things. 'Cause I don't like to tell her no. And it's not her fault why I'm in this predicament and she didn't ask to be here. I brought her here so it's my responsibility to look after her, whether … I've got it or not.' (W1)

Not being able to treat his daughter affected how James felt about himself:

'It makes me feel down as shit, it's horrible.' (W3)

James emphasised his responsibilities as a parent and how his poverty undermined his ability to fulfil these responsibilities. Rosie echoed this:

'[My son] has been asking me for the past three days if we can go swimming. And I can't even afford to go swimming with him … It's getting the bus, he'll probably want a chocolate bar … It's hard. I know sometimes it's only a fiver to go but it's not. It's bus fare and other stuff. It's just expensive, even just to go swimming. Even just to go to the park, it's a bus. Everything seems to be about money. The responsibility that he gets fed, he gets washed, he gets clothed, you know, that's all there. … But the stuff that I'd like to do with him, there's a big stop on it and that upsets me sometimes.' (W1)

Poverty made it difficult for Sophie to afford fresh food for her children:

'They go on about children that are obese … Well, the bit of benefits that you do get once you've paid out on your bills and that lot you might have 40 quid left. What else do you buy? You can't go and buy all fresh stuff and meat and stuff like that. It is more freezer stuff than 'owt, to last you.' (W1)

The public health agenda has focused considerable attention on the problem of child obesity and called for individual behavioural change. In so doing, it has sometimes mirrored the individualising narrative of the 'welfare' 'problem'. Sophie's account illustrates how poverty and benefits receipt can make healthy eating difficult, as well as leaving individuals feeling unable to meet what they see as their responsibilities to their own children.

The work involved in 'getting by'

The work involved in managing on benefits was often time intensive, including activities such as hand washing clothes, collecting and selling scrap in an attempt to make a few pounds and going to several shops to try to pay the lowest price possible for day-to-day essentials. Cath spoke about going to a number of shops in her effort to get the best deal, as well as shopping almost daily in order to take advantage of supermarkets' reduced shelves of food fast approaching its use-by date. As well as being time intensive, getting by often required considerable ingenuity in trying to find creative solutions to make limited financial resources last as long as possible. Examples included parents asking friends to have their children over for tea when the money had run out and using electric blankets rather than heating bedrooms. Some reported resorting to crime, most commonly shoplifting for basic essentials when these could not be bought with existing funds:

'A few week ago I only had six or eight pounds ... I were in Asda just getting a couple of bits for the weekend for when [daughter] come, and I spoke to her on the phone and she said "dad, oh will you get me some cheese?" But cheese is like, it can be like £2 a block and that, so I pinched it because I thought she wanted it but I couldn't afford to buy it. Imagine going to prison for a block of cheese? It would be stupid, wouldn't it [laughs].' (James, W1)

'This is going to sound really bad but sometimes, for my kids' clothes or even for myself, I actually steal them and I got caught a few week ago stealing but that's the only way I can see to get the things ... I want for my kids. And that's just general things like – because they grow too quick – or like [son] now his shoes are talking to him but I can't afford to buy him no shoes until I get my big money in another two weeks. It's embarrassing when you have to steal to get the things that you need because you haven't got enough money because you need your shopping and your gas and your electric.' (Chloe, W1)

There has been a rise in reporting and concern about 'survival crime' (Dwyer and Bright, 2016; Fitzpatrick et al., 2016), which is how the shoplifting activities of James and Chloe are best described.

The active work involved in getting by on benefits is a pertinent challenge to notions of the inactive out-of-work benefits claimant and a clear example of the mismatch between citizenship from above and below. At the same time, it is important to acknowledge that individuals did sometimes describe their benefits receipt and daily lives in terms of inactivity and even boredom:

'I'm bored at the minute … when I'm sat about I seem to drink more … and it's running my bills up and stuff just sat in the house. It's sheer boredom, just sat about, doing nowt.' (James, W2)

Chloe captured the dualism between boredom and hard work, which she saw as characterising her own benefits reliance:

'It's boring staying at home all the time but it's also hard work.' (W1)

The common association between benefits receipt, poverty and boredom is perhaps best understood as one of the negative psychological effects of poverty, which can also include anxiety, depression and a feeling of powerlessness (Beresford et al., 1999). The dominant narrative narrowly focuses on the boredom – and occasional inactivity – that can characterise benefits receipt, mobilising these to support a 'welfare dependency' thesis. Simultaneously, this narrative neglects the other aspects of day-to-day realities that fit less well with the policy agenda; for example, the work that getting by on benefits involves.

Debt and financial exclusion

Getting by on benefits almost inevitably entails an acceptance of some degree of debt (Macmillan, 2003; Harrison, 2013; Walker et al., 2013;

Hickman et al., 2014). Experiences of debt were common among participants, whose finances fluctuated over a very short timeframe or cycle, almost always directly tied to the dates of benefit payment(s). Individuals would frequently speak of "pay day" – when they received their benefit money – as the time to immediately settle all key outgoings before the money ran out:

> 'My money – as soon as it's come in – I've got three 20-pound notes … that's all it is … Gas and electric, bills, food, that's it, it's gone. And then I don't get paid for another week.' (Rosie, W1)

There are particular financial penalties attached to living in poverty, sometimes described as the 'poverty premium' (Schmuecker, 2013). These include the higher energy costs associated with prepayment meters, difficulties accessing affordable credit and short-term budgeting making it difficult to bulk-buy groceries to save money. The 'poverty premium' makes the struggle to get by even harder and stretches already tight finances even further.

Chloe became trapped in a cycle of debt:

> 'When I get paid, that's it, my money's gone. And then I have to start borrowing again for other things that I need. It's hard … When I first moved in I weren't on a [gas] meter, and so I got a bill through and I couldn't afford to pay it. So now they've put me a [prepayment] meter in and they're taking a lot of money off me [to repay debt]. And when I put a tenner in they give me like £2 gas. I don't get no emergency and they take the rest off. So, I'm forever putting money on gas and I need that for my cooking.' (W1)

Small changes could have a very significant impact on individuals. For Cath, a free bus pass significantly improved her life, meaning she could now make healthcare appointments she previously could not afford to attend. She said the bus pass was the "biggest gift ever" (W1). Any unplanned-for additional expenditure could also have serious consequences, potentially tipping individuals and their families into further debt and financial difficulty. The precariousness of individuals' financial situations contributed to a pervasive sense of insecurity and an ever-present worry about how they would cope with unanticipated and unplanned financial demands. Budgeting and managing small sums of money in the immediate term was time-intensive, emotionally draining and often distressing.

Research shows that low-income families actually tend to do better than wealthier families at budgeting and that the debt problems of those on the lowest incomes are rarely the result of 'bad' financial management or a deficit in individual financial capability (Financial Services Authority, 2006; Ben-Galim and Lanning, 2010). Nonetheless, there remains a persistent sense of failure associated with debt and borrowing. Individuals certainly did not seem to derive pride from their ability to manage on very small sums of money; rather, they often talked about their debts as symptomatic of their being "bad with money" (Rosie, W1).

Informal chains of borrowing and lending

Family and friends commonly played vital roles in informal lending and borrowing; if anything, this was more widespread than reliance on formal forms of credit. A number of individuals spoke of borrowing money from their family very frequently (some daily, many weekly or fortnightly):

> 'It's "dad, can you lend me, can you lend me, can you lend me?" [laughs] all the time.' (Chloe, W1)

While these sources of financial support were commonly appreciated, they were often a source of embarrassment and shame, reinforcing the findings of other research (Lister et al., 2014; Fitzpatrick et al., 2016). Hall and Perry (2013) describe the 'relationship premium' of necessary borrowing from friends and family, which centres on the additional relational strain that these chains of borrowing and lending can cause. 'Sharon' experienced this 'relationship premium':

> 'I were [borrowing] ... money off people and stuff like that and it just got really degrading. One time I had to ask my little brother and ... I was so embarrassed to ask him. I had no other way.' (W1)

Borrowing money from her ex-partner left Karen feeling worse about her own parenting abilities, suggesting that the relationship premium can extend to not only those from whom one has to borrow, but also those for whom one is caring:

'It feels like I'm not a good mum 'cause I can't provide for him.' (W2)

James and Sophie had learned to manage their budgets by loaning out some of their benefit payment to friends who were also receiving benefits. As James explained:

'I get paid, I like to [lend] to people that get paid the following week. It's like saving, keep safe ... I try to [lend] out every pay ... If I [lend] it, I know that they won't get paid till the week after so if I want it back they 'aven't got it.' (W2)

In this way, James was able to 'bank' some of his benefit money with a friend in an effort to manage his very limited funds. He felt that if he kept all his money he would not be able to stop himself from spending it, so the informal lending arrangement was a way of self-regulating his behaviour in an effort to get by.

Resilience

The literature on poverty and social exclusion has frequently explored people's capacity for 'resilience' in the face of the everyday struggles that inevitably accompany reliance on benefits for all or most of one's income (Lister, 2004; Aylott et al., 2012; Harrison, 2013). Resilience is commonly understood as 'the capability to "bounce back" from adversity' (Harrison, 2013, p. 98). This research found that high levels of resilience were built upon a variety of skills, knowledge and experiences that helped individuals navigate their lives. These skills – including close financial budgeting, managing relationships with benefit officials and developing and utilising informal networks and chains of support – were rarely sources of pride or esteem. This is perhaps unsurprising given that the activities associated with benefits receipt are now arguably too heavily laden with negative connotations linked to the ongoing stigmatisation of those on out-of-work benefits (see chapters one and six).

Cath attributed her own resilience to having always had to manage without:

'I'm all right. I'm still here ... once you've had nothing if there comes a time when you've got nothing again, I think you can handle it better. But if you're brought up with everything, and then you end up with nothing, I think it's harder for them people to handle.' (W1)

The resilience that people sometimes displayed was often combined with both an acceptance that life on benefits was difficult and an associated sense of powerlessness:

'We are finding it [managing on benefits] hard. It's not easy ... we have ... to persevere don't [we], take it one day at a time ... Sometimes we look at [being on benefits] and be judgemental and sometimes we look at it and think ahh ... It's something, we have to take the hard time with the good ... It could be better, it could be worse.' ('Dan', W1)

'You just have to live with it. You know there's nothing you can do. You just have to carry on.' ('Susan', W2)

Dan and Susan's acceptance of their lot might perhaps be interpreted as a passive reliance on benefits, but it was in fact accompanied by continued efforts to get off benefits. In his interview, Dan spoke of previous efforts to secure employment, while Susan spent the whole of the initial research period trying to find work despite repeated setbacks and the challenge of trying to combine her parenting responsibilities with work-search activities (see Chapter Four).

Alcock (2006) has suggested that people's experiences of poverty may change over the time in which they experience it. In considering the differing levels of resilience evident within the sample, it was notable that those who had been on benefits the longest had the most developed and routinised strategies for getting by, while those who had spent less time on benefits were still navigating how best to manage on a low income. This is not to say that the strategies employed were always effective or likely to improve individuals' prospects in the long term. However, they were mechanisms that enabled individuals to get from one day to the next, which was often the only time frame on which they could concentrate given the severity of the challenges and financial insecurity they faced.

'Amy', who had been on benefits for 14 years, explained how she and her husband were trying to manage while they waited for a benefit change to be processed. They had been left with £12 to last them 11 days:

'We can get like a bag of sausages for £1, just like 20 sausages which will be like five meals between us because we've got till ... a week on Wednesday to survive till Steven gets his DLA ... We've got one food parcel [which had] a bag of pasta, some soup, some beans, some hot dogs, we already had a tin of new potatoes in the cupboard. And a little bit of pasta and things ... We've managed ... We've had to sell our brand new TV, we've had to move that one [little TV] out of the bedroom into here, sell our brand-new widescreen TV. We'll do it on buyback at Cash Converters and our PlayStation and PlayStation games and everything. And tomorrow we might have to [pawn our] mobile phone and other stuff.' (W1)

By contrast, 'Josh' – who was much younger and had been on benefits for three years – seemed less confident in knowing how to manage on a very small income:

'Since I've been living here I've just racked up debts and debts and debts. I mean it got to about £1,000, £2,000, and being on benefits is kind of difficult, being able to pay for everything.' (W1)

Getting by entails hard choices, constant juggling and simply having to go without (Lister, 2004). It creates daily demands that make planning for the future much more difficult, as people in poverty so often have to operate within very short timeframes. This research demonstrates the agency, ingenuity and domestic management work required in order to live on a low income (Ridge, 2009; Batty and Flint, 2010; Flint, 2010). Further, this research has also been able to track engagement in this work over time and the toll that getting by while living in persistent poverty takes. It documents some evidence of an erosion of the capacity to sustain resilience as individuals face repeated changes to their benefits and linked reductions in their income, living standards and sense of security (see Chapter Seven).

Although it is important to recognise that getting by entails agency, it is crucial not to romanticise this agency, particularly given the strain that the 'work' of managing involves (Harrison, 2013). Not everyone has the capacity for the same degree of resilience; there is a risk that, in foregrounding the resilience of some, we tacitly judge and even blame those who do not show the same tenacity and resourcefulness (Harrison, 2013). There is an allied danger that, by focusing on individuals' agency as they demonstrate resilience in the face of adversity, we overemphasise the individual to the neglect of the structural factors that constrain – and often cause – the living circumstances that demand such a resilient response (Harrison, 2013). Highlighting evidence of resilience is important as it serves as a rebuttal of dominant politicised accounts of benefits reliance. But, at the same time, it is also critical to detail the broader structural conditions and challenges that face individuals struggling to manage on out-of-work benefits.

Not working but still contributing

The work that getting by on benefits entails is a pertinent counter to the dominant characterisation of out-of-work benefit claimants as inactive and passive. Exploring the various forms of socially valuable contribution in which many individuals were engaged further undermines this characterisation. While none were in paid employment at the time of their first interviews, they were often active as volunteers, carers, parents and givers of informal forms of support.

'Adrian' volunteered between five and seven days a week at a local homeless persons' hostel:

> 'I proper love it [volunteering]. You feel satisfaction as well if someone's coming in really hungry. Give them some food, at least they've eaten for the night.' (W1)

Although individuals often attached value to their volunteering work, they also often felt it went unvalued and unrecognised by wider society. In her efforts to find work, Susan started volunteering at a church listening service, as she was keen to get experience as a counsellor:

> '[I'm] happy that I'm helping someone ... [but] it's not even that I get my transport costs or nothing ... My time, it should be valued more.' (W2)

Care work, particularly looking after family members, was also a common experience. Within the sample, seven were engaged in care work. Jim, who himself had serious mental health issues, spoke about caring for his partner and brother, who both also had mental health issues:

'That's [caring's] all I do. I don't get any time apart from it, you know.' (W1)

'Beckie' described the daily work that caring for her adult daughter involved:

'I keep in touch with her on a daily basis; make sure that she's all right. Make sure she's had a bath and eaten ... I have to carry her more or less.' (W1)

This care work was rarely described as a source of self-esteem, but instead simply a component of their everyday lives, which often entailed substantial work but was rarely conceptualised as such. The fact that individuals did not speak of their care work in these terms is perhaps connected to the extent to which it is rarely recognised or prioritised in government and media discourses.

Latest estimates suggest that 1.2 million carers are living in poverty (Aldridge and Hughes, 2016). The carers at highest risk of poverty are those who live with the people for whom they care and who spend long hours caring, as was the case for Jim. Research shows the financial value of the informal care and support provided in England – estimated at £55 billion in 2011 (National Audit Office, 2014a) – but this vital care work all too often goes unvalued and even unseen.

In contrast to how individuals characterised their care work, it was common for parenting of children to be described as a source of self-esteem, coinciding with findings from other studies (Batty and Flint, 2010; Duncan and Edwards, 1999):

'Like my mum and dad, I know that they are so proud of [son] because of how I've brought him up, and that's a buzz to me is that.' (Rosie, W2)

'I think I was put on this earth just to be a mum. I think I were. That's probably the only job I'm good at.' (Chloe, W1)

While the single parents interviewed attached value to their parenting roles, they said that this work went unvalued by wider society and often felt stigmatised (see Chapter Six). This was often a source of anger but it did not stop them from seeking to prioritise their parenting activities, often in the face of opposition and obstruction from agencies associated with the welfare state (see Chapter Five).

Individuals also provided informal support to friends, family and neighbours, again often reported as simply part of everyday life. Examples included helping decorate friends' homes, raising money to support local food banks and informal assistance with childcare. Sophie helped out with childcare for friends:

'If they [friends] need help, then obviously I'm there. So like my friend up the road, she's been poorly so I've been watching her son.' (W3)

Many also described receiving informal support, which often made a decisive difference in their everyday struggle to keep afloat, particularly during times of crisis. Neighbours supported 'JD' when his wife suddenly died:

'If it weren't for them, I don't know what the hell I would have done ... They were feeding me [points to one neighbour], and they were feeding me [point to other neighbour].' (W1)

Sophie frequently washed her clothes at a neighbour's house to save the expense of using a launderette. She felt guilty about relying on her neighbour in this way:

'You can't keep putting it on her because she's on benefits, same as me. You know, it's gas, electric and that lot so ... I'm like "do us that bag and I'll give you a fiver or something", and she's happy with that so that's all right, but you can't keep putting on your neighbours. It's hard.' (W1)

Such informal chains and networks of support in which individuals are both givers and recipients of 'mutual aid' (Oxfam, 2010) are indicative of the 'bonding social capital' of families and friends (Forrest and Kearns, 2001, cited in Shildrick and MacDonald, 2013) on which they could draw. Mutual aid work is more common in low-income communities than in more affluent communities (Williams, 2005); this research found a relative abundance of these forms of unpaid yet critically important exchanges. These exchanges are arguably now more vital than ever, given the ongoing impact of welfare reforms and consequent growing reliance on community networks (Kuper, 2014). It remains to be seen, however, whether the provision of such informal support in low-income communities will itself be threatened due to the increased pressures that welfare reform places on affected households (see Chapter Five).

Political (dis)engagement

While individuals were often active in their local communities as volunteers and neighbours, there were very few signs of formal political participation and engagement. Nine members of the longitudinal sample were not registered to vote: a finding that reflects the nationally low rates of formal political participation among those living in poverty (The Electoral Commission, 2005; Flinders, 2014). When describing why they did not vote, individuals frequently mentioned that they saw it as a pointless action that had no capacity to engineer positive change:

> 'I don't even vote. I don't think it's worth it.' (Chloe, W1)

> 'Whoever I vote for, the country's going to the dogs anyway, so I don't bother.' ('Sam', W3)

Individuals regarded politicians' lives as far removed from the everyday lived experiences of struggling to get by on benefits – a criticism those living in poverty commonly level at politicians (Perry et al., 2014, Roberts and Price, 2014):

> '[Politicians] haven't got a clue how people live. I don't know what planet they're on.' (Isobella, W2)

Responding to a quote from David Cameron about the need to change the benefits system, Cath suggested:

> 'Tell him "walk a year in my shoes" and then we'll talk about this statement that you've just made.' (W1)

Widespread distrust and dislike for politicians was evident:

> 'I don't have any faith in any of them [politicians] because they're all alike. They say this, that and the other to get in and when it comes to the stick and lift, they don't deliver what they say.' ('Terri', W1)

Individuals spoke of being marginalised from the political process while also feeling that their views and opinions were neither valued nor sought by officials and decision makers, reflecting the extent of their exclusion from mainstream political engagement. When asked whether there had been a time in the past two years when someone at the DWP or JCP or another official had been interested in their views on an issue, not a single individual said "yes", illustrating the extent of this disenfranchisement. It was common to greet this question with laughter, as if the very idea of officials being interested in their views was comical. Susan laughed when asked this, responding:

> 'I haven't even tried because I'd probably think, hmm, who cares?' (W3)

The disenfranchisement these individuals experienced is symptomatic of the degree of citizenship exclusion of those on benefits and living in poverty and reinforces the ways in which political citizenship rights can be undermined when individuals have weaker social rights.

Aspirations and imagined futures

Popular notions of benefit claimants as a culturally distinct and separate underclass often suggest that those living in poverty also have a poverty of aspiration, which is tied to their dependence on 'welfare' and passive acceptance of their lot (cf. Murray, 1984; Mead, 2010). Having outlined individuals' past lives and difficult presents, it is important to explore their imagined futures and aspirations. Strikingly, most of the sample (15 of the 22) listed getting off benefits as their primary hope for the future:

> 'My aim or my plan is not to be on benefits in a year's time.' (Susan, W1)

> '[My hope for the future is] to get a decent job, that's well provided for.' ('Robert', W1)

The centrality of the aspiration to move off benefits and into employment was reflective of the importance placed on paid employment and the values individuals attached to it (see Chapter Four). Several emphasised their wish to leave benefits permanently, reflecting their previous negative experiences of transitioning on and off benefits through a low-pay, no-pay cycle:

'Hopefully … I might get a full-time job and stick at it. Then not be on benefits ever again.' (Amy, W1)

A notable and recurrent feature of participants' aspirations was a desire to be "normal" (James, W3) and to lead a "normal life" (Chloe, W1):

'Getting up, going to work, coming home and having me tea and a shower and watching telly. I know it sounds sad, but just a little life like that'd be lovely. Have a bit of money in bank where I don't have to worry about things. "Yeah, all right, we'll get a takeaway this weekend' or "yeah, go and get them shoes that you want".' (James, W3)

'[In the future] I'd like a nice house; I'd like stability, money and just a nice house, that's really all I want.' (Chloe, W1)

As well as these aspirations, individuals frequently expressed a desire for a future life that was secure, stable and without worries – characteristics they often felt to be missing from their present lives. Individuals imagined a future that might include "a stable routine" (Chloe, W3), "a nice life … Peaceful, no stress like this" (Adrian, W1) or "being financially stable" (Rosie, W1). As Kempson (1996, p. 163) concluded in her study of those living on low incomes almost 20 years ago: '[people on a low income] have aspirations just like others in society: they want a job, a decent home, and an income that is enough to pay the bills with a little spare'.

Two reflections on the mainstream aspirations of those living on low incomes emerged from this study. First, while both the government and underclass narratives characterise those relying on out-of-work benefits as cut off from the mainstream and with different values (Murray, 1984; Prideaux, 2010; Duncan Smith, 2011b), this research found individuals who share the hopes (and fears) of the majority of the population. They are notable in their ordinariness. Cameron's governments frequently suggested an association between income poverty and poverty of aspiration (BBC News, 2010; DWP and DfE, 2011). This association was notably absent in this research, which reinforces findings from research with young people that the notion of 'poverty of aspiration' is a myth (Archer et al., 2014). Second, the fact that a number of individuals explicitly expressed a future wish to be "normal" and enjoy an "ordinary life" is perhaps reflective of the extent to which they currently feel unordinary and set apart from the mainstream (see Chapter Six).

The future: a resource or something to fear?

While there were commonalities in aspirations, there were also notable differences regarding how individuals approached and considered their imagined futures. Some saw the future as a resource on which they could draw to hope for a better, more positive life, while others saw it mainly as something to fear or something simply impossible to envisage. Given the prevalence of extreme difficulties in their present lives, individuals sometimes found comfort in carving out different future lives that did not feature the struggles of their current lived realities:

Adrian: 'I live in the future sometimes in my head, but then when it comes to the future it doesn't exactly come out how you expect it to.'

Ruth: 'And does that help you cope with the present?'

Adrian: Yes, 'cause I'm happy about what might come in the future.' (W3)

'I always think about [the future]. Like when I apply for jobs I think me head goes wild wi' meself and I think "If I get this I'll be able to do that", I get carried away wi' meself in me little head ... I always think of [the] future, what'll 'appen and where I'll be.' (James, W1)

Some, however, really struggled to actively engage with their own futures. This was particularly common for those whose lives were most challenging:

'I take one day at a time, see how we go and then think about tomorrow tomorrow. And I think that's the best way to do it.' (Chloe, W1)

'A person told me: "don't worry about tomorrow, 'cause tomorrow may never come". It's just taking each day at a time, that's all you can do nowadays.' (Dan, W1)

Dan made a link between his experiences of poverty and benefits and what he described as the difficulty – even the pointlessness – of planning for the future, given how hard it felt to realise positive change in his own life:

'You're just existing, innit, but then you think well let me try and then you can't try 'cause they've got you in that trap, haven't they. You know when you see a hamster running around? You're trying and you go down and you think, I mean getting a job you have to pay your rent, you have to work, you're like flipping hell, and then the bills.' (W1)

For others, while the future did preoccupy them, it was as something to be feared. Isobella described anxieties about her health deteriorating:

'I suppose one of the things which I don't want to do is end up in a wheelchair which may be a possibility ... So I'm looking at the future and it doesn't look particularly rosy.' (W1)

Cath simply felt unable to see a future and she explicitly linked this to her struggle to manage on benefits:

'I don't have a future. I don't have one. You can't have one on benefits. How could you have a future? You can't save up for a holiday, you just can't do it.' (W1)

For most, future occasions generally seen as a source of welcome anticipation were associated with dread, anxiety and worry because of the extra expenditure they entailed. Christmas and family birthdays were often seen as particular flashpoints at which the pressure to buy presents and cook special meals became unmanageable:

'When it comes to Christmas and stuff, that's when you get yer kick in your teeth. Because you know it's coming and you know you can't provide for it. When your kids are expecting and you can't do it. That's the worst part.' (James, W3)

This was a recurrent theme in the interviews, with parents particularly struggling with their feelings around Christmas time and birthdays when they simply could not afford to treat their children as they wanted. They were unable to take pleasure in planning and looking forward to these annual events – an indication of the relational and psychological harm caused by their poverty and social exclusion. This is also perhaps another example of the way in which poverty impacts on an individual's citizenship status; while the rest of society is included in a celebration of Christmas, for example, they are excluded by their poverty and inability to fully participate in the material consumption that contemporary Christmas celebrations entail.

A particularly notable finding from this research is the ways in which being on benefits in general – and experiencing welfare reform in particular – impacts upon and constrains individuals' capacities to plan for and look towards their future (see chapters four and five). The short-term demands associated with welfare-to-work policies and the insecurity created by welfare reform leads to a climate in which it becomes more difficult to mobilise the future as a resource. Writing about her experiences of persistent poverty in the US, Linda Tirado (2013) explains: 'We don't plan long-term because if we do we'll just get our hearts broken. It's best not to hope. You just take what you can get as you spot it.' Many of those interviewed hoped for a better future, but at the same time – and reflecting Tirado's account – they commonly described the necessity of living day to day and a fear of doing otherwise. This inevitably made active planning and the realisation of positive change harder to achieve.

Conclusion

This chapter has introduced the participants and detailed the everyday realities for a small group of individuals in receipt of out-of-work benefits. What this illustrates is the hard 'work' that being on benefits entails – work that is almost completely concealed in dominant depictions of benefit claimants as inactive. Further, the evidence of the various forms of socially valuable contributions in which so many of the participants were engaged is a pertinent challenge to not only the assumed passivity of benefit claimants, but also their supposed non-contributing behaviours via their non-engagement in the formal labour market. This points to a wider problem with the dominant citizenship narrative, which so firmly and narrowly equates responsible behaviour with engagement in paid work (Lister, 2003; Patrick, 2014a). Recent governments' policy focus and emphasis on paid work overshadows and undermines the economic, social and moral value of the various forms of unpaid work and contribution undertaken in communities across Britain (Bailey and Tomlinson, 2012; Coote and Lyall, 2013; MacDonald and Shildrick, 2014). These forms of contribution are not only unrecognised in government characterisations of inactive out-of-work benefit claimants, but also sometimes made more difficult to fulfil due to low rates of benefits and the inflexible demands made of claimants by JCP staff and welfare-to-work programmes (see Chapter

Four). The caring, volunteering, parenting and informal aid in which many of those interviewed were involved is evidently of real social and economic value, but this value is obscured and neglected by the dominant citizenship narrative from above.

The findings detailed in this chapter also describe the hard work and active agency so closely bound up in out-of-work benefits receipt. These findings show the hard choices individuals on out-of-work benefits so often face and the strategies they adopt to get by, which include 'radical economising' (Fitzpatrick et al., 2016). Historically, social policy analyses have been criticised for focusing either on structural forces to the detriment of agency, or – at the other extreme – on individual behaviours and actions while neglecting how the broader structural context shapes, enables and constrains them (Williams and Popay, 1999; Lister, 2004). There are evidently risks associated with romanticising or overemphasising individual agency (Lister, 2004, 2015), particularly in the context of an individualisation of responsibility, but such agency is nonetheless a critical area for social policy analysis. Indeed, it is important to foreground the exercising of agency so often in evidence, particularly as this counters portrayals of 'welfare dependants' as passive and inactive. But it is simultaneously critical to recognise that the agency and resilience that getting by on benefits demands are closely tied to structural forces that constrain individuals and all too often lead to their facing persistent poverty and hardship.

Further, this chapter has illustrated how individuals' poverty and benefits receipt often serve to cut them off from wider society, which is symptomatic of the citizenship exclusion of those living in poverty. Overall, these lived experiences contrast starkly with stereotypical images of welfare reliance enabling a life of relative ease – even comfort. The dominant citizenship framing from above implies that those on benefits are irresponsible (even feckless) individuals with culturally distinct and problematic values and beliefs, whose non-working behaviours are just one indicator of the extent to which they are detached from mainstream society. Countering this, the aspirations of those interviewed were remarkable only in their ordinariness. Engaging with individual claimants' aspirations for the future enabled another important dimension of the lived experiences of benefits receipt to emerge – namely, the ways that poverty and benefit receipt can constrain people's capacities to plan for the future, as well as making the future seem more insecure and fearful. This is explored further in the next chapter, which details individuals' relationships and experiences of paid work over time and shows how policy interventions can sometimes make it harder to achieve work-related aspirations.

Note

[1.] 'W1' is used to denote first-wave interviews, 'W2' second wave, 'W3' third wave and 'W4' fourth wave.

FOUR

Is welfare-to-work working? Relationships with work over time

The dominant framing of the 'problem' of 'welfare' emphasises the non-working behaviours of out-of-work benefit claimants. This then serves to demarcate those who rely on 'welfare' from the 'hard-working majority' seen to be busy earning a wage, providing for themselves and their families and securing a fêted (if illusory) independence. Familiar and well-worn archetypes of the inactive benefit claimant do considerable rhetorical work in creating and reinforcing divisions between those in and out of work, and suggesting the need for corrective policy action to move 'welfare dependants' from welfare-to-work. But to what extent does this narrative fit with the lived experiences of out-of-work claimants themselves?

This chapter details the employment journeys of those interviewed, showing dynamic processes of engagement with and disengagement from the paid labour market. Following individuals' experiences over time moves us beyond static demarcations between 'workers' and 'welfare dependants', enabling a better understanding of individuals' uneven and often insecure relationships with paid employment. It becomes possible to tease out the extent of the mismatch between dominant representations of 'work' and 'welfare' and lived experiences on the ground. There is also scope to better understand how far the dominant citizenship narrative from above, which valorises and promotes paid work, fits with experiences from below. The policy approach emphasises welfare-to-work and activation policies as mechanisms that support transitions into employment, enabling greater social and citizenship inclusion for those so targeted (Patrick, 2014b). A key finding from this chapter is that the promised 'world-class' support from Job Centre Plus and the Work Programme is often experienced as ineffectual and unsupportive, sometimes even operating to undermine rather than enable work-related aspirations.

Critiquing recent work in this field, Andrew Dunn (2013, 2014) has argued that Left-leaning social policy academics too often selectively present evidence to dismiss ideas of a 'welfare dependency' culture and to undermine the rationale for welfare reform. Dunn suggests that some academics tend to only present their data on the majority of claimants who want to engage in paid work, while glossing over – even concealing – findings on the minority who do not show these same orientations. In a direct response to this critique, this chapter also explores the experiences and attitudes of the small minority of those interviewed who expressed reservations about engaging in the paid labour market. Following a discussion of individuals' orientations to employment, the employment journeys of those interviewed during the initial research period are detailed. This chapter then looks at experiences of welfare-to-work support, encompassing the Work Programme and Job Centre Plus provision.

Orientations to paid employment

All but four of the 22 participants first interviewed had previous experiences of employment. Most had had a variety of jobs that were generally low skilled, low paid and insecure (for example, retail, cleaning, catering and labouring). James' employment history was fairly typical: he had worked in warehouses, bakeries, gas companies and on building sites:

> 'I've been all over [with work] … like a gypsy, yeah [laughs].'
> (James, W1)

Three of the disabled individuals – Cath, 'Tessa' and Isobella – had lengthy working experiences, which were suddenly interrupted when they became ill. These included better-paid and higher status roles, spoken about with particular pride:

> 'My last job in the past was PA to Senior Vice President
> in [a] legal [firm], which was very exciting.' (Isobella, W1)

Individuals were often nostalgic about their working histories, which they compared favourably with their current receipt of benefits:

> 'I loved it [work]. Absolutely loved it … I had a busy work
> life and I did enjoy it.' (Cath, W1)

For disabled people, a narrative of loss emerged and they compared their current benefits receipt unfavorably with their working histories:

'If you asked me and [partner]. We'd rather be well and working. We didn't say ten years ago: "Oh, great, I hope I don't have to work again". I had a good job, I were happy. I had good money – more than I get on benefits – a lot more. And then you just, it just hits you.' (Tessa, W1)

While Cameron's governments described a 'culture of worklessness' in areas of high economic inactivity (DWP, 2010b; Duncan Smith, 2014b) and suggested that some out-of-work benefit claimants lack the motivation and drive to enter employment, most of those interviewed wanted to work (see Chapter Three). These aspirations typically endured over time. Even those who experienced frequent rejections and unsuccessful job searches retained a strong commitment to finding employment. Susan spent all of the initial research period of 2011-2013 seeking employment without success. She tried a number of different strategies, participating in welfare-to-work courses and volunteering to try to gain additional experience:

'And still the jobs are not coming [laughs]. I'm trying and trying, and still I can't get a job. I am trying.' (W2)

The effort to stay positive and hopeful was evidently a challenge:

'I really hope I will get a job ... I dream of it [finding work] and I don't see it happening soon. I don't know. But I'm trying really hard to achieve it.' (W2)

Participants often explicitly contrasted the life available on benefits and the hoped-for life that might be theirs if they found employment. Indeed, paid employment was often characterised as the antithesis of unemployment. In constructing a visual timeline of her hopes and fears for the next 12 months, Sophie placed "to get a job" as her primary hope; her fear was that she would "stay on benefits" (W2) (Figure 4.1).

Valuing work: beyond monetary gain

The political agenda prioritises 'making work pay', suggesting that people often decide whether or not to work based on a calculation of how much financially better off they will be in employment. However, this research found that motivations to work are 'far more complex and varied than a simply utility-maximising response to a pecuniary

Figure 4.1: Sophie's timeline

My timeline

incident' (Dean, 2012, p. 355). Sophie wanted to work despite recognising that she was no financially better off in employment:

'It's not the money [that's motivating me].' (W3)

'I would say [working was] about the same [financially] once I'd paid out for my bus fares and that, it were the same as on [benefits] but I were doing something. It were a get up and go.' (W3)

While others did speak of the financial rewards of employment, there were also examples of individuals emphasising paid employment as a way in which they could become included and accepted by mainstream society. Paid employment was seen as being important for self-reliance and independence. Again, a contrast was often made here between the independence of employment and the necessary dependence of benefits receipt. Individuals described aspirations to find employment and become "self-reliant" (Josh, W1), able to "support myself" (Susan, W2) and "independent" (Chloe, W2; Sam, W2). In terms of the social advantages of employment, Sophie spoke of the possibilities employment provided for some "me time" (W2) while Karen felt it could "get me out of the house for a bit" (W1).

The decisions the parents in the study made regarding paid employment were typically combined with their desire to be a good parent, and so were more complex than a narrow rational economic calculation of the financial costs and benefits of entering paid employment. Four of the five single parents saw paid employment as compatible with good parenting, although each aspired to find paid work sufficiently flexible for them to be physically available for their children as and when required. Some of the single parents were partly motivated to enter employment in order to provide strong role models for their children:

> 'I do want to work. I don't want him [son] to think that I'm a lazy mum. I'd like him to think: "Oh, my mum's at work". I don't want him to grow up and think that you can manage in life without a job because you can't.' (Rosie, W1)

As well as evidence of efforts to balance paid work with competing responsibilities, there were also some signs of resistance to a dominant focus on paid work as *the* primary activity shaping a productive life:

> 'Just at the moment I think getting more well is a priority and not work really. I do want to work in the future, that's what keeps me going ... You can have a purpose in life and not be working. You could have a purpose to get better, to improve your quality of life.' (Tessa, W2)

This resistance to paid employment as the primary duty of a responsible adult was most apparent among disabled individuals. For them, employment was arguably not currently a realistic option and their focus on other responsibilities and values needs to be understood against this context. There is broader evidence of disabled people's resistance to the idea that paid work is necessarily and always the solution (Macinnes et al., 2014b) – a narrative that remains ever present in political accounts.

Job 'choosiness'

In terms of the types of jobs that individuals sought, some expressed job 'choosiness' while others described themselves as willing to accept anything they could find. Dunn (2014) drew on quantitative analysis and interviews with JSA recipients to distinguish between determined job seekers and those who display 'choosiness' and a reluctance to undertake what are seen as less attractive jobs. For Dunn, evidence of 'choosiness' provides a justification for welfare conditionality and sanctions in order to undermine claimants' capacity to be 'choosy'.

Among those interviewed, some showed almost no job choosiness, often reflecting their determination – and sometimes desperation – to find a job:

'I'd do 'owt, cleaning the toilets or anything as long as I knew that we had enough to pay the rent. Then I'm not bothered what kind of work I do.' (Sophie, W1)

Others did express a desire to find good work:

'You've got a long life. You don't want to be stuck in a job that you don't like for the rest of your life. You want to be doing something you're enjoying.' (James, W1)

However, after two years of unemployment and struggles to find appropriate training and support, James considerably scaled back his ambitions:

'I'm going for all different things now [like] warehouse ... looking at retail. I've even looked at cleaning.' (W3)

James had been frustrated in his attempts to secure training to become a support worker by the Job Centre's demand that he be permanently occupied in job searching, as well as restrictions in the amount and nature of training permitted while on benefits. Over time, and as a result of these experiences, his employment aspirations changed and were reworked in ways that suggested a gradual diminishing of choosiness in response to policy interventions and structural factors.

JD, a disability benefit claimant, also expressed 'job choosiness':

'I don't see why I can't be picky. All I'm saying is I don't want [a shift] that's 12 hours and I don't want one that's underpaid. I don't think that's asking too much.' (W1)

Later in the interview, JD detailed particular ambitions to find work as a street cleaner or in a new supermarket that was going to open close to his house in the coming months, showing that his choosiness was fairly limited. Indeed, JD's 'choosiness' was incredibly modest and would be regarded by most as completely reasonable, especially given his enduring health problems.

Rosie tied her own choosiness to wider efforts to secure employment that contributed to her self-esteem and was part of a longer-term goal to develop a career:

'I'm not asking for a snobby job. I don't want to be a secretary or a solicitor ... I've been in a sandwich shop and a fish and chip shop to get some money. [Now] I want to do something for myself and to feel a bit better about myself.' (W1)

As we will see later, Rosie's motivation to find 'good' work led to her undertaking work experience, subsequently moving into relatively secure work with opportunities for progression and development. As such, her initial choosiness reaped clear rewards, raising questions about work-first policies that do not always allow individuals to make these kinds of choices.

When discussing evidence of job 'choosiness', academics and policy makers need to carefully define what the nature and extent of this choosiness is, as well as considering the ways in which choosiness may be a positive aspect of individuals' efforts to secure 'good work' and thus something that should be encouraged rather than curtailed. Displaying job 'choosiness' can be a constitutive part of individuals' planning for the longer term in order to realise positive career ambitions and choices. Such choosiness may help prevent individuals from becoming stuck in long-term precarious work, something increasingly common in Britain's polarised labour market (Goos and Manning, 2007). There is an argument that the social rights of citizenship should encompass the right to a certain degree of 'choosiness', especially where individuals are otherwise compelled to accept insecure, low-paid employment.

Actively seeking 'work'?

While individuals expressed clear aspirations to enter work, it did not necessarily follow that they were actively engaged in seeking employment. All five of the disabled people followed over time felt unable to participate in paid employment due to their significant impairment(s) and/or illnesses:

'I can't work full time and ... well, who's going to employ me? Again, that comes down to I don't think I'm employable.' (Isobella, W3)

The five jobseekers within the longitudinal sample expressed clear aspirations to enter paid employment – although one (James) did have periods when he was not actively seeking paid employment. For the five single parents, four had clear aspirations to enter work, although only three were taking active steps to find paid work throughout the period of the study. The longitudinal sample can be segmented into three categories: active jobseekers, those who felt unable to enter paid employment due to illness and disability and those with a more ambiguous relationship to paid employment. As a short hand, these three groups can be classified as 'employment seekers', 'employment unrealistic' and 'employment ambiguous'. The spread of the three groups according to benefit type is outlined in Figure 4.2.

Figure 4.2: Orientations towards employment among longitudinal sample

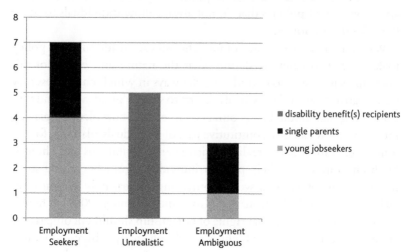

Three individuals might be crudely categorised as 'employment ambiguous'. Cameron's governments would have seen such individuals as particularly likely to require welfare conditionality and the threat of benefit sanctions; these are exactly the people that Dunn claims academics tend to ignore. All three had previously worked and so did not fit into a neat characterisation of out-of-work claimants completely detached from the paid labour market. James was living in supported housing when he was first interviewed following a period of homelessness. His high rent made paid employment financially unsustainable:

> 'At the minute ... I know I'm on Jobseeker's but I don't seek work because if I got work I couldn't afford my home so I don't go looking ... We worked it out before in the [support worker's] office and they said ... "you couldn't afford to live in one of these and [be] working full-time on minimum wage".' (W1)

James' support worker advised him to hold off seeking paid employment until he secured affordable housing, which he managed to do between the second and third interview. By the time of the third interview, James had started to actively seek work, given that he would now be able to afford to pay his rent if he were to find paid employment. James' experiences demonstrate the barriers to paid employment that can sometimes impact upon and shape people's choices and orientations towards employment:

> '[The] cost of living [is] stopping me from going to work. … It sounds stupid, don't it … Go to work and can't afford to live. Go on benefits and barely, you can, but only just, but you can do it.' (W1)

James' relationship with paid employment changed over time in close conjunction with broader changes to his circumstances, which were also linked to social welfare provisions (in this case, housing). What James needed was not compulsion and conditions, but a benefits system sufficiently personalised to recognise how his additional housing costs made transition into paid employment unaffordable.

Chloe and Karen, both single parents, had more complicated relationships with employment. Karen described wanting to enter paid employment but did not seem to be taking any active steps to find a job, perhaps linked to her poor self-confidence and fear of change. She had been a victim of domestic violence and had to move around several times to escape her violent ex-partner. Karen reflected:

> 'It feels like a long time for [work] to come … It's getting out there, finding jobs, applying for them, doing interviews. Trying to make yourself look smart when you've got nowt to wear [laughs]. It's just things like that really.' (W1)

Difficult life experiences and challenging present circumstances inevitably impact – often in complex ways – on individuals' readiness and capacities to participate in paid employment (Shildrick, 2012; Shildrick et al., 2012a). Significantly, as discussed later, Karen was offered only very limited welfare-to-work support.

Actively choosing benefits? Chloe's relationship with work

Only one member of the longitudinal sample, Chloe, could perhaps be described as actively choosing benefits over paid employment:

'I won't be able to afford [to go back to work]. I'll have to go move in with my dad or summat because I can't afford to pay rent and everything and work. Because then I'll have to pay council tax, water rates, rent and then pay for school dinners and ... it will be hard ... I don't want to go to work.' (W1)

'[Work] wouldn't pay. It'd be good to go back to work 'cause it would get me out of the house, give me a break from the kids but ... it isn't worth it so I don't see the point in it.' (W1)

Chloe felt she would need to earn significant sums of money to be better off in paid employment and displayed a lack of awareness of the availability of in-work financial support. When asked what wage would make employment worthwhile, she replied:

'Four, five hundred pound a week would do it ... But what job is going to pay you 400 or 500 pound a week?' (W1)

Over time, Chloe's position changed:

Ruth: 'What's the one thing you most want to change about your current situation?'

Chloe: To already have a job and ... a routine. I need a stable routine. ... When you go out to work and everything, it gives you a sense of wellbeing ... don't it. You're fitting into the world, you do what everyone else is doing. But when you're on social [benefits], you're just, not like you aren't good enough for any job, but like you feel less skilful and less confident.' (W3)

Chloe clearly had an ambiguous relationship with paid employment. Indeed, those who defend work-related welfare conditionality to compel people into work might well highlight her fluctuating but (at times) evident resistance to paid employment. The impact of work-related conditionality on Chloe is explored in Chapter Five.

What is evident in Chloe's account – and indeed in all three of those categorised as 'employment ambiguous' – is that each still sometimes discussed their aspirations to enter paid employment and mentioned its various non-pecuniary advantages. As other research has also found

(Webster et al., 2004; MacDonald and Marsh, 2005), such experiences do not fit with neat (but simplistic) characterisations of individuals completely removed and detached from the labour market. This reinforces the central place that individuals commonly reserve for paid employment in their imagined futures – as well as the valorisation of the social and psychological rewards of employment – which ties in with recent governments' emphasis on employment's transformative potential.

Employment experiences

Paid employment journeys: moving into (and out of) work

While the political narrative implies distinct categories of out-of-work claimants and hard-working families, the lived reality for many is of frequent movements in and out of work and on and off benefits (Shildrick et al., 2010). Four individuals within the longitudinal sample found employment at points during the initial research period of 2011 to 2013, but this was sustained in only one case. Robert and Josh both had a series of spells in and out of work, with their experiences characteristic of the low-pay, no-pay cycle identified by Shildrick and colleagues (2012b). The employment was insecure, temporary and badly paid – in each case well below the National Minimum Wage (NMW) – and did not enable them to escape poverty. Both Robert and Josh were exploited in some of the roles they took on. Robert did a temporary "crappy job" (W2) in water chlorination on a "fixed" rate of £30 a day, even though he sometimes had to work 12–14-hour days. Josh received just £80 for working approximately 35 hours a week in a corner shop (£136.65 less than he was entitled to under the 2012 NMW rate of £6.19 an hour).

Josh's role in the corner shop developed and evolved over time, starting while he was still claiming JSA:

> 'Before he wasn't paying me, he was just paying me in kind, groceries etc. and now he's paying me … but that's only because I told him that the Job Centre were forcing me to do [the] … Work Programme and he said, "right I want you here rather than doing work for them" … so he offered me some cash for it.' (W3)

For Josh, a Work Programme referral precipitated his signing off benefits and instead moving into the informal economy. This is an example of conditionality operating to reduce benefit take-up but not necessarily to support people into long-term, sustainable employment – something highlighted in the research evidence on conditionality and sanctions (Watts et al., 2014; Loopstra et al., 2015).

Josh knew that his employment in the corner shop was "kind of a rip off" but was determined to keep the role:

> 'It's all I can get at the minute. I can't seem to find anywhere else. I keep applying and nowhere seems to want me so I'll take what I can get really.' (W3)

As well as the shop, Josh had two spells of temporary seasonal employment with Royal Mail, arranged by an employment agency. Josh described many problems with this temporary, insecure employment, including uncertainty over the number of hours to be worked, long delays in receiving pay and low wages.

For Robert, temporary roles in water chlorination and on a building site were secured in addition to a permanent part-time role as a steward at the local football stadium. Robert averaged only about ten hours of work a month in his stewarding role and so had to claim JSA when he could not find any additional employment – a classic example of the common, and growing, issue of underemployment (Harkness et al., 2012; TUC, 2014). Robert was so keen to work that he also occasionally helped his friend out "for nothing" with his water chlorination business; he preferred this to the inactivity he associated with benefits and saw it as a "favour for a favour" (W3), as his friend sometimes lent him money.

Sophie also secured work, finding a sales job that she could initially combine with the parenting of her three children:

> '[I] found it through [local newspaper], phoned them up, they rang me back, interviewed and then ... got the job, which I were quite proud. First interview in five years and got the job straight away.' (W3)

Although Sophie enjoyed the job, when the school holidays arrived she was unable to find childcare and so had no choice but to leave. She described the difference between being in and out of work:

> 'When I were working, it was something to tell the kids about when I come home from work. Just sit at the table, have our meal as normal and they'd be like "oh, what did

you do at work? Did you get any sales mummy?" And the kids used to buzz off of it, and we'd buzz off of each other. And now it's just, "oh no, cleaned up, went shopping", same, same.' (W3)

For Robert, Josh and Sophie, it was demoralising to find work only to lose it shortly afterwards (in each case due to demand-side and structural barriers rather than the individuals' behaviour or conduct in work). However, they remained committed to "getting off" benefits and into employment. At the time of the third interviews, Robert had just finished working on a building site and was busy trying to secure a new position, ideally as a security guard. Sophie was also actively seeking employment, with Josh still employed at the shop and preparing to start another contract with Royal Mail.

In many ways, Josh, Robert and Sophie's working experiences closely match the defining features of what Standing (2014) has characterised as 'the precariat', a new class in the making:

> a multitude of people living bits-and-pieces lives, having short-term or casual jobs interspersed with periods of unemployment or labour market withdrawal, with insecure incomes, few assured enterprise or state benefits, and a lack of occupational careers. (Standing, 2011, p. 11)

Rosie's employment journey

While Josh, Robert and Sophie experienced short-term employment and then re-entry onto benefits, Rosie moved into fixed-term employment with the prospect of career development and advancement. She received employment-related support from her housing association, which led first to voluntary work experience and then the offer of paid work:

> '[The housing association] picked me up and helped me along ... and they put me on the [employability] course which is all about improving your confidence and things ... they've just given me that push and I kept going and going.' (W3)

She saw the shift from benefits to employment as transformative:

'It made a big difference [getting a job], especially to me, because I've worked all my life, and I don't do very well not working, because I feel like I've not got anything going for me, and I need something to keep me going, otherwise I end up in a bit of a depression state. It just felt amazing, the money as well, the fact that you're getting up and getting dressed to go out the door, and you're coming home and you're glad to be at home, rather than sick of being stuck in the house. It's great. I couldn't ever go back to it [benefits].' (W3)

Rosie's enthusiasm for working was in notable contrast to her earlier description of out-of-work benefits receipt:

'It's not even about the money [being on benefits]. It's just this, not doing anything. I'm sick of it. I'm sick of not doing anything ... Even like going out. It's not a rush to go anywhere ... I feel like I want a routine in my life and it's just not happening on benefits.' (W1)

In each case in which an individual found employment during the initial research period, it was the result of their own efforts; there was no evidence of welfare-to-work providers or Job Centre Plus advisers assisting in the transition to employment. Rather, it was the result of active and determined job searches, with support agencies and informal networks often playing a particularly critical role.

Experiences of 'poor work' and 'exclusionary employment'

Significantly, while all four who found work described it positively, in no case did their employment income enable them to escape poverty – or even to become significantly financially better off. In-work poverty remains a significant problem and one neglected by the welfare-to-work policy narrative (Lister, 2004; Crisp et al., 2009; Wright, 2009; Newman, 2011; Hill et al., 2016). In Britain, one in five workers is classified as low paid, with low pay often persisting over time due to a proliferation of low-skilled, insecure jobs that offer little chance of progression (Corlett and Whittaker, 2014).

Recent analysis of the large-scale Poverty and Social Exclusion survey described the prevalence of what Bailey (2016) termed 'exclusionary employment': work that fails to deliver security, stability and/or an income that takes you out of poverty. Bailey found that one in three adults in paid employment is experiencing exclusionary employment, suggesting that these individuals are not receiving the rewards that the dominant narrative implies come with paid employment. One in six working adults is in poverty, one in six is in poor quality work and one in ten is in highly insecure employment, having experienced at least six months of unemployment over the past five years. Bailey's findings point to the need for more policy attention to be paid to the problems with a labour market that is so dominated by badly paid, insecure and low quality jobs.

Importantly, though, his suggestion that such work is 'exclusionary' in the sense of failing to provide socially inclusionary outcomes needs to be treated with some caution. Findings from this research show the rewards individuals associated with engaging in paid work, even when such work did not enable them to escape poverty or to move into more secure and stable forms of employment. Although the employment that Sophie, Robert and Josh secured could be described as exclusionary, even 'poor' work (low paid, poor quality, insecure and low skilled), they each described deriving satisfaction from their jobs. As Shildrick et al. (2012b) found in their study of the low-pay, no-pay cycle, 'poor work' is still attractive to many people, generating a range of social benefits even when it also contains negative aspects. The conclusion of Batty et al. (2011, p. 25) is pertinent:

> Labels such as 'poor work', 'donkey work' or 'junk jobs' fail to capture some of the value attached to work at the lower end of the labour market. While it is certainly the case that such forms of employment can involve low pay, long or unsocial hours and pervasive insecurity, it is also evident that these jobs can still generate esteem and provide the basis on which dignified working identities can be constructed.

Work on the margins: experiences of informal work

As well as formal experiences of paid employment, several of the participants described informal work they had experienced either historically or during the course of the research. Informal working while also claiming out-of-work benefits has been described as a (sometimes critical) mechanism of survival for those living in low-income neighbourhoods (Smith, 2005; Crisp et al., 2009; Katungi et al., 2012). While 'working on the side' is condemned in political and media narratives, the individuals interviewed commonly described it as a necessary aspect of efforts to get by on a very low income:

> 'I was working at this fish and chip shop … just cleaning and stuff … It was all right because I needed the money … a fiver an hour. I know it's not much but it were cash in hand.' (Sam, W3)

Dan (a member of the original sample) felt he had no choice but to continue to claim benefits when he initially secured paid employment:

> 'I got my job, but they didn't pay you, like a month in hand … So I was … in a Catch 22, I didn't have no money. I couldn't sign off because I would have had no money to get to the job, so what I did was went to the work … then I had to sign on just to cover rent and to get me food … And then I got caught, working and signing on … I told them, I was just going to do it until I get my first pay and then tell them … And they says "oh, all right", and they … gave me a slap on the hand. So … what can I say? … How do you win in this time?' (W1)

As a result of this experience, Dan terminated his paid employment. He described feeling stuck in a system that made it financially difficult to secure paid work. There are particular financial challenges and costs associated with frequent moves between out-of-work benefits and low-paid temporary work (Shildrick, 2012). This sometimes creates a 'precarity trap' (Standing, 2011) – as in Dan's case – that prevents people from successfully making the transition into employment.

Barriers to employment

While four people did find work during the initial research period, the same number were actively involved in looking for work – albeit unsuccessfully. The experiences of unsuccessful job searches, rejections and often simply silence in response to applications and enquiries had a negative effect on individuals' self-esteem and confidence:

> 'You sort of give up on yourself I think.' (Susan, W2)

'I'm sick of going around town and handing out my CVs and getting nothing back.' (Adrian, W3)

As part of her effort to secure paid employment, Sophie tried unsuccessfully to find voluntary work as a bridge to more formal employment, applying to a local homeless hostel but hearing nothing back. This was disappointing for Sophie:

'I'm handing it out for free and no one's contacting me back.' (W3)

The work of finding employment was experienced as demanding and often associated with frequent disappointments and setbacks. Lack of success in securing employment was rationalised by discussing the various barriers to paid employment that individuals faced.

Here, it was common for individuals to highlight a lack of jobs and the state of the economy in post-2008 Britain:

'I'd take any job at the moment but there's no jobs.' (Adrian, W1)

'How can you go back to work if there's no jobs out there?' (Sophie, W2)

The difficulty of competing against those recently made redundant was noted:

'There's so much unemployment that the competition is too high ... You see stores being closed all the time and ... I can't compete with them because they've just been employed.' (Susan, W3)

Several thought that migrant workers were willing to work for less than British nationals and were sometimes preferred by employers:

'The reason me and a lot of people can't get a job is 'cause they give them to the immigrants first ... Mainly because they think they can pay them less [laughs] and walk all over them more.' (JD, W1)

The single parents – all women – spoke repeatedly about the barriers to employment that they associated with issues such as a lack of appropriate childcare, the demand from employers to work flexibly and outside school hours and their own wishes to work part-time to combine responsibilities to their children with a desire to work. Susan attributed her failure to find retail work to being unable to work at weekends:

> 'Supermarkets: the moment you mention you cannot work weekends because of childcare, they don't want to take you on. So this is really hard.' (W1)

Over time, Susan retrained as a teaching assistant, hoping it would enable her to juggle parenting and employment:

> 'It's hard to find a part-time job in retail ... if it wasn't for childcare ... it would be, I think, better in retail because with my experience in the bank I'm used to dealing with customers rather than children in school. But ... I'll have to adjust.' (W3)

The difficulty in finding paid employment that could be effectively combined with parental responsibilities – as well as the lack of availability of suitable childcare and flexible part-time roles – were recurring themes in the interviews, highlighting the gendered nature of barriers to employment (Gingerbread, 2010a; Millar and Ridge, 2013).

All of the disabled people in the longitudinal sample described their impairments as the greatest barrier to their engaging in paid employment and did not feel ready to enter work. In recent years, there has been a particular focus on efforts to address the 'disability employment gap'; that is, the difference in employment rates between disabled and non-disabled people. In 2015, Cameron's Conservative government pledged to halve this gap, which would require 1.2 million more disabled people to enter employment. While efforts to support disabled people into employment are to be welcomed, it is important that these work with (and not against) the views of disabled people themselves about their capability and readiness to engage with paid employment. The disabled participants in this study were resistant to and questioning of efforts to move them into employment. Isobella was frustrated at having to participate in work-related activities when she felt her impairments meant that any move into employment was unrealistic and unfeasible. She also felt that employers would be unlikely to employ her:

'If I was an employer looking for ten people, and if I had a skill, or the skills that they needed, I still would be bottom of the list because of my condition … I wouldn't employ me because if I want my business to succeed, I want people who are going to be there, which may be the wrong attitude but people are out there to make money, if you've got to then consider someone having a rest, so you have a room for them it all adds to the costs that they may not recoup by the work that they do.' (Isobella, W1)

While individuals' assessments of their employment barriers placed much more emphasis on structural, demand-side issues than the dominant political narrative, many also detailed individual and supply-side barriers. Barriers mentioned included a lack of training, qualifications, skills and experience, as well as poor self-confidence:

'[The barrier is] just your confidence really, 'cause you've not worked for so long. It's that confidence to go for an interview and to apply for a job.' (Karen, W1)

Susan felt her age was an additional factor in her struggles to find employment:

'I've also got that at the back of my mind thinking "oh who's going to employ me at my age".' (W2)

This illustrates the ways in which experiences of paid employment and work search are differentiated by factors such as age and gender – factors not always taken into account in policy responses, which tend to treat all out-of-work claimants as a broadly homogeneous group.

Recent governments' characterisation of the 'problem' of worklessness implicitly suggest that it is a 'problem' of individuals either choosing not to work or lacking the skills and (often financial) motivation to make the transition from out-of-work benefits into employment (Wright, 2009; Newman, 2011) (see Chapter Three). The supply-side of the labour market is emphasised, with a concurrent neglect of demand-side barriers to employment, such as an absence of jobs, shortages of suitable affordable childcare and the endurance of discriminatory practices towards disabled people (Wright, 2009; Deacon and Patrick, 2011). In fact, as this book shows, individuals face both demand-side and supply-side barriers to employment but the structural issues they experience are too often concealed by a politicised focus on what individuals need to do to become 'work-ready'.

The provision of welfare-to-work 'support'

The 2010–15 Conservative-led Coalition government promised that their flagship new welfare-to-work programme – the Work Programme (WP) – would deliver personalised, effective support to claimants on a payment-by-results basis (see Chapter Two). All four of the longitudinal sample referred onto the WP were on JSA and none displayed particularly entrenched or severe barriers to engagement in the paid labour market. None of the disabled participants were referred to the WP, despite four spending time in the WRAG of ESA. Adrian – the jobseeker who faced the greatest barriers to employment, including criminal convictions and no paid work experience – was not referred onto the WP during the initial research period, although this may have been partially due to him frequently being subject to benefit sanctions. This limited engagement in the WP is itself revealing, given that those facing the most significant barriers to employment were not referred onto the programme.

Susan's Work Programme journey

To better understand the experiences of those who did participate in the WP, Susan's engagement with the programme is now explored as a case study of its processes and impact. On being referred, Susan was eager to participate in the WP:

> 'I was happy to go because I'm happy really to try anything that can get me to work because I really, really want to go to work.' (W2)

She found aspects of the programme useful:

> 'It was helpful. They were nice people, they lift you up … When I was thinking "who can employ me", that kind of views, they teach you "don't say that". I have a better CV and [know] how to do better applications.' (W2)

However, Susan became frustrated when a work placement she was promised as part of the programme failed to materialise. Instead, she managed to secure her own placement, volunteering for an agency from which she had previously received support. Susan needed a Criminal Records Bureau (CRB) check for this placement. She arranged with the WP provider for this to be undertaken, completing all the necessary forms and travelling into the WP provider's offices twice to submit necessary paperwork. When the CRB check had still not been received several months later, Susan spoke to her adviser, only to find out that they had never sent it to be processed:

> 'It really made me upset because if they didn't want me to find my own placement, if they weren't happy about it, they only had to say.' (W3)

Following the end of the fieldwork, Susan wrote to me:

> The Work Programme didn't give me any help at all to find work; from job search, applications, interviews, I did everything myself. All they did was put me down, asking me why I was not getting jobs while I was getting interviews, to the point where I was feeling scared to attend my appointments whenever I failed an interview.

While Susan initially spoke positively about how WP advisers boosted her self-esteem, this changed over time, perhaps as the emphasis shifted towards critiquing her perceived failure to secure employment. Reflecting back on her experiences, Susan felt the WP increased the employment-related barriers that she faced, with advisers questioning of her failure to secure a job reducing her self-esteem and self-confidence.

Susan's WP advisers also undermined her own longer-term work-related aspirations, in particular her ambition to become a teaching assistant (TA):

> The Work Programme people were getting impatient with me as I was getting interviews but no job ... The woman who was running the office told me that I needed to get a job ASAP, that I needed to start looking for any job, especially care work because TA jobs were very competitive because of holidays. I felt so demoralised, I started to doubt myself and the decision I had made to pursue that [TA] job, which I chose to do because of being a single mum. I started getting anxious every time my appointment was coming up. At some point I believed that I was never going to get it. (written communication)

After the initial research period ended, Susan did manage to secure a TA assistant job but this was arguably despite, rather than because of, her engagement in the WP.

An absence of innovative support?

Susan described marked similarities between the support provided by the WP and the support she had previously received from JCP. This was also emphasised by Robert and James. Robert's WP experience seemed almost identical to a typical signing-on appointment at the Job Centre, with an emphasis on policing the requirements that claimants are available and actively seeking employment:

> 'They go "sign a little piece of paper" … of what jobs you've applied for, and that's it. Then they give you another date. What's the point in that? There's no point.' (W3)

This overlap and continuity – what Whitworth (2013) characterises as a 'Groundhog Day approach' – is a notable contrast to the personalised support the Coalition government promised the WP would deliver (DWP, 2011b).

Brief appointments left individuals feeling that advisers' main purpose was to 'hassle' them to apply for more jobs:

> 'All I get told nowadays, not as in help-wise, but all my adviser says to me is "I want to see an interview from you". Not to help me get an interview … no, "I just want to see an interview from you", and that's it.' (James, W3)

Overall, there was little evidence of innovation in the support provided. Individuals were commonly referred onto basic skills courses, provided with help to redo their CVs and occasionally offered work experience. Particular examples of bad practice included James' experience of participating in a training qualification in which the answers to a test were written on a whiteboard to be reproduced in "your own words" (W3). James was also frustrated by what happened when he was put forward for a job interview:

> 'I did an Aldi's group interview and I got through to the next part of it and they promised me that I'd get a one-to-one and I ain't heard 'owt, and I've chased it up, chased it up and I'm now apparently getting told that the [WP]

person that's meant to be running it can't be bothered. So if they can't be bothered, why should I be bothered?' (W3)

While the WP was heralded as an innovative programme of work-related support, those interviewed experienced a programme that in many ways simply replicated what was previously provided by JCP. Further, there was little evidence that those referred onto the WP viewed the support provided as actually moving them closer to the paid labour market.

Work-related 'support' from Job Centre Plus

Much more common than participation in the WP were regular appointments with JCP via fortnightly signing-on appointments or occasional Work-Focused Interviews (WFIs). However, individuals were often failing to receive even this relatively minor level of input. For example, Karen – a single parent who had been on IS for four years when first interviewed – was invited to attend her first WFI only when her transition onto JSA approached (when her son was almost five). She was a participant who could be classified as having an ambiguous relationship with employment and she expressed a range of fears and concerns regarding making the transition into paid employment. Karen was in particular need of meaningful help and support and it is thus notable that none was forthcoming.

Others requested assistance from JCP but were refused. Sophie asked for an additional WFI:

'I went in a few weeks back, before the kids broke up from school, to ask for a lone parents' adviser meeting to get ready for September when my daughter ... starts school. And like, "oh, well you have to wait for your appointment. We can't just hand them out like that". I'm like, "one minute I'm asking for help to go back to work and you're telling me I have to wait for me appointment".' (W1)

Here, Sophie was trying to plan for a move into work when her youngest child started school – an effort that went unsupported by JCP.

In addition to a lack of support with realising aspirations and work-related goals, this research also found some evidence that the constant short-term demands the WP and JCP made of out-of-work claimants interfered with and even prevented more strategic, long-term thinking and planning. Individuals were often occupied with trying to meet the demands made, while facing the constant threat of sanctions for non-compliance. Efforts to prove job-search activities – part of what Standing describes as 'work-for-labour' (Standing, 2014) – reduced the time individuals had available to devote to longer-term thinking about work and their employment-related aspirations. In this way, the process of engagement with both the JCP and WP only contributed to a further shrinking of people's time horizons.

Individuals commonly thought the role of advisers was to police and manage their claim(s) and often did not even consider the Job Centre as somewhere they might go for employment-related assistance. Josh described how he saw his Job Centre adviser's role:

> 'Just trying to make sure you are actually looking for jobs and if you're not, then, suffer the consequences kind of thing [laughs].' (W1)

Overall, individuals were negative about and dismissive of the support provided by JCP:

> 'I feel like as soon as you've been for your appointment they've forgotten about you. Even though they've promised that they'll do all these [things for you]. You know, "you're on the waiting list and we'll get back to you next week, we'll ring you", and no, you don't ring me. They've never rung me. It annoys me … It's like as long as … you've signed on, that's it, you're done, next customer, that's how I feel it is.' (Rosie, W1)

There is a tension between JCP's dual roles of providing employment-related support and policing eligibility for financial support (Fletcher, 2011). There has been growing recognition that JCP is no longer fit for purpose (Bright, 2014; Graham and McQuaid, 2014; Lammy, 2014; Miscampbell and Porter, 2014). Its role of providing employment-related support has been particularly criticised – criticisms that the findings from this research only reinforce. These findings are particularly pertinent given that, with the closure of the WP, the JCP will actually take on a greater role in back-to-work support – something it is perhaps not currently particularly well-equipped to deliver.

Inconsistent messages about work-readiness

A further problem with the nature of welfare-to-work support provided was the inconsistent messages individuals received about their judged work-readiness. Three of the disabled people within the longitudinal sample spent some time in the WRAG of ESA, and so were expected to comply with work-related demands or risk benefit sanctions. Despite being in the WRAG, 'Kane' was never invited to attend an in-person WFI or to participate in any other forms of employment support:

> 'They never sent me for any job focused interviews or anything like that. [I was] a bit pissed off really ... They were meant to be trying to get people into work and they weren't – didn't seem to be trying to get me into work at all.' (W3)

After being placed in the WRAG, Sharon was required to attend just one WFI. Her adviser then suggested that future appointments be by telephone, as he did not feel she would benefit from more active work-related activity given the extent of her impairment(s):

> 'He said, "from what you say you're definitely not ready for work so I'll just ... write on to leave you alone for a bit", which I really appreciated.' (W1)

While the WCA process placed both Sharon and Kane in the WRAG and thus found them to have limited capability to work, JCP staff appeared to feel differently and so did not prioritise them for support or interventions.

Inconsistencies and contradictory suggestions about work-readiness seem to extend to other benefits. Sophie, a single parent, explained how JCP advised her that she was perhaps not yet ready to enter paid employment at the point at which she was about to be transferred onto JSA. This was despite Sophie wanting to move into paid employment:

> '[The Job Centre adviser said] "aw well we don't think you're ready [to work]". And ra ra this and ra ra that. "What about some voluntary work" ... It was one minute on my case go back to work and now I'm telling you I can go back to work, you're telling me I can't in a way.' (W2)

Given the recent policy focus on closing the disability employment gap, the evidence of a lack of support being offered to disabled people and inconsistent messages around work-readiness is troubling. Set against an ongoing focus on the need to support welfare-to-work transitions, it is particularly surprising that some of those deemed 'work-ready' by the benefits system were being discouraged from entering employment by frontline advisers. The behaviour of JCP advisers, who quickly moved disabled people onto less intensive and demanding forms of welfare conditionality, is a pertinent reminder of the discretion of street-level advisers (Lipsky, 2010; Fletcher, 2011) and the ways in which their own agency and practices can mediate (and sometimes soften) the policy intent.

Street-level bureaucracy and individual agency

The extent to which individual advisers sometimes translated work-related demands in particular ways or advised claimants (such as Sophie) that they were not work-ready – despite their being placed on a benefit premised on the requirement that an individual is actively seeking and available for work – are examples of the agency and discretion operational by those working on the frontline (Riccucci, 2002; Fletcher, 2011). While the agency of benefit claimants themselves is endlessly analysed and critiqued, much less attention is paid to how those working in 'welfare' services – street-level bureaucrats – utilise available discretion in ways that may affect policy implementation and the experiences of individual claimants. Media reports over recent years (Domokos, 2011) have highlighted that JCP advisers are now subject to targets and much greater performance monitoring, and suggested that advisers are set particular targets for the number of claimants sanctioned (a suggestion consistently denied by government ministers). It is possible that this cultural change is reducing the scope for individual advisers to exercise discretion and deliver more or less support to their 'customers'.

However, what was clear from this research was the importance claimants attached to their relationship with their JCP and/or WP adviser(s). As Susan put it when asked how she was treated at the Job Centre:

> 'It depends on who you see. Some people are nice, some people are helpful and some people, when you ask them they just. Pfff. There are some people who don't give you information. They just maybe say "talk to your adviser next time you come". I find some people are not helpful.' (W1)

Robert recounted being put on a back-to-work course with one adviser who put him down and belittled him. He reported being repeatedly sanctioned due to his inability and unwillingness to establish a positive working relationship with her. When Robert returned onto the course with a different adviser, he described it much more positively, hinting at the impact the nature of the relationships established can have on employment support experiences and the continued importance of discretion and agency at the frontline.

Research has consistently found that what matters in the delivery of truly effective welfare-to-work support is the relationship between advisers and individual claimants and that the best outcomes are recorded when this relationship is positive (Walker and Wiseman, 2003; Hasluck and Green, 2007; Toerien et al., 2013). There were few signs of positive relationships in this research, with consequences for the likely success of welfare-to-work interventions.

Imagining better support

Given the extent of dissatisfaction with the back–to-work support received, in their second interview participants were asked to draw an imaginary back-to-work adviser, listing the qualities such an adviser might have as well as the types of help, support and assistance they would provide. Individuals emphasised how they would like to be treated by advisers and the degree to which this contrasted with their previous experiences. They commonly described an ideal adviser who would treat them with respect, speak to them politely and be "smiley, not condescending" (Isobella, W2). The pictures of advisers drawn by James and Karen are reproduced in figures 4.3 and 4.4 respectively. James (Figure 4.3) highlighted his desire for advisers to "be understanding", "polite" and "less forceful" – and to "listen", while Karen (Figure 4.4) wanted advisers to display friendliness and say "would you like to" rather than "you must".

Individuals expressed a desire for a more collaborative and equal working relationship rather than the current emphasis on compulsion and instruction. This could include what might seem like fairly basic requests; for example, that advisers make an appointment *with* the claimant rather than *for* them, thus acknowledging and respecting their other commitments. Individuals (such as Karen) frequently requested more assistance, such as weekly signing in appointments. Again, this adds weight to the argument that out-of-work benefit claimants are strongly orientated towards paid employment. These findings further reinforce the importance of the nature of the relationship between benefit officials (and related agencies) and individual claimants.

Figure 4.3: James' perfect back-to-work adviser

Figure 4.4: Karen's perfect back-to-work adviser

Conclusion

Through focusing on relationships with paid employment, this chapter has provided a dynamic picture of participants' past experiences of work, current orientations and movements in and out of work. It has illustrated the prevalence of the low-pay, no-pay cycle and the difficult 'work' of seeking employment. Further, this chapter has provided detailed accounts both of individuals actively seeking employment and those with more ambiguous relationships to employment, including one participant – Chloe – who at times expressed an active preference for benefits over paid employment. What emerges from this is a picture far more complex than that suggested by neat dichotomous divisions between 'strivers' and 'skivers', between the 'hard-working majority' and 'welfare dependants'. Are those that move into and out of work only citizens when they are in employment? The stereotype of two static groups of 'hard-working families' and 'welfare dependants', citizens and non-citizens, collapses when we look at dynamic relationships between employment and out-of-work benefits receipt over time. Furthermore, the active efforts of many of the participants to secure employment, albeit often without success, suggests that the dominant model of inactive benefit claimants requiring conditions to make them move from welfare-to-work is flawed (Wright, 2016).

Engaging with lived experiences on the ground enables us to see the extent to which people move in and out of work, on and off benefits, with these transitions often affected by structural factors outside of their control. We also see that orientations and values around employment are far more complicated and nuanced than a simplistic case of valuing work when, but only when, it provides greater financial rewards than those available on out-of-work benefits. While this chapter has highlighted evidence of some individuals who, at certain points, expressed resistance to engaging in paid employment, it is unclear whether work-related conditionality and sanctions are the appropriate policy responses – especially given the various and often entrenched barriers to employment such individuals so often faced. There is also a related question about whether a whole social security system should be designed around the presumed irresponsibility of a small minority therein (Wright, 2013), particularly as conditionality and compulsion may actually undermine the scope for more effective welfare-to-work support to be delivered (see Chapter Five).

In policy terms, we also need to question the validity of a continued emphasis on making work pay (and by default making sure that 'welfare' does not). We have seen measures that reduce benefit entitlement –

such as the announcement to reduce the level of ESA to the equivalent of JSA for those in the WRAG – justified on the basis of a need to sharpen financial incentives to work. But this is problematic if one accepts first that decisions about whether to enter work are not always made on this basis and second that individuals so often face enduring barriers to paid employment – barriers that are sometimes simply not (or even not capable of) being addressed. Further, it is important to look much more closely at whether the work-first approach and immediate and short-term demands with which it is associated can interfere with – and even interrupt – the realisation of longer-term job aspirations. This is tied to questioning the place for 'job choosiness' within the welfare-to-work policy frame and whether a right to a degree of choosiness should be defended, both on citizenship grounds and in terms of promoting transitions into sustainable, 'good' work.

A number of citizenship implications flow from the mismatch between the dominant narrative of benefit claimants' labour market detachment and the lived realities reported in this book (see Chapter Eight). These are reflective of the disjuncture between citizenship narratives from above and citizenship as it is lived and experienced from below. At the same time, the individuals interviewed did seem to valorise paid employment and associated it with a wide range of non-pecuniary rewards, mirroring politicians' endless focus on the value inherent in paid work. While those who moved into employment typically entered low-paid, unskilled and even exploitative roles, they still described positive advantages flowing from these experiences, particularly when contrasted with their experiences of out-of-work benefits. This finding is consistent with many other studies (Dean and Taylor-Gooby, 1992; Crisp et al., 2009; Haux et al., 2012; Shildrick et al., 2012b; Hickman et al., 2014; Hussain and Silver, 2014). Taken together, this evidence suggests that an overarching focus on enabling transitions into employment dovetails with the aspirations of those on out-of-work benefits. It does not, however, suggest that a work-first focus is the right one, or that enough is currently being done to protect those who receive out-of-work benefits from poverty or to provide effective support to make such transitions.

In their welfare-to-work efforts, recent governments have introduced a range of welfare reforms that they have justified on the basis of making work pay, tackling 'welfare dependency' and creating clear financial incentives for moving into employment. The individuals interviewed for this book were directly affected by some of the welfare reforms undertaken by the 2010–15 Coalition government. The next chapter outlines and considers these experiences.

FIVE

Ending welfare dependency? Experiencing welfare reform

Since the 1970s, mainstream politicians have been concerned with addressing what they have described as cultures of 'welfare dependency': the notion that for many people it has become the norm to 'choose' benefits receipt over paid work (Dean and Taylor-Gooby, 1992; Hills, 2015). Successive waves of welfare reform have sought to undermine this supposed 'welfare dependency' and 'activate' benefit claimants by introducing policies designed to support transitions from 'welfare' into 'work' (see Chapter Two). Measures introduced have included the increased and extended application of welfare conditionality and sanctions; changes to the eligibility conditions and levels of benefits; the development of new forms of back-to-work support; and policies designed to 'make work pay' by increasing the gap between the 'rewards' of benefits receipt and those of paid employment. Under Cameron's governments the mantle of welfare reform was taken forward with renewed vigour and zeal, with policy changes defended on the basis that they would help affected individuals to lead more responsible, independent lives as dutiful, hard-working citizens.

This chapter details dynamic experiences of welfare reform and maps the cumulative impact of such reform on individual lives. This provides a fluid, textured and rich picture of individual responses and experiences, which very often clash with the political narrative and policy framing. Individuals were variously affected by the migration of IB claimants onto ESA and the intensification and extension of welfare conditionality (including a ratcheting up of the severity and frequency of benefit sanctions). Experiences of the IB–ESA migration, increased conditionality and benefit sanctions are explored in turn, with individual case studies detailing how they were anticipated, experienced and responded to over time. This is followed by a summary of the 'work' and 'costs' associated with welfare reform, which can together be described as the 'burden of welfare reform'. First, individuals' expectations about welfare reform are discussed, illustrating how concern about future benefit changes seeps into and impinges upon individuals' present lives.

Anticipating welfare reform

When the first interviews took place in 2011, many of the Coalition government's reforms were yet to be rolled out, but welfare reform and proposals to modernise the benefits system featured prominently in newspaper headlines and television news bulletins. Universal Credit was being heavily trailed, although it was unclear when and how those interviewed would be affected. This created a climate of uncertainty and fear in which individuals were often unsure about how the reforms would impact upon their own lives.

Knowledge about welfare reform was frequently garnered from friends and 'the grapevine'; rumours were circulating, some of them inaccurate. Official governmental communication – when it came at all – was difficult to understand. Cath's fear about welfare reform increased over time:

> 'It's more scary [than when we last met] because it's been a bit of a silence. Loads of scare stories but silence from government. We all know it's going to happen, but they've sort of said it, then gone quiet. Not talking to us.' (W2)

Word-of-mouth communication, albeit an important source of information, sometimes added to the anxiety and unease around forthcoming benefit changes – particularly when rumours included the suggestion that ever harsher and more punitive changes were being introduced. In a particularly common area of misinformation, three of the four single parents anticipating a move from IS onto JSA assumed that this would lead to a reduction in the income they received, when in fact the change was not a financial one but rather the introduction of the obligation to be available for and actively seeking work. These single parents were therefore often worrying – unnecessarily – about how they would manage with less money when they were moved onto JSA. Karen explained:

> 'I'll have to manage my money a bit better until I find a job ... [because] I think it's a lower income on it [JSA] ... I'm sure it is.' (W2)

By following people over time it was possible to explore how far people's anticipations of welfare reform's impact coincided with their experiences. There were some notable divergences here, particularly among disabled individuals. Tessa expected the ESA reforms to be targeted at "others", primarily those "playing the system" by abusing the disability label (W1). These expectations proved incorrect:

> 'I didn't worry when they were on about all these new reforms ... I knew I had treatment-resistant paranoid schizophrenia. And I thought ... most people know that's a serious illness ... people around me got worried, and I said "it'll be fine, it's for those who've got a bad back and they're playing football on the weekend." I never thought I'd be fighting.' (W2)

In contrast, Kane was very anxious that the reforms would see him lose his eligibility for disability benefits. In fact, he was awarded ESA:

Kane: 'I thought they'd send me onto Jobseekers. I were
            pretty pessimistic really.'
Ruth: 'So how did you feel when you got the letter saying
            you're in the WRAG?'
Kane: 'Surprised more than anything. Surprised and then
            pretty pleased.' (W2)

For Kane, being awarded ESA was "like a weight off my shoulders" (W2), hinting at the many months of anxiety and worry he had experienced as he waited to be assessed. Kane's experiences also illustrate the impact these reforms can have even when eligibility to benefits is sustained. While Kane was awarded ESA following his attendance at a WCA, others had more difficult experiences of the IB–ESA migration. It is to exploring these experiences that this chapter now turns.

Redrawing of eligibility for disability benefits

Shortly after entering office in 2010, the Coalition government committed to keeping to its predecessor's timetable by migrating all existing IB claimants onto ESA by 2014 (see Chapter Two). This was despite the expression of considerable concerns about the accuracy and effectiveness of the WCA, the in-person medical at which a claimant's eligibility for ESA is determined (Citizens Advice Bureau, 2010; Harrington, 2010; Gentleman, 2012). After a WCA, applicants can either be found fit for work (FFW) and so ineligible for ESA (and likely to instead claim JSA) or placed in the Work-Related Activity Group (WRAG) of ESA, where they receive the benefit but on condition of participation in work-related activity. Those judged to have the most serious impairments are placed in the Support Group (SG), where they receive a higher level of ESA with no conditions attached.

All five of the disabled individuals in the longitudinal sample were reassessed. However, only two experienced a face-to-face WCA; the eligibility of the others for ESA was determined by their completion of an initial questionnaire (ESA50) and – on occasions – supplementary written information. Three of the five were unhappy with the initial decision made about their entitlement to ESA. All three successfully challenged these decisions. The ESA journeys of the five disabled individuals are outlined in Table 5.1.

Table 5.1: Experiences of migrating from Incapacity Benefit onto Employment and Support Allowance

		Had a face-to-face WCA	Initial decision	Outcome appeal	Support with appeal	Experienced repeat assessments in research period
Happy with initial decision	Kane	•	WRAG			
	Cath		SG			
Unhappy with initial decision	Isobella		WRAG	SG	•	
	Tessa		WRAG	SG	•	•
	Sharon	•	FFW	WRAG	•	•

Table 5.1 shows that, in each of the three cases in which the initial ESA decision was challenged, individuals were supported with the appeals process – in two cases by welfare rights officials and in one by a specialist health support worker. Individuals described this support as critical; two said it had made a decisive difference to their feeling able and confident to actually go through with the challenge. The Coalition government subsequently withdrew Legal Aid support for all benefit cases (except those involving the Upper Tribunal and judicial review), meaning there is no longer any financial support from the state to enable advice agencies to represent and support people seeking to challenge benefit decisions (Ministry of Justice, 2014). The Coalition also legislated for mandatory reconsideration of benefit decisions, so that claimants must first put in a request for the decision to be reconsidered before they are allowed to lodge an appeal (DWP, 2013). This creates an extra process with which individuals have to comply

before their appeal can be formally heard at a tribunal. To explore the IB–ESA migratory process and provide a detailed understanding of how this reform can be experienced, Sharon's 'welfare reform journey' is outlined as a case study.

About a year before her first interview, Sharon attended a WCA, at which she was found fit for work:

'I think I answered about two, three questions and the other two were yes or no answers so I don't feel that I had enough time in the interview for him to assess me. I didn't feel like I had a chance really to explain my side, and my point of view … To actually explain how I feel and how hard it is just for me to go outside.' (W1)

At the WCA, claimants are awarded a number of points based on the extent of their capability to work; a threshold of 15 points is necessary for a WRAG ESA award (DWP, 2012a). Sharon was awarded zero points:

'He [the assessor] wrote down that I had anxiety but he wrote down that I had no points … the decision really, really upset me.' (W1)

'When I went to [assessment centre] I had no idea that he were scoring me … putting points on me 'cause I felt that it were a bit degrading.' (W1)

Disability activists and disability studies academics have long called for disabled people to be recognised as experts on both their own impairments and the consequences of living in a disabling society (Stone and Priestley, 1996; Barnes and Mercer, 1997). These assessments appear to cast disabled people as passive participants in the process of determining eligibility for disability benefits and to provide little scope for individuals' own expertise to be recognised.

With support from a welfare rights adviser, Sharon challenged the initial WCA decision. She had to wait almost a year between the WCA and the tribunal hearing of her appeal:

'I was just fed up waiting for … [the tribunal], I just wanted to get it over and done with 'cause I were dreading the day it came 'cause I knew that I had to sit there in front of

two complete strangers and basically ... explain everything.'
(W1)

Sharon described how difficult it was to attend the tribunal and how the emotional and practical support of her adviser enabled her to do so. The tribunal overturned the original decision and Sharon was instead placed in the WRAG of ESA. Sharon drew an explicit contrast between the tribunal, in which she felt she had an opportunity to fully describe the nature and extent of her health issues, and the medical, which she experienced as rushed and impersonal.

Significantly, Sharon's negative experiences of claiming ESA affected her readiness to put in a claim for another disability benefit (DLA). Despite being told by her DWP adviser that she might be entitled to DLA because of the additional costs associated with her impairments, Sharon delayed putting in a claim for DLA by almost a year. Sharon was fearful that the process of claiming would be a repeat of her difficult experience with ESA:

'I dread going through [it again] ... It gets me right upset.'
(W1)

Following input from her support worker, Sharon did eventually put in a DLA claim and was awarded the benefit without having to go through the appeals process. Sharon used the additional money to pay for taxis so that she could take her three-year-old son to nursery, which her agoraphobia and anxiety had previously prevented her from doing.

Less than a year after being awarded ESA at the tribunal, Sharon was told that her claim was to be reassessed:

'You worry about it ... are they going to say no again and we're going to have to go through all that again or I've just got to go see someone who's judging you and ... you know that they're looking at you and staring ... it puts you down really.' (W2)

Despite Sharon's worries she was re-awarded ESA. However, she was then informed that her eligibility for DLA was under review. Once again, Sharon was left in a state of anxiety and worry:

'I'm really really anxious about it 'cause with them stopping a lot of people I can see them just stopping it and me having to go through the appeal and all that again and it's just really uncomfortable basically.' (W3)

Sharon was concerned about what would happen if she were reassessed and found ineligible for DLA:

'I use a lot of [DLA] for taxis to get me around ... I get taxis for him to school. So the first thing I worried about is he wouldn't be able to get to school ... at least while I'm on this I can say well I'm taking him to nursery, and I'm doing that. So if it stopped I don't know what I'd do.' (W3)

Sharon feared that the withdrawal of her DLA would undermine her capacity to fulfil her parenting responsibilities, with adverse consequences for both her and her young son. For Sharon, claiming disability benefits was associated with a persistent experience of stress, anxiety and the repeated need to share personal medical circumstances with strangers – something she found particularly difficult.

The assessment process for ESA, combined with regular reassessments, can cause recurrent anxiety, stress and worry for disabled people, many of whom are already living with mental health issues (Barr et al., 2015; Dwyer et al., 2016). ESA operates to reclassify and redraw eligibility for disability benefits, with many individuals judged to require activation, conditions and compulsion to enable transitions from benefits into paid employment (Puttick, 2007; Piggott and Grover, 2009). After her tribunal, Sharon was placed in the WRAG, where she was expected to participate in work-related activity or risk benefit sanctions. In this way, she became subject to an expanded conditionality regime – something that affected almost all of the individuals interviewed for this book.

Lived experiences of 'ubiquitous conditionality'

A notable feature of welfare reform over the last 35 years has been the increased reliance on behavioural conditionality in efforts to 'support' claimants off benefits and into the formal labour market (see Chapter Two) (Deacon and Patrick, 2011; Dwyer and Wright, 2014). This continued under Cameron's governments, which extended both the reach of conditionality and the possible consequences of failing to comply with the regime. Despite the consensus across all the main political parties on the central place of welfare conditionality in policy responses to unemployment and economic inactivity (as well as in a range of other policy domains), the efficacy and ethicality of conditionality remains contested, particularly in the academic community (Dwyer, 2010; Patrick, 2011; Grover, 2012; Whitworth and Griggs, 2013; Standing, 2014; Dwyer and Bright, 2016).

By tracking experiences of welfare conditionality over time it has been possible to explore both immediate and longer-term responses to conditionality and compulsion. The following outlines some of these responses and highlights how conditionality operates in various and sometimes contradictory ways, often simultaneously. Given that those interviewed encompassed disability benefit claimants, jobseekers and single parents moving from IS to JSA, the forms of conditionality experienced included mandatory attendance at appointments, demands to change and/or increase job search activities and the requirement to participate in welfare-to-work programmes, training courses and unpaid work experience placements. Throughout, sanctions operate as the ever-present threat for noncompliance with these demands.

Documenting individuals' experiences illustrated how far conditionality has become mainstreamed and 'ubiquitous' (Dwyer and Wright, 2014), with 13 of the longitudinal sample experiencing at least one form of conditionality during the initial research period. The most commonly applied form of conditionality was mandatory attendance at appointments, which included signing on at Job Centres and WFIs for disability benefit claimants and single parents not yet migrated over to JSA. Five experienced at least one benefit sanction during the initial research period. For three of these it was their first sanction, while two of the jobseekers – Adrian and Robert – experienced multiple sanctions. Ten described being threatened with sanctions, illustrating the embedded nature of sanctions as a policy tool and threat within today's social security system.

Kane and Cath were the only individuals not to be made subject to any form of work-related conditionality. While Cath was on IB before being transferred to the SG of ESA, Kane was placed in the WRAG of ESA, where he would have expected to experience some conditionality as part of efforts to support him into the paid labour market in the longer term. Kane spent over six months in the WRAG, yet for unknown reasons he was never invited to attend a WFI or offered any other work-related support, which he expressed disappointment about (see Chapter Four). The fact that Kane felt let down, even excluded, by not being asked to attend the JCP suggests that some individuals welcome – or at least want to be included within – the conditionality regime, while also indicating the broader issues with the limited provision of employment support to those in the WRAG (Hale, 2014).

Individuals' responses to work-related welfare conditionality were often ambiguous and complex; they were simultaneously resistant to and partially welcoming of the compulsion and demands being made of them. To understand these responses, they must be situated within the context of individuals who in most cases displayed strong and clear orientations to engagement in the paid labour market (see Chapter Four).

Karen felt both excited and frightened about moving onto JSA and the additional conditions this would involve:

> 'It's good to get out of the house, not to be stuck at home all day, but at the same time I'm scared to get out there and do it all again ... It's going to push me to get a job, but at the same time it's pushing me too fast.' (W2)

For Sophie and Sam, both on JSA by the time of the third interview, conditionality was viewed as largely unproblematic – not because it was not affecting them, but because they were both actively seeking paid employment and so were relaxed about fulfilling work-related demands. Anticipating being moved onto JSA, Sophie explained:

> 'It don't bother me one bit.' (W2)

A year later, she reflected on her transition from IS to JSA:

> '[It's made] no difference 'cause I were looking for work before anyway.' (W3)

Negative experiences of conditionality

More negative experiences and responses to conditionality were widespread. These encompassed the denial of agency conditionality was seen to entail, the fear of hardship and destitution underpinning it, a resistance to the language and operation of compulsion and negative consequences for relations between street-level advisers and claimants founded on conditionality and the threat of sanctions. Finally, several saw the benefits system and its constant conditionality as being so demanding and unpleasant that it served as an additional motivation to transition into paid employment. Evidently, this last response may be one some politicians would welcome, especially when viewed within the rubric of benefits as a 'lifestyle choice' (cf. Osborne, 2010).

Susan grew increasingly weary of her interactions with the JCP and the WP. As such, a major advantage of moving into paid employment became the opportunity it would provide to escape from the welfare conditionality regime. She repeatedly described her aspiration for a future:

> 'Getting off benefits and being able to support myself, where no one is going to say "do this", "come here", none of that.' (W1)

Resistance to the language and operation of conditionality was particularly common and a dominant theme to emerge from all four waves of interviews. Individuals often picked up on the lack of choice that conditionality entailed. A narrative that simply said 'you must do this' left no room for their own preferences to be expressed and valued. This was experienced as a denial of agency:

> 'It's like, when you're on benefits, they're controlling what you do and when you do them. You haven't got your own mind, you've got to do everything by what they say … And sometimes you don't want to.' (James, W1)

It was common for individuals to also describe conditionality as a paternalistic practice that treated them as children to be directed and controlled instead of adults with a right to make their own choices:

> '[On benefits] you're not getting spoken to like a person … [you're] getting told to like a child. Saying "you will do this, otherwise…".' (James, W1)

The logic of contractualism so often used to defend conditionality suggests two parties freely entering into an agreement, with the right to benefits contingent on the responsibility to comply with work-related demands (Deacon, 2002; Dwyer, 2010). However, the reality is that claimants often have little real choice, particularly when they are completely financially reliant on their out-of-work benefits (White, 2003; Fitzpatrick, 2004). Robert was made to sign a contract saying he would apply for ten jobs every week:

> Robert: '[If] I haven't found ten jobs to apply for then they'll sanction my money … I don't know how they can force you to sign a contract for that.'

Ruth: 'Did you sign the contract then?'

Robert: 'Yeah 'cause I had to, otherwise I would've got sanctioned.' (W2)

Robert also recounted particular frustrations when his WP adviser handed him a ream of paper with around 70 jobs to phone and apply for, threatening him with a sanction if he did not apply for them all. The roles were in security – the sector Robert wanted to work in – but he was unable to ring each of the potential employers because he had no phone credit. Robert's poverty and the structural constraints it placed on him made it impossible for him to comply with this work-related demand, for which he potentially faced a sanction.

Robert also felt less inclined to comply with his adviser's demands because of how she interacted with him:

'It's how she spoke to me about it. Now if she would have said, "would you", not "you have to", that's where they go wrong. If they say "you have to do it", then no, I won't do it. But if it's "would you do it", then yeah I would. But I'm not having somebody telling me to do summat.' (W3)

Robert repeatedly refused to fulfil the demands made of him, sometimes leading to confrontation and open conflict with his JCP and WP advisers and – of course – benefit sanctions. In these encounters, Robert was seeking to assert his individual agency – to make choices – albeit from within a relatively powerless position. Robert's active response and resistance reinforces Wright's (2016) conclusion that benefit claimants often experience powerlessness and a lack of choice and control, but simultaneously try to take active measures to change and challenge their situation. It also demonstrates the ways in which conditionality and compulsion can have perverse consequences, whereby individuals resist the demands made of them because of the supervisory nature of the encounters with their advisers.

Perverse consequences are also in evidence when conditionality operates to push people further away from, rather than closer to, the paid labour market. Isobella was on IB and doing permitted work – making and selling gift cards – at the time of her first interview. Over the course of the research, she was migrated onto ESA and initially placed in the WRAG, with her benefits time limited to a year. Isobella feared that her engagement in permitted work was making her look a "soft target":

'Because I'm on the permitted work scheme I do worry that, merely being on it, they're going to think, "oh, she can work", and put you in that group.' (W1)

By her third interview, Isobella had decided to stop this employment – partially due to other health-related issues, but also because she wanted to do everything she could to make sure she was not incorrectly classified as capable of participating in the formal labour market. In this way, Isobella's transition from IB to the more conditional ESA, and the related questioning of her eligibility for unconditional disability benefit, perversely meant that the small amount of paid employment in which she had been engaging came to an end. Evidently this was not the policy intention, but it demonstrates the complex and sometimes unexpected nature of responses to welfare conditionality.

Reasons for resistance to conditionality

Over time, a majority of the longitudinal sample (ten of 15) described how conditionality forced them to do things they would not have done if they had been given the choice. Typically, this involved activities such as applying for jobs they did not want, attending appointments and participating in training and welfare-to-work programmes that they found unhelpful. Evidently, welfare conditionality is explicitly designed to compel out-of-work claimants to participate in work-related activity that the government deems will help move them closer to the paid labour market, with compulsion intended to counter any resistance to engagement (Gregg, 2008; DWP, 2010b). Individuals commonly linked their unwillingness to attend appointments and courses to their perception that these activities were failing to move them closer to work or were inappropriate, given other barriers to their participation in paid employment:

'[The course] didn't really help me at all … I'll do anything I can just to not go on it … I just didn't see the benefit to it at all.' (Josh, W1)

'It's quite irritating really because if you have a medical report saying one thing, and then the system forces you to attend these interviews or have these appointments, you're thinking … "I'm not fit for work, so why are you wasting time, effort and money forcing me to do these kind of

things when life would be a lot simpler [without them]".'
(Isobella, W3)

As with ESA and the WCA, conditionality undermines and even ignores the expertise of individuals themselves, whose own understandings of their barriers to work and the help that would be most beneficial for them rarely seemed to feature in officials' setting of work-related demands and activities.

There is a particular ethical issue when welfare conditionality compels people to participate in activities that actually conflict with individuals' own sense of responsibility and duty. There were several examples of the duty and obligation individuals felt as parents being undermined and challenged by the expectations of work-related welfare conditionality. Sophie found the JCP inflexible, with advisers displaying a lack of understanding towards parents' particular needs and undervaluing the parenting work in which she was engaged. She recounted being given an appointment for 5.40 pm:

'When they make a time for you, you have to go. I'm like "my kids are in bed at half past six". They're like "but that's not our problem, you have to come or we'll take so much off your benefits".' (W1)

Susan explained how the JCP had tried to make an appointment for her that clashed with the time of her daughter's swimming lesson:

'And then she [Job Centre adviser] said, "are you aware you have an appointment on Friday at twenty past four?" And I said, "oh, ok". And then I remembered, I had just enrolled my daughter in swimming lessons on Fridays, 4.30. So I said "Oh, no I can't. I've just enrolled my daughter" and I think that Friday was going to be the first lesson … And then she went and talked to someone. And then she came back, she said, "Sorry, we cannot accept such excuses". I said, "It's not an excuse. Look, I've got her swimming costume and all that with me." I got out the receipts. They were still in my purse, and I said, "there's the receipts as well." Because it's not easy for me, to pay like £50. And then the man came as well, and he said, "do you know that your priority is attending these appointments?" I said; "I don't think so," I said, "My priority is being a mother". Because whether I'm

drawing Job Seeker's Allowance, whether Income Support,
nothing, my daughter will always be there [crying].' (W1)

Susan experienced conflicting demands from her dual responsibilities
as a parent and a jobseeker, which were not always easily reconciled.
She was frustrated and angry that JCP staff assumed that the jobseeker
role should be prioritised, given that this was out of step with her own
interpretation of her responsibilities.

What is notable about both of these examples is that the individuals
did want to enter paid work but experienced a JCP environment that
refused them flexibility over appointment times – a perhaps small but
significant manifestation of a broader ignoring and undervaluing of
their parenting work. When the conditions of out-of-work benefits
compel parents to put work-related demands before their parenting, and
when this is out of line with their own moral ordering of priorities, the
policy agenda is significantly infringing upon and limiting individuals'
citizenship rights. Affected individuals experience a policy regime that
undermines their own moral rationalities of parenthood (Duncan and
Edwards, 1999): how they understand their responsibilities as a parent.
This is all the more important because it is not equally experienced
by all parents in society but only by those at the bottom end of the
income spectrum, whose reliance on the most stigmatised and overt
form of state assistance means they are also most subject to the state's
punitive and coercive gaze.

Chloe's 'welfare reform journey'

Chloe has already been highlighted as an individual who described
preferring to stay on benefits rather than seek paid employment (see
Chapter Four). Her experiences of and interaction with welfare
conditionality as a single parent are particularly interesting, especially as
she most closely fits recent governments' characterisation of claimants
who 'choose' a life on benefits and so need conditionality and the threat
of sanctions to activate them into paid employment. At the time of her
first interview, Chloe was anticipating being moved from IS onto JSA
and the extra conditionality this would entail. She appeared resigned
that this would see her move into employment:

'You've got no choice ... You're going to have to go and
find a job ... If they're going to send you to work, they're
going to send you to work, aren't they?' (W1)

In this interview, Chloe was fairly upbeat about how she currently managed on IS:

> 'It [benefits] just makes you plod along and gets you your essentials.'

Little had changed by the second interview and Chloe was still waiting to be migrated onto JSA:

> 'I'm a bit nervous [about the changes] but I've got no choice have I.' (W2)

A year later, Chloe had been on JSA for a little over two months. She had immediately struggled to comply with the conditionality regime and had missed several appointments:

> 'They were adding more stress to me life ... asking me about computers and all that. I don't know how to do it. They want me to go on courses to learn how to do it and to put my CV out there. But if you haven't worked for like, God, five or six years it's hard. It's nerve wracking to go back out to work.' (W3)

Chloe's JCP adviser sanctioned her for not doing enough to seek paid employment and failing to attend several appointments. When she found out she had been sanctioned, Chloe:

> 'Cried. Phoned everybody possible and just tried to get it sorted out ... I think I cried solid for, like, two week. I couldn't cope.' (W3)

The sanction meant real hardship for Chloe and her two children:

> 'Four weeks with no money is pretty alarming when you've got kids and bills and a house to run.' (W3)

Chloe's mental health appeared to have significantly worsened, and she described her struggle to cope with day-to-day life:

> 'We're paupers, we're so poor. It's like we're living in – you know where you see all these adverts – please feed our children – feed my bloody children ... Me Dad asked me

if I were on drugs the other day, and I said, "No." He said I'm looking right withdrawn in face. I said, "Dad, I am stressed, you have to have money to get drugs, Dad". So at the end of the day, no, it's stress, can't cope.' (W3)

As a result of the sanction, Chloe sought advice from a charity that had previously provided her with support following domestic violence. Given Chloe's deteriorating mental health, the charity advised Chloe to put in a claim for ESA, which was successful. Although Chloe's narrative perhaps suggested someone for whom the conditionality regime was designed, the various barriers she faced to paid employment as well as her significant situational vulnerabilities (including poor mental health, history of domestic violence and periods of substance misuse) meant it actually operated to push her further away from the paid labour market. There are real questions with the ethicality and efficacy of sanctioning such individuals, especially given the risk of third-party harm to others (White, 2003), in this case Chloe's two children. Being sanctioned adversely affected Chloe's mental health and made it harder for her to fulfil her parenting responsibilities. Even if one were to take the view that Chloe's failure to fulfil work-related demands required a disciplinary, punitive response, there remains a question about the appropriateness of this being a financial sanction that directly and negatively affected her children as well as herself. Single-parent charity Gingerbread (2014) has warned that benefit sanctions can adversely affect children, whose health and ability to concentrate at school can be undermined when their household income falls following the loss of income that sanctions cause.

Benefit sanctions: Adrian's 'welfare reform journey'

To look more closely at benefit sanctions, the experiences of Adrian – who faced both lengthy and repeated sanctions – are now outlined. The other individuals who were sanctioned faced shorter periods without benefits; but, like Adrian, they highlighted the hardship sanctions caused and the lack of clarity behind sanction decisions – something reinforced by the existing research evidence into their operation and impact (Watts et al., 2014; Dwyer and Bright, 2016; Fitzpatrick et al., 2016).

Adrian was one of a small number of the sample (two of the 22) who had virtually no experience of paid employment. He had been sanctioned numerous times in the past, often due to miscommunication and misunderstandings rather than a deliberate failure to comply with work-related activity and requirements. He spent almost a year without any money during a succession of sanctions:

> 'When they didn't tell me about Hardship, I had to go into town every day stealing sandwiches and stuff. And I got caught for this. They sent me to court and I just thought to myself, "well, this is maybe what they want me to do", you know what I mean? I can die or I can commit crime so I thought, "well I'm not letting them win", so I didn't commit a crime after that.' (W1)

At the time of the first and second interviews, Adrian was on a six-month sanction:

> 'I did get this, kind of a job, it was door-to-door sales but it was on commission so I tried it out for a week and then I just ... [gave it up] because ... what I was trying to sell nobody ... were buying it. But what the Job Centre have done – they've given me a sheet – the sheet says I have to apply for this [cafe] job but I already applied for that [sales] job and got that job ... so they sanctioned me for not applying for this [cafe] job even though I already had that [sales] job.' (W1)

Adrian found the logic for this sanction difficult to understand. His experiences tally with what Alison Garnham, Chief Executive of the CPAG, has called the 'frail grounds' behind many sanction decisions (cited in Ahrends, 2015).

Although Adrian sometimes tried to appeal the sanctions he faced, he struggled with the impersonal bureaucracy of the process:

> 'My sanction, when they make the decision themselves, it's not the person you're speaking to, it's not even really a fair trial. What they do is they write down [their decision] and just fax it off to someone in Doncaster or Sheffield that's not even sat next to me, and then they say well sanction for a year. They're just reading it off a bit of black and white paper ... Something like that, it's like the court sentencing me to a crime when I'm not there.' (W2)

The contrast Adrian draws between the sanctions system and the criminal justice system is also drawn by Webster (2015), who describes the former as 'Britain's secret penal system', which lacks the safeguards designed to protect offenders in the mainstream judicial system.

When asked how he felt when he realised he had been sanctioned, Adrian responded:

> 'Phew, not very good, really. I mean in my head, somewhere in my head I were like "well I'm going to have to go back into crime again" ... Just to survive. I'll keep out of it though. But it's a horrible feeling.' (W1)

After three months on this sanction, its adverse effects on Adrian were clear:

> 'I've lost a lot of weight because of it. That's really put me down ... I'm having like one, one and a half meals a day.' (W2)

Ironically, Adrian felt that sanctions made it harder for him to seek employment:

> 'You'd ring them [employers] up and they'd say "oh, come down, we'll go for an interview". You'd go for an interview and if it's a point where you're being sanctioned, you're all ... skinny and everything, you look proper ill. They look at you and go "nah, you look like a crackhead or something".' (W1)

As a result of the non-payment of a fine relating to his shoplifting when on a previous sanction, Adrian spent a short period of time in prison between the second and third interviews. During this time, arrears built up on Adrian's housing association flat when his Housing Benefit was stopped due to his sanction. He did not realise he had to complete additional paperwork for his claim to continue and was subsequently evicted from his home.

By the time of the third interview, Adrian was no longer on a benefit sanction and was living in a homeless hostel, where he also volunteered. He had managed to stay clear of shoplifting and petty crime, instead relying on support from the hostel. Looking back at his experience of benefit sanctions over the time of the research, Adrian concluded:

> 'Say my life in the last year and a half, everything that's gone on, if I just take everything out that's gone on apart from

the benefits, the benefits issues and just leave that there, I'd call it hell.' (W3)

His experience of sanctions – in conjunction with interactions at the Job Centre, which he described very negatively – hardened Adrian's resolve and determination to leave benefits behind and secure paid employment:

'I don't even wanna be anywhere near the Job Centre, I just want a job.' (W3)

However, Adrian arguably needed personalised and dedicated support if he was to find paid employment – support that was not forthcoming during the initial research period. Research suggests that the most vulnerable are the most at risk from benefit sanctions (Peters and Joyce, 2006; Griggs and Evans, 2010; Finn and Casebourne, 2012; Manchester CAB, 2013; Oakley, 2014; Welfare Reform Committee, 2014; Dwyer and Bright, 2016). Adrian could be described as vulnerable and he had experienced considerable disadvantage, including time in care as a child, a history of offending as a teenager and young adult and very limited educational opportunities. Adrian's case study illustrates the cumulative adverse effects of repeated sanctions on individuals' lives. It also demonstrates the extent to which the promise of a social security 'safety net' is now being withdrawn from those judged not to be complying with the conditionality regime.

Exploring experiences of welfare conditionality and benefit sanctions shows that, while individuals occasionally welcome what they regard as the "extra push" provided by conditionality, it regularly operates in more perverse ways: preventing people from engaging in or welcoming back-to-work support and even pushing them further away from, rather than closer to, the labour market. The findings from this research correspond with the evidence emerging from a large-scale qualitative longitudinal study of conditionality's impact across a diverse range of claimants groups (Dwyer and Bright, 2016). Following the first wave of interviews with almost five hundred individuals, Dwyer and Bright concluded that there was: 'limited evidence to date of welfare conditionality bringing about positive behaviour change. Evidence of it working to move people nearer to the paid labour market was rare' (2016, p. 1).

The work associated with welfare reform

Living through welfare reform and engaging with the demands made by the conditionality and sanctions regime can be time intensive, emotionally demanding and repetitive, requiring the completion of endless forms, appearances at interviews and appointments and the provision of proof of work-search and activity. While there is growing media and political interest in the adverse financial consequences of welfare reform (cf. Jones, 2015; Robinson, 2016; Stone, 2016), there has been less recognition to date of the work it entails for those directly affected – work that creates an extra burden on those already struggling to get by on benefits (see Chapter Three).

Particular work is required to challenge decisions with which individuals disagree, for example regarding eligibility for disability benefits or sanctioning. Isobella had a long struggle with the DWP following an initial decision – made without a WCA – that she should be placed in the WRAG of ESA. As Isobella was a homeowner with fairly substantial savings, this outcome meant she was subject to new rules limiting entitlement to contributory ESA to 12 months for those in the WRAG. At the same time as disputing her ESA eligibility, Isobella was also appealing a decision on DLA and so was in frequent communication with the DWP. She described the toll this was taking:

'It [challenging the DWP] does take a lot out of you. I mean I think especially with the rheumatoid arthritis because it's a fatigue side as well so I do get very tired very quickly … when you're in the system like this it can be very down-heartening, time consuming and energy sapping.' (W2)

'I think this [benefits] system sometimes becomes bigger than the problem that I've got health-wise because you're fighting a big system, and that's more difficult to do.' (W2)

Isobella sometimes put off making phone calls to the DWP:

'It's got to be on a good day for me [to ring them] … I've got to think, oh right, okay, I … feel … ready to fight … you need that push, that energy.' (W3)

Another disability benefit(s) claimant, Cath, was eventually awarded DLA after a successful appeal (and following two previously unsuccessful applications). For Cath, the benefits system:

'grind[s] you down. That's the system, it's designed to do it. Yeah ... and they do it well as well.' (W2)

After finding out about her second unsuccessful application, Cath burnt all her papers:

'When I got home that evening I burnt 'em and I thought, "that's it, I'm finished with [them]. You can't fight 'em".' (W2)

Despite wanting to "give up", with the support of a welfare rights adviser Cath appealed this decision, attending a tribunal where she was awarded DLA. She described how she drew on her reserves of strength and resilience:

'I get bursts of, we'd say 'spunk and grit' ... and it comes from inside, and [you think] "just yes and do it".' (W3)

The DLA award made a significant difference to Cath's life, giving her a small financial cushion and helping her to meet the extra costs associated with her impairments. Cath reflected on the difference it had made:

'Worry. Gone. Gone. No more stale bread, no more off milk, no more going without ... a conversation of lack, constant lack is not here anymore ... The worry has just gone, the constant worry. It was like constant rain.' (W3)

While Cath was pleased to have been awarded DLA, at the time of her third interview she had just been told she could be affected by the bedroom tax. Cath was also aware of the planned replacement of DLA with PIPs and was concerned that her recently awarded DLA would not be available to her under the new regime. When asked what she expected to happen to her benefits in the future, Cath replied:

'I expect them to take it all back off me.' (W3)

In this way, just as anxiety over one welfare reform was temporarily resolved another took its place, leaving Cath in a constant loop of fear, anxiety and stress.

The work of challenging benefit decisions demands considerable energy and resilience. Individuals demonstrated active resistance to officials' judgements and classification, with the hard work involved in making these appeals yet another counter to the notion of inactive benefit claimants. As a result of this work, individuals often experienced significant qualitative improvements in their circumstances in relation to benefit entitlement. This has particular implications for others who are perhaps less able or willing to pursue benefit appeals and challenges.

The Legal Aid reforms and new rules on mandatory reconsideration of benefit decisions are likely to make the work of challenging decisions more difficult and they could mean some of the most vulnerable simply feel unable to and/or not fully aware of their rights to do so. There are fears that the Legal Aid reforms will create a 'justice gap', with some of the poorest and most vulnerable in society unable to challenge benefit decisions due to an 'advice desert' following the withdrawal of funding (Legal Action Group, 2013). A recent survey of advice workers in Liverpool found that 94% of those who responded did not agree that all those who needed advice were able to access it, suggesting a high level of unmet need (Organ and Sigafoos, forthcoming).

To fully assess the impact of welfare reform it is critical to consider the ways in which it adds to the work associated with benefits receipt. The work that welfare reform demands may reduce the time available for individuals to actively engage in job-search and long-term future planning, which could make entry into employment less rather than more likely. Although this chapter has focused on the work welfare reform requires of those affected, it also – of course – creates considerable work for welfare state officials, support agencies and local authorities, with inevitable (but arguably neglected) cost and resource implications.

The costs of welfare reform

Clearly, welfare reform also incurs considerable human costs. These are not just financial but also extend to its emotional effects, impacts on health and the ways it infringes on an individual's capacity to think about and plan for the future. These costs, in conjunction with the work it entails, can together be described as 'the burden of welfare reform'. The financial costs of welfare reform were most stark when individuals had been sanctioned due to the impact of being expected to manage on zero income. Rosie, a single parent, reflected on the impact a sanction had on her and her young son:

> 'They're all right saying that [a sanction] is a punishment for
> not going in but what are me and my son meant to eat for

the rest of that week? Really, they were quick enough to take our money but if that's the only money we're getting, what are we meant to do?' (W2)

Single parents reported particular difficulties managing with the shift from weekly to fortnightly payment of IS:

'Ever since it's gone fortnightly it's so hard. I've never been so skint in my life. I've never got any money.' (Chloe, W3)

'You could manage it easier [when it was weekly]. It were like you got paid every week, you paid everything off every week.' (Karen, W2)

Stretching the budgetary period from a week to a fortnight was associated with increased debt and financial hardship. Under Universal Credit, payment is made monthly to encourage recipients to get into the 'habit' of monthly money management, which the Coalition government described as the norm for 'working families' (DWP, 2010c). In fact, many employees – particularly in low-paid sectors – are still paid weekly and fortnightly (Bennett, 2012). Individuals were resistant to a future of monthly payments:

'It's the worst thing you could do. I understand why they're doing it 'cause they're trying to get people used to monthly wages but not people on benefits. Not on what we get.' (Karen, W2)

In this instance, the government's reform trajectory is out of step with families' own strategies for managing to get by on out-of-work benefits, with negative consequences already noted in the shift to fortnightly payments and further negative implications anticipated as monthly payments under UC is rolled out (Bennett, 2012; Tarr and Finn, 2012).

Reforms such as the bedroom tax, abolition of the Social Fund, roll out of Universal Credit and localisation of Council Tax Benefit were only just starting to be implemented at the time of the third interviews, meaning that individuals were yet to feel some of the most substantial financial impacts of the Coalition's welfare reform programme. Individuals' growing awareness of the tenor and pace of welfare reform meant they anticipated future financial consequences, which sometimes led them to change their current financial management as well as further adding to feelings of fear and unease about the future:

'I have been ... looking at essentials myself ... food and electricity and things like that so I'm conscious that everything's going up but my money isn't so I will have to take some measures to cut back. Whether that be on food or putting another woolly on instead of putting the heating on.' (Isobella, W2)

A climate of ongoing welfare reform and the politicians' repeated promises to make further changes to the benefits system seemed to have created a new status quo of anxiety and insecurity for the individuals interviewed. Some drew an explicit contrast between a previous period of relatively stable benefits receipt and their current uncertainty about future eligibility and levels of benefits. Tessa had been on IB without interruption for almost ten years prior to being migrated onto ESA. She was then assessed twice in the course of just 18 months and on one of these occasions placed in the WRAG, before appealing and being moved over to the SG:

'They check them [benefits] more than any time in the past and ... [benefits] can just be taken away ... I'm really anxious about [another medical], I'm just trying my best not to think about it and sort of focus on it, 'cause if I do focus on it, it just gets me really upset.' (W3)

A pervasive fear about the consequences of welfare reform was heightened by the rhetorical backdrop of government and media pronouncements on the need to get 'tough' on 'welfare' and finally end 'welfare dependency'. Many felt targeted and that their deservingness of benefits was being undermined:

'[the government] does seem to be picking on the most vulnerable, they pick us off one at a time. That's how they get us.' (Cath, W1)

Anxiety and worry were particularly notable among disabled individuals:

'I've been thinking if they did stop my benefits, I don't know what I'd do. I know for a fact I'd end up poorly and in hospital again.' ('Jessica', W1)

'[I'm] frightened. Frightened because if I'm going to be any worse off I might as well move onto a park bench. Where do you go from here?' (Cath, W1)

Given a sense of uncertainty around future benefit entitlement and eligibility, individuals often explained how the ever-present backdrop of welfare reform was making it harder for them to plan for the future. Experiences of welfare reform added an extra layer of insecurity and uncertainty to the already challenging context of getting by on benefits and made planning much more difficult. This made taking active steps to make changes in their lives less likely – an outcome that goes against the broader remit of welfare reform.

Many feared that in the future their benefits would end or be reduced. As a result, they simply felt unable to implement positive changes in their lives in case these unravelled and became unsustainable when further reforms took effect. James made an explicit link between the ongoing reforms and his uncertainty about his options for the future:

'You're thinking, if I stay on benefits, they're making all these ... cuts and stuff, you don't know what your options are.' (W1)

The combination of uncertainties around her benefit entitlement and a feared further deterioration in her health left Isobella simply not wanting to think about the future:

'I can't think about [the future] because that just depresses me because I can't envisage my situation changing dramatically for the better. And obviously if it doesn't change dramatically for the better [laughs], then the likelihood is that it's going to get worse. And that's a bit scary.' (W3)

This demonstrates how processes of welfare reform affected people's ability to mobilise the future as a resource for trying to imagine a more positive future life, as well as hinting at the reach of the negative consequences of welfare reform.

Inevitably, perhaps, the climate of anxiety and uncertainty around welfare reform often had a negative impact on individuals' health and wellbeing. In correspondence following her third interview, Susan reported that she had been prescribed antidepressants for the first time – a decline in her mental health she directly attributed to the stress and pressures of dealing with the welfare conditionality regime. Isobella and Sharon also described how their health was adversely affected by welfare reform:

> 'I have felt quite depressed with this ... it's not been the best few months.' (Isobella, W2)

> 'It's just made my depression worse.' (Sharon, W1)

For Isobella, completing her disability benefit claim forms took a particular toll:

> 'You want to forget [how bad it is] you don't want to dwell on the bad things. But [the form is] designed that you've always got to think well, this is on a worst day. And, of course, by the end of the form you've got yourself in such a bleak mood that the only thing that can get you out of it is coffee and cake ... I think it took me about four days to fill the form in because I could only do so much before thinking, I'm fed up with this. Fed up with feeling low and having to write this so that they'll understand it.' (W3)

Tessa and her psychiatrist were concerned about the worry and anxiety the ESA migration was causing her, given that experiencing stress could lead to a worsening of her paranoid schizophrenia:

> 'I told my psychiatrist, "I've not heard anything [about ESA]". And she was saying "well, look, you need to keep your stress levels down" ... and it does stress you out. You've got a partner who's not well, you're not well yourself every day, and you get benefit letters and if you're not careful your schizophrenia goes through the roof, your voices, your hallucinations, your paranoias ... And I don't think they [DWP] realise that. We're just a name on a page, just no one.' (W2)

Tess and Isobella were already living with severe impairments. Their interactions with the benefits system placed additional strain on their mental health – an indication of the health costs welfare reform can incur.

Conclusion

This chapter has explored the lived experiences of welfare reform for a small group of directly affected individuals. It has shown the ways in which the ever-present threat of further welfare reform impacts and impinges upon their capacity to plan for and look forward to the future. By detailing experiences of disability benefit reform, intensified conditionality and sanctions, this chapter has also highlighted how conditionality can have the perverse consequence of moving people further away from, rather than closer to, the paid labour market. These perverse consequences suggest a flaw with the current policy approach, which sometimes appears to undermine rather than support welfare-to-work transitions.

A detailed examination of Chloe's experiences of conditionality showed how its application to an individual who expressed a 'preference' for benefits over work did not create the circumstances from which she could move from 'welfare' and into 'work'. Chloe was simply unable to meet the demands that being on JSA made of her and so applied successfully for ESA, where she was subject to less intensive conditionality. Chloe's welfare reform journey reminds us that the policy intent of welfare conditionality and its actual effects do not always correspond.

The emotional, health and financial costs of welfare reform have also been detailed, as have the ways in which processes associated with benefits changes – and challenging decisions with which individuals disagree – only add to the work that getting by on benefits demands. Taken together, there is evidence of a significant burden caused by welfare reform – a burden inevitably most strongly felt by those who are the targets of the changes. Often, what was particularly notable in the day-to-day lives of individual benefit recipients was a combination of constancy and flux: constancy in the relentless, repetitive struggles to get by and cope with and sometimes challenge welfare reforms; flux given the backdrop of welfare reform and ongoing, cumulative changes to benefits entitlement.

The policy narrative suggests that a drive to reform welfare will reap rewards by making our 'welfare' budget more affordable, transforming individual lives and returning 'fairness' to the benefits system. However, lived experiences of welfare reform challenge each of these claims. While money may be saved by restricting eligibility for benefits, more needs to be done to estimate the human and financial costs that are the by-products of the endless drive for reform – costs that extend to the state resources required to administer checks on benefit eligibility and appeals of benefit decisions. There is very little evidence to suggest that welfare conditionality and sanctions are effective tools in the 'welfare-to-work' effort (Watts et al., 2014) – and yet they remain central to the approach pursued. On sanctions, in particular, there is mounting evidence instead of the very real hardship that they cause and the lack of a causal link between imposing sanctions and supporting sustainable welfare-to-work transitions. A National Audit Office investigation into the value for money provided by the sanctions regime found that sanctioned claimants were as likely to stop claiming benefits as they were to move into paid work, while, for disabled claimants, being sanctioned actually made finding work harder (National Audit Office, 2016). Against this context, politicians continue to emphasise the central place of sanctions in a well-functioning benefits system, with Damian Green using his first major speech as Secretary of State for the DWP to argue: "we need sanctions, and I don't agree with those who would abolish them" (Green, 2016). In this case, the policy approach continues *in spite* rather than *because of* the available research evidence of its impact.

Finally, on the question of 'fairness', the public and its political representatives have to decide what type of social security system they want to provide and whether they are comfortable with one that takes as its starting point the assumption that individuals requires compulsion and condition to 'help' them off benefits and into work. Welfare reform operates to undermine the social rights of citizenship in ways that make remaining rights ever more conditional, fractured and contingent. There are evident citizenship implications that flow from this, not least with regard to the extent to which citizenship processes now operate to exclude rather than include citizens who are living in poverty and subject to welfare reform (see Chapter Eight). The policy rhetoric implies that welfare-to-work measures and associated reforms will lead to the inclusion of targeted individuals. But this masks the excluding and exclusionary effects these policies can and do have. The exclusionary potential of social citizenship and welfare reform is only hardened by a popular narrative that so often blames individual benefit recipients for their own poverty, targeting them with a stigmatising and demeaning rhetoric. In the next chapter, the impact of the pervasive stigma around benefits receipt is examined and its reach and effects detailed.

SIX

Scroungerphobia: living with the stigma of benefits

In seeking to justify and defend their programme of welfare reform, Cameron's governments repeatedly stereotyped and stigmatised recipients of 'welfare' (Baumberg et al., 2012; Daguerre and Etherington, 2014). In speeches, policy documents and media interventions, they characterised 'welfare dependants' as 'languishing' on benefits, all too often exhibiting a host of problematic and deficit behaviours (cf. Cameron, 2014b; Duncan Smith, 2014a). Through repeat interviews with out-of-work benefit claimants, this research allowed us to see how individuals were affected by the dominant narrative on 'welfare', which influences how they saw themselves and – importantly – how they saw and regard 'others'. As Hans Gerth and C. Wright Mills (1953, pp. 88–9) wrote more than 60 years ago:

> If the upper classes monopolise the means of communication and fill the several mass media with the idea that all those at the bottom are there because they are lazy, unintelligent and in general inferior, then these appraisals may be taken over by the poor and used in the building of an image of their selves.

Theorists have repeatedly emphasised the importance of thinking of poverty and social exclusion not only as states of material deprivation, but also as ones with significant relational and psychological consequences and costs (Lister, 2004; Levitas, 2006; Walker, 2014; Wright, 2016). This chapter examines the relational dimension of out-of-work benefits receipt and explores how individuals respond to being at the receiving end of a punitive and demeaning rhetoric. It demonstrates the consequences this can have for individuals' identity and sense of self-worth, as well as the ways in which the benefits system itself so often reproduces and reanimates benefits stigma. Following an outline of experiences of benefits stigma, this chapter goes on to look at how individuals challenge and manage this stigma – most commonly through engagement in a defensive 'othering' of those judged less deserving of state support. Attitudes towards welfare reform and conditionality are then outlined, showing how individuals are often receptive to the case being made for welfare reform despite being adversely affected themselves by the changes introduced.

How benefit claimants see themselves

In the UK today, stigma and shame are very commonly associated with benefits receipt and the poverty it so often entails (Macmillan, 2003; Batty and Flint, 2013; Shildrick and MacDonald, 2013; Garthwaite, 2014; Graham et al., 2014; Walker, 2014; Wright, 2016). Distinctions drawn between 'them' and 'us' operate to determine who has lower and higher social status and feed into a shaming process that has negative implications for those judged to be at the bottom of the social hierarchy (Walker et al., 2013, 2014). Shaming that is backed by the power of the state is best described as 'stigmatisation' (Walker et al., 2014).

In his classic work, Goffman (1990) defines stigma as: 'The phenomenon whereby an individual with an attribute which is deeply discredited by his/her society is rejected as a result of the attribute. Stigma is a process by which the reaction of others spoils normal identity' (p. 3). Goffman's theoretical account of stigma recognises how people with deviant or discredited identities and behaviours (which he terms 'attributes') can be rejected and excluded from society. It focuses on the relational and the consequences of having particular characteristics that set one apart from the 'normal'. The process of stigma 'spoils' affected individuals' identities and casts them as deviant and 'other'. This is of clear relevance for out-of-work benefit claimants, whose non-work and out-of-work benefits receipt are so often seen as problematic 'attributes'.

Baumberg's (2016) study of stigma and benefits describes how stigma and shame operate on three levels. 'Personal stigma' is a person's 'own feeling that claiming benefits is shameful' (Baumberg et al., 2012, p. 5). 'Stigmatisation' is the view that others see claiming benefits as shameful, while 'claims stigma' refers to the shame and stigma attached to the processes of claiming benefits (Baumberg, 2016). These three categories are closely related and often difficult to disentangle because, for example, processes of stigmatisation and experiences of claims stigma often feed into and directly contribute towards personal stigma. Rather than thinking of them as separate categories, they are best understood as dimensions of an overarching experience of stigma. As useful concepts for better understanding the drivers behind stigma, they are employed here to explore individuals' experiences and understanding of the stigma(s) they faced.

Personal stigma

Ten individuals in the longitudinal sample described living with the personal stigma of benefits receipt. They frequently tied their feelings of shame regarding benefits receipt to the lived realities of getting by on benefits. Particularly negative associations were attached to having to go without, occasional engagement in criminal activity such as shoplifting and being unable to participate in social events and family celebrations. There were signs that individuals internalised and perhaps partially accepted processes of stigmatisation, with some appropriating the derogatory words associated with benefits reliance to describe themselves:

> 'I feel like a bum. I feel useless. When you're walking around the streets … everybody knows that you're not a worker because you're out and about through the day so you feel worthless. … You feel like some people are looking at you as if to say "fucking, he's taking piss, he's another one that just sits about and does nowt". And then when you go shopping and you're having to buy all the cheapo stuff, you feel, I don't know, you feel ashamed. That's how it is. You see people putting nice products in their trolleys and you can't, you've got to get the minimum and it's tough if you like it or not because that's all you can afford.' (James, W1)

Here, James describes how his feelings about his benefits receipt are bound up in his assumptions about how other people perceive and judge him, illustrating the close links between personal stigma and stigmatisation. James explained earlier in the interview that he had no direct experience of being treated differently due to his benefits receipt. This suggests that he was projecting his own views about being on benefits, perhaps combined with a broader awareness of the stigmatising of 'welfare dependency', onto an expectation that others would also be critical of him.

Individuals often talked about their benefits receipt negatively; some self-described it as 'scrounging'. In particular, young jobseeker Sam replicated dominant narratives, describing herself as a "scrounger" in two of her three interviews. This critical self-description emerged over time and seemed to correspond with her transition from IS onto JSA and into the world of job search and Job Centres, again showing how the different dimensions of stigma intersect. In her first interview, Sam, a recent care leaver, had just secured an independent home and was at college full-time. Due to benefit changes, she was in the process of being moved off IS and onto JSA. At this point, Sam made no reference to 'scrounging'. By the time of the second and third interviews, Sam had left college and was trying – without success – to find paid employment:

> 'I feel a bit weird when it comes to the jobseekers bit because I don't like scrounging off of people ... I don't like scrounging money.' (W2)

> 'I need a job; because I'm sick of scrounging. That's how I think of it, anyway, I'm sick of scrounging.' (W3)

I asked Sam if she had felt like she was 'scrounging' when she was on IS:

> '[Before] maybe because I was a teenager and I didn't see it like that but now I've got more awareness that [benefits] come from the government. That's how I see that I'm scrounging money really.' (W2)

Sam saw a future move into paid employment as having the potential to "get that feeling of being ashamed off of me" (W3), and so her experiences of the shame and stigma of benefits receipt contributed towards her motivations to enter employment. Over time, as Sam continued to vocalise her experience of personal stigma, she demonstrated the extent to which benefits receipt can cause psychological and relational harm as well as material hardship (Lister, 2004).

Individuals' negative feelings about benefits receipt directly contributed to broader critical assessments of self, which were damaging to self-esteem and emotional wellbeing. This was evident in the cases of both Kane and Cath. Kane's third interview took place in prison, where he was serving a custodial sentence. He reflected on his previous spell on disability benefits:

> 'Being sat at home doing nowt, and your self-esteem, it doesn't do much good for your self-esteem, you feel useless.' (W3)

Kane sent me a letter from prison in which he described feeling "useless" and "like a burden" (see Figure 6.1). Kane suggested that the associations he attached to his benefits receipt actually contributed to a worsening of his mental health. This again highlights the personal stigma of benefits receipt.

Figure 6.1: Extract of letter from Kane

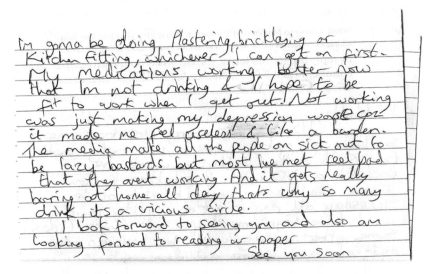

Cath also described her receipt of benefits as unwelcome and in all three of her interviews explicitly equated making a claim for DLA with "begging". Filling in the benefit claim forms makes "you feel like you're begging" (W1), she said; and she later reflected: "I'd like to be working … it is begging [being on benefits]" (W3). She explained:

> 'If I stay on benefits for the rest of my life then it's going to affect me for the rest of my life. It's going to keep me down, and a feeling of worthlessness as a human being. Like my life's not worth anything but theirs [the government's] and their families' lives are.' (W1)

For individuals like Cath, being on benefits has become a byword for a whole range of negative experiences and circumstances, which are all connected in some way with receipt of benefits and the poverty that entails. These include being economically inactive and seeing oneself as a 'welfare dependant' as well as the material manifestations of poverty and resultant societal exclusion.

Cath, Sam and Kane all saw being on benefits as inevitably bound up with feeling negatively about themselves and implied this could only be addressed by moving off benefits. Following people over time showed how changes in employment status affected experiences of personal stigma, with some welcoming the loss of stigma they associated with a move from out-of-work benefits into paid employment. This was particularly notable in Rosie's account. She started the research in receipt of out-of-work benefits but, by the time of her third interview, had just secured full-time employment (see Chapter Four). In this interview, Rosie reflected on her experiences on out-of-work benefits:

> 'I've been poorly through depression every time I've been on benefits, because my mum and dad have worked hard all their lives to be where they are now, so that's the impression I get, that you need to work hard and earn your money.' (W3)

> 'Benefits just isn't for me at all. I don't think I've got the mindset to be lazy because it'd just make me feel depressed. Some people don't mind being on benefits and watching TV or doing their own thing all the time and I just couldn't live like that anymore, so things are definitely better.' (W3)

Rosie felt as if she was a failure when she was receiving out-of-work benefits; she also seemed to associate benefits receipt with passivity and even laziness. Her narrative is an example of individuals internalising the dominant characterisation of 'welfare dependency' in ways that are perhaps indicative of a wider shift from conditionality to conditioning, whereby individuals self-regulate and critique their own non-working behaviours (see Chapter Eight).

Rosie contrasted this sense of failure and the depression she experienced with her changed situation on the cusp of secure, full-time employment:

> 'When you work for your money it's a lot different to receiving benefits, because you kind of feel better to spend that money because you've earned it.' (W3)

In this way, Rosie's intersecting 'welfare' and employment journeys illustrated the dynamic nature of the personal stigma around benefits, as well as the value attached to paid employment as a means of shedding such stigma.

Stigmatisation

Alongside expressions of personal stigma, it was common for individuals to experience the effects of stigmatisation; that is, the view that others see benefits receipt as shameful (Baumberg, 2016). Obviously, these subjective perspectives are themselves framed and interpreted through the lens of individuals' attitudes to their benefits receipt and so are closely connected to personal stigma.

Many appeared to understand – and even accept – what they perceived as people's antipathy towards benefit claimants:

> 'I think a lot of people who work do resent people who are on benefits 'cause it's like they're getting a chunk out of their wage ... getting put into the system for the benefits ... I'd probably feel the same.' (Sharon, W3)

> 'A lot of people don't like paying their taxes and it's going towards somebody who's not doing anything ... [and] I do tend to agree.'(Josh, W3)

At the same time as accepting resentment towards benefit claimants, individuals spoke of the impact of stigmatisation on their own lives, highlighting interactions with members of the public and shop staff and consequences for familial relations. Individuals felt they were treated differently because of their benefits receipt:

> 'I always feel like you get looked down on and stuff 'cause you're on benefits.' (Sophie, W1)

> 'People stare at you in the street like you're summat they stood on. I think it's just wrong.' (Karen, W1)

Karen highlighted the role social media increasingly plays in constructing and circulating critiques of out-of-work benefit claimants (Jensen, 2014; Tyler, 2014c), while also showing a resistance to the popular portrayal:

Karen: 'A lot of people just slag us [people on benefits] off. Like we don't work, we don't need to work 'cause we get paid for it and I want to work. I want to get off benefits but it's hard.'

151

Ruth: 'When you say people slag you off do you mean like to your face or ...'

Karen: No, it's all over Facebook like "oh, look at people on benefits, they get everything". But we don't.' (W1)

Three participants – Amy, Cath and Jessica – sometimes felt excluded from their families because, as benefit claimants, their poverty meant they could not participate in family celebrations; their benefits receipt was also perhaps shameful because it deviated from the family 'norm'. When asked if she felt being on benefits affected the way she was treated, Cath answered:

'Yeah, of course it does. In my own family ... I've had things like "how long you been on benefits now" ... across a room.' (W1)

The fact that Cath interpreted such a question as an attempt to differentiate her from the rest of her family, even to stigmatise her, demonstrates the extent to which benefits receipt is now mired in negative associations and bound up in feelings of stigma and shame.

It was common for some individuals to face double and even triple stigmas due to their identities not just as 'benefit claimants' but also as single parents and/or disabled people. Rosie explained how she felt stigmatised as a single parent living in social housing:

'I don't think you get treated differently [on benefits] but I think that you're put into a category. I think you're kind of stereotyped into "single mum on benefits", just by a lot of people. Having your own house with a little child and [they] think that it's all free and you've got this house free, and it's not like that.' (W1)

Several of the disabled individuals spoke of the stigma attached to disability, particularly mental health issues:

'Even if you're just speaking to somebody and you say "oh, I'm on benefits", especially if you say you're on disability money ... If you tell somebody that you're poorly and that you've been in and out of hospital ... you can tell that they're sort of like; "weirdo, weirdo".' (Jessica, W1)

Later in the same interview, Jessica continued:

'Even if I'm just walking about town I do sort of feel lower than everybody else, not as privileged. Because obviously being on benefits and having an illness you're sort of stuck.' (W1)

Jessica's narrative demonstrates the harm and distress that can be caused when people internalise the stigmas surrounding disability and benefits, which leaves affected individuals feeling excluded from wider society.

Claims stigma

Alongside experiences of personal stigma and stigmatisation was widespread evidence of claims stigma. Individuals frequently described the processes of benefit claiming and receipt as dehumanising and alienating. Interactions with JCP and WP advisers were characterised by judgemental and disrespectful treatment:

'[Job Centre staff] do look down at you ... last week when I went down, she went, "have you applied for any jobs?" I went "yeah, 23". And she looked at me as if to say, "right okay, whatever" ... basically they look at us like rubbish 'cause we are on benefits ... it's like they put you in a category or something ... like lowlifes or something like that. It does get you mad.' (Sophie, W3)

Individuals sometimes explicitly picked up on the dehumanising nature of the claims process:

'You're just another number, you're not a person. That's how I feel about it [being on benefits].' (James, W3)

Cath and Isobella both highlighted the impact of the security guards present at Job Centres:

'When I started to go in the Job Centre again there were guards. Security men, and I'm thinking what a thing ... It's wordless, It's a silent, och, I don't even have the words. It's the image ... They're symbolising the fact that they're the big superpower and we are powerless and we've got to do as we're told, when we're told.' (Cath, W1)

'I assumed perhaps to some extent, obviously erroneously, that [the Job Centre] was an office that wanted to help you ... [but] of course, you've just sort of got burly security guards patrolling up and down, and you just think, what do they think I'm going to do? Pull out a gun?' (Isobella, W3)

The presence of security guards reflects the ways in which claimants are characterised and managed as 'threatening' populations (Fohrbeck et al., 2014), while Cath and Isobella's narratives illustrate how individuals so targeted can in fact feel "threatened" by the JCP environment. Individuals also often mentioned aspects of the physical environment of the JCP – the absence of toilets; a ban on attending appointments with hot drinks – that added to their feelings of being stigmatised as an unwelcome, deviant and potentially dangerous population. Such feelings negatively impacted on the scope for individuals to build positive relationships with their advisers and the likelihood of their seeing the JCP as somewhere to go for help and/or support.

Robert described how he felt a JCP adviser's treatment towards him changed once she realised he was actually engaged in some part-time employment, with the suggestion that he became more deserving and less stigmatised once his status as a 'worker' was realised:

'She started getting snotty with me ... Basically [saying] get off your arse and find jobs. So I said to her ... "are you going to give me the form so I can do my hours?" [to record paid work], right, and she turned around and she goes "oh, do you work?" and her tune changed then.' (W1)

Importantly, processes of welfare reform and changes to benefit entitlement were sometimes experienced as extending the reach of this claims stigma, particularly around the questioning of eligibility that the reforms so often entail. Isobella repeatedly explained that she was uneasy about claiming benefits. She believed she ought to be able to manage on her own and so found the constant struggle to prove entitlement especially difficult to sustain:

'I was always brought up that ... you paid your own way so that's the other thing that I find is difficult as well, especially with the questionnaires that you have to fill in, because I feel I shouldn't be having to fill them in, because I should be able to manage. Of course, I can't. So that is also something else that wars with me and again a lot of confidence I think is lost because I feel almost as if I'm saying "oh please give me something", instead of saying "look I'm entitled to this" so I think that can have a big impact.' (W2)

The continuing requirement to demonstrate deservingness impacted negatively on her:

'You do feel a bit like a washed up ... sponging off society, even though for years and years I've paid in and have been a good girl, and done what I was told to do. And now it's all blown back in my face.' (W3)

Isobella's personal stigma regarding claiming benefits was only reinforced and intensified by the demands of a benefits-claiming process that required her to complete lengthy forms as part of an effort to 'prove' her own entitlement. In this way, the personal and claim dimensions of stigma operated together to entrench and deepen her feelings of shame and stigma. Isobella had to manage this stigma while simultaneously facing an ongoing struggle to demonstrate her eligibility for disability benefits. In this way, the stigma only added to the emotional strain she already faced (see Chapter Five).

Undoubtedly, processes of welfare reform are adding another layer to experiences of claims stigma. The constant demand to demonstrate deservingness is experienced as a questioning and undermining of one's own entitlement, which inevitably – even as it is resisted – impacts on how affected individuals feel about themselves. There are clear risks that the presence of claims stigma – as well as processes of stigmatisation and personal stigma – will lead some people to underclaim benefits to which they are entitled; there is evidence of this in both this research and the wider literature (Baumberg et al., 2012; Shildrick et al., 2012b; Garthwaite, 2014).

Managing and deflecting stigma

Not claiming all the benefits to which one is entitled is one way to manage and seek to deflect the stigma associated with benefits receipt. In this research, some people also sought to 'pass' as non-benefit claimants, concealing their stigmatised identity – a classic strategy for managing stigma (Goffman, 1990; Tyler, 2013, 2014b). Tessa, who was living with paranoid schizophrenia, described how she preferred not to disclose either her impairment or her benefits receipt:

'I don't tell anyone I'm on benefits, apart from me close mates and stuff ... Well I don't tell them about me illness 'cause everyone reacts wrongly when they hear "schizophrenia" ... people do judge, if you're on benefits and stuff.' (W2)

Reflecting active agency, there were also limited forms of resistance, with some individuals challenging the stigma and negative associations of benefits reliance. Susan challenged what she experienced as the dehumanising processes of benefit claiming:

'I might be on benefits but I'm also a human being.' (W2)

In a different vein, Sophie repeatedly questioned the characterisation of benefit claimants as passive by emphasising the hard work associated with being a single parent:

'[The government] just think that we [single parents] sit at home on our backsides all day. They don't realise the cooking, the cleaning, looking after the kids and that lot. That's a full-time job in itself I think.' (W2)

Others appeared less able to challenge the stigma and instead spoke of simply trying not to think about it:

'People are full of assumptions and judgments. I've come to realise that recently a lot and it sickens me and it gets me angry to be honest. I just try and block it out.' (Adrian, W3)

A recent survey that explored the consequences of benefits stigma for out-of-work benefit claimants found that 38% said worrying about what others thought of them harmed their confidence and self-esteem, while 31% felt such worries adversely affected their mental health (Who Benefits?, 2014, p. 4). Certainly, the findings from this research demonstrated the extent to which people internalised negative characterisations of 'welfare dependency' in ways that were profoundly damaging to self-esteem, self-confidence and self-worth, indicating the psychological and relational harm that can be caused by poverty and social exclusion. The findings also suggest that today's out-of-work claimants are conditioned to view their own benefits receipt as inherently problematic, possibly undermining the logic and need for conditionality.

Are benefits ever a 'lifestyle choice'?

Cameron's governments repeatedly returned to the idea of benefits as a 'lifestyle choice' in their attempt to justify tightening welfare conditionality and reducing the real value of many benefits. Speaking at his first Conservative Party Conference as Chancellor of the Exchequer, George Osborne (2010) argued that benefits had become a 'lifestyle choice' for too many, while David Cameron asked in a high profile speech on 'welfare': 'Why has it become acceptable for many people to choose a life on benefits?' (2012b). This suggestion of 'choosing' benefits also provided justification for measures that sought to compel out-of-work benefit claimants to prepare for paid employment, with enforcement required to persuade individuals to make the better 'choice' of finding a job. While this narrative may have been utilised in efforts to defend recent welfare reforms, it is not one supported by the empirical findings of this research. Individuals scoffed at the idea of benefits as a 'lifestyle choice', commonly employing strong negative language to describe the reality of life on benefits:

> 'People don't choose to live on benefits – it's not our choice. It's just the way that things have happened. We don't choose to live on benefits, we don't want to live on benefits.' (Sophie, W1)

> 'I wouldn't opt for [benefits] if I had a choice ... because one, you're perceived like a scrounger ... and secondly, there are things you can't do because that's the only money you have.' (Susan, W3)

All of those interviewed saw their own receipt of benefits as not a 'lifestyle choice' but a necessity, given their individual circumstances. Several actually questioned whether it was possible to have a 'life' on benefits:

> 'It [benefits] ain't a life choice, you don't want to be living like that. It's like a pigeon, innit, you're just there pick pick pick, and that's it really. You're just existing.' (Dan, W1)

> '[On benefits] you're just existing, not living. That's all you're doing.' (James, W3)

'You can't really have a lifestyle on benefits … Me, being on benefits, I don't really have a life … If someone is on benefits then what life is that? That's not a real life, really, you're just wasting away slowly.' (Josh, W1)

Significantly, though, while individuals did not think the notion of benefits as a 'lifestyle choice' applied to them, they often thought it applied to some 'other'. It is to an exploration of this 'othering' – arguably the primary mechanism utilised to try to manage and deflect the shame of benefits receipt – that this chapter now turns.

How benefit claimants see others

Participants very commonly described some 'other' who did regard benefits as a 'lifestyle choice' and whose deservingness of benefits was questionable. The widespread examples of this 'othering' needs to be set against a context of enduring hostility towards those on out-of-work benefits. In popular imaginings, those living in poverty and in receipt of out-of-work benefits are themselves conceptualised as 'other' and set apart as culturally and behaviourally distinct from the hard-working majority (Lister, 2015).

When they critiqued the behaviours of those judged undeserving, individuals frequently pointed to immigrants, those with substance misuse issues, fraudulent disability benefit claimants and those with no previous employment experience. Immigrants came in for censure and there was often significant anger expressed about what was seen as politicians' continued support for immigrants, which was sometimes explicitly contrasted with politicians' apparent lack of support for British out-of-work benefit claimants. This was particularly notable in Chloe's narrative and featured in each of her three interviews:

'I'm doing this basically all by myself on what they give me and it's ridiculous. And then there's people like Zara next door and she's from a different country, she's from Pakistan and she's a lovely, lovely woman but she gets free gas, free electric and Home Office pay her shopping. She gets everything for nowt, and they still get money [too].' (W1)

'These Pakis get to sit on their arses all day, get paid, get free gas, get free electric and they're not even allowed to go out to work.' (W2)

'I'm not racist, I really aren't, but I don't agree at all with the way that we're living in our country compared to what other people [from other countries] are living. I really don't. And it gets me really angry ... so help me that I want to go out and punch some Polish or darkie.' (W3)

Chloe's anger towards immigrants appeared to grow over time, perhaps corresponding with the decline in her own material and psychological circumstances, which was itself linked to experiences of welfare reform (see Chapter Five).

There were clear correlations between individuals' own benefit-claiming identities and those whom they identified as undeserving. Specifically, there was implicit evidence that individuals sought to shore up their own deservingness by critiquing and 'othering' those with different characteristics to themselves (Chase and Walker, 2013). Both Robert and Isobella highlighted their previous working experiences as justification for their own deservingness of benefits and suggested that 'others' who had never worked were less entitled to the same social welfare. As Robert explained:

'If you haven't put nowt into country you shouldn't get nowt off country. Like I still pay me tax on [stewarding job].' (W3)

In addition, the disabled participants were particularly likely to talk of undeserving disability benefit claimants who were not *really* disabled. Sharon was "offended" when she received a questionnaire to reassess her eligibility for disability benefits:

'There's so many people out there that are just lazy and don't want to work and they ... won't get questioned and sent to [ATOS].[1] They'll just get left. And there's people out there that are on disability that don't deserve it. I mean I've seen a man a couple of weeks ago that was on disability and had a disability badge and everything, and he was just walking normal and swinging his walking stick about like it was nowt. And I thought there's people there that actually really deserve it that could do with the money, and they're not even getting it and it just winds me up.' (W2)

There is the possibility that welfare reform will only extend 'othering', as individuals who find their own benefit eligibility questioned become increasingly resentful about the 'deservingness' of others. Certainly, several said they felt that, with benefit changes, 'deserving' benefit claimants were being punished for the actions of those not behaving as they should. As Susan put it:

'People who need help ... are punished by those who just want to abuse the system.' (W2)

To differentiate between the undeserving 'them' and the deserving 'us', individuals commonly made a broad distinction between those who 'choose' benefits or were to 'blame' for their own situation and those who were reliant on benefits due to factors beyond their control – such as impairments, unemployment and caring responsibilities. In making this distinction, individuals re-emphasised their own lack of choice over their situation and highlighted that many did actively choose to stay on out-of-work benefits. In this way, individuals accepted the 'benefits as lifestyle choice' rhetoric when applied to some 'other'. Sometimes the contrast drawn was explicit:

'Some people choose it [benefits], some people think "I'll have a kid and go on benefits and that'll be me". Some people are used to it, but I'm not. Well, I never have been.' (James, W1)

By employing 'othering', individuals were asserting 'bad-people-exist-but-I'm-not-one-of-them', which Kingfisher (1996) also observed in a study of US female welfare recipients (cited in Garthwaite, 2014).

Understanding 'othering'

The 'othering' in which individuals engaged was part of an effort to resist and challenge being judged and condemned as part of a homogenous group of out-of-work benefit claimants. In their accounts, individuals described politicians' tendencies to generalise about the benefit-claiming population:

'[David Cameron] puts us all into that category which is wrong because there are people like myself that are looking for work, that want to go back to work. We don't want to just sit at home and do nothing. Obviously, where on the other hand there is people that do sit at home and do nothing, and they're happy with that.' (Sophie, W3)

'They shouldn't tarnish us all with the same brush. We're all individuals, they should look at people as individuals instead of putting us all in that same "oh, they're on Jobseekers"' category, so it's like you're all useless. And that's how they look at you.' (James, W1)

They also highlighted the dominant portrayals of benefit claimants in the media, sometimes explicitly linking these portrayals with the ways they were treated. Sophie described how programmes such as *The Fairy Jobmother* were giving benefit claimants a "bad name":

'They [participants on *The Fairy Jobmother*] all sit down and they don't want to do this and they don't want to do that and it gives other people that are on benefits a really bad name. "Oh you scruffy little scroungers", it's not easy you know. We wouldn't be on it if we had a choice.' (W2)

Individuals' awareness of these negative portrayals, as well as their own re-creation and utilisation of them via 'othering', may be part of their broader acceptance of a new framing consensus on welfare (see Chapter Two). By 'othering', individuals implicitly suggest that the dominant portrayals and stereotypes are correct but simply do not apply in their own individual cases. This could be evidence of a broader process of 'conditioning', in which such individuals are persuaded – even co-opted – to accept the hegemonic narrative that problematises 'welfare' and those who receive it. Ironically, as the 'othered' themselves 'other', they inevitably become active in circulating notions of benefits receipt as shameful and inherently negative and problematic (Chase and Walker, 2013). When combined with the power and purchase of the current hostility towards 'welfare', the absence of resources and the structural barriers faced by out-of-work claimants perhaps make a more sustained challenge to the overarching narrative simply unfeasible.

'Othering' serves as an attempt by out-of-work benefit claimants to distance themselves from society's negative and condemnatory gaze by delineating and creating separations between 'us' and 'them', the deserving and undeserving. 'Othering' represents a form of 'identity work', which constitutes a (not always successful) effort to construct a more positive identity (Ronai and Cross, 1998; Elliott, 2005). The stereotypes and critical depictions of benefit claimants can thus be seen as simultaneously a threat to claimants' own identities – as well as a discursive resource that can be mobilised to defend their own entitlement by emphasising that, while 'others' may fit this portrayal, they themselves do not (Fohrbeck et al., 2014).

'Othering' occurs alongside what must sometimes feel like a struggle for limited resources. Social welfare in particular is being increasingly withdrawn and made conditional on behaviours and assessments of 'deservingness' as part of processes of welfare reform (Patrick, 2014a; Wright, 2016). In this context, 'othering' also needs to be understood as part of claim-making, with individuals emphasising their own entitlement to social welfare by means of undermining the rights of an 'other'. 'Othering', then, can be recognised as an aspect of getting by on benefits (Lister, 2004) and even as a form of (admittedly very defensive) citizenship engagement (Ellison, 2000). Defensive forms of citizenship engagement encompass activities that seek to defend the real or perceived erosion of social rights (Ellison, 2000; Cook et al., 2012). They can be contrasted with more proactive forms of citizenship engagement, in which individuals and groups feel able to mobilise in efforts to extend their entitlement and even to make demands for new rights (Ellison, 2000; Cook et al., 2012). 'Othering' as a form of defensive citizenship engagement and claim-making is inevitably negative in tone. It can also have repercussions for claimants' own citizenship inclusion, given that it serves to reanimate and strengthen the dominant, problematizing narrative.

Constructing positive moral identities in difficult times

While 'othering' was common, there were also limited signs of attempts to carve out a more challenging form of claim-making that highlighted the 'deservingness' of most, if not all, benefit claimants. This could be seen as an explicit challenge to the dominant narrative and particularly a rejection of the new framing consensus on 'welfare'. It was most notable in the accounts of Cath and Isobella, both of whom were also the only participants to be critical of some of the behaviours and treatment of the 'undeserving' rich. Cath reserved particular censure for British pensioners living abroad and yet still claiming their Winter Fuel Payments:

'I think if your belly's full, put your plate down, get your finger out of the bowl.' (W3)

Cath also challenged the 'them' and 'us' dichotomy:

'I believe, in all walks of life [there are] people swinging the lead.' (W2)

Isobella made a link between the 'undeserving' behaviours of the poor and the rich, arguing:

'I'm willing to concede that there's an awful lot of people claiming benefits that perhaps shouldn't, like there's a lot of bankers claiming bonuses who shouldn't.' (W2)

Interestingly, Cath and Isobella were also the most vocal in their resistance to the government's welfare reform agenda, showing a clear link between their rejection of both the dominant narrative and the reforms for which this narrative provides a justification.

For Isobella, describing social security support as 'benefits' is misleading:

'I don't like the word benefit actually. I'd like to call it entitlement because I do think I'm entitled. A benefit to me is something that you have as an add-on and is almost like a bit of a treat. So I don't see Incapacity, or the money that comes through it as a treat. It's actually what I'm due because I've paid in for 200 years all my National Insurance.' (W1)

In Cath and Isobella's accounts there is an attempt to construct an alternative narrative about benefit claimants' deservingness and ongoing rights to social welfare. This narrative is potentially inclusive (of out-of-work claimants, if not the rich) and contributes to their own attempts to create and sustain positive moral identities as benefit claimants who are entitled to – and need – support. While Cath and Isobella challenged aspects of the government's welfare reform approach, it was notable that most of those interviewed seemed persuaded by the need for changes to the benefits system.

Attitudes towards welfare reform and conditionality

Despite being directly affected by some of the benefit changes taking place, individuals were commonly supportive of the central tenets and underlying principles of welfare reform. Indeed, of the longitudinal sample, nine expressed some agreement with aspects of the welfare reform approach. What is evident in this seemingly contradictory position is the impact and reach of 'othering'. Processes of 'othering' provide a rationale for the overarching direction of welfare reform; namely, efforts to activate the 'irresponsible' and to make sure that the 'choice' of benefits is no longer available to those judged not to deserve or 'need' state support (Cameron, 2010b; Duncan Smith, 2010a; DWP, 2010c). This was evident in people's accounts:

> 'There is quite a lot of people faking having bad backs and stuff. So I think [the government have] got to do something really.' (Kane, W1)

> 'In some ways [welfare reform] is a good idea because maybe there is people who don't need to be on certain benefits that could go out to work. Not like me but people that are just playing on it or something to get money out of the social.' (Amy, W1)

In these narratives, individuals' continued deservingness is emphasised – just as 'others'' undeservingness is seen as providing a justification for welfare reform.

Individuals' attitudes to welfare reform sometimes seemed to be fluctuating and unstable. This could be linked to their conflicting perspectives as both observers of the benefits system as a whole and as individuals targeted by some of the changes. Over time, there was also some evidence that support for welfare reform was weakening. This often occurred in tandem with the realisation that these reforms were causing significant hardship and difficulties for many, including themselves. While critical of the pace of change and its perceived targeting of many 'deserving' groups, Isobella did initially see some potential in the welfare reforms being introduced:

> 'I suspect there are lots of people who probably could go to work who are on something like Incapacity Benefit but on the other hand I think there are vastly more people who do need it who can't work. And so I think they're sort of being penalised for the fact there are some people who don't [deserve benefits], perhaps because in the past governments have been lax and the legislation hasn't been tight enough, or the claims have been less strong.' (W1)

However, over time, as she saw her own entitlement to benefit questioned, she started to rethink her attitudes to the Coalition government's approach and become increasingly angry:

'I've got probably worse at feeling angry at what they're doing.' (W2)

'I am far more critical of the [government] of what they've done ... and the problems that they've put people through.' (W3)

Isobella's changing stance towards the reforms suggests that, as individuals experience the direct impact of benefit changes, their attitudes and willingness to defend the approach may alter.

As well as frequently being persuaded by the case for welfare reform, individuals were often supportive of an emphasis on welfare conditionality and employed contractual, paternalist and communitarian arguments to defend the attachment of conditions to benefits receipt. While they were often resistant to the application of conditionality to themselves, they could still see clear arguments for it being applied to an undeserving 'other'.

In the first and third interviews, individuals were presented with vignettes describing the application of work-related conditionality to a single parent, a young jobseeker and a disabled person. When discussing these vignettes, individuals tended to engage in a consideration of the individual circumstances of the claimant in question and an assessment and exploration of their 'behaviour' and 'deservingness'. There was comparatively little evidence of a broader questioning of the whole premise of attaching conditions to benefits receipt.

Chloe felt it was fair for a young person to be compelled to take part in mandatory, unpaid work experience:

"Cause he's a boy, he's 19 year old and he should go out to work ... If I had a full-time partner and I lived with him I'd expect him to [work] ... He's a young lad on his own. Get out to work you lazy little shit [laughs].' (W1)

James defended conditionality's applicability to a single parent whose children were both at primary school:

'She could get a part-time job within them [school] hours. Ten till two or owt like that ... I understand it would be hard for ... but she should look for summat.' (W3)

It seemed that – perhaps through familiarity and repeated imposition – the overarching conditionality framework had become accepted and viewed as largely unproblematic. Some even called for conditionality to be extended further:

> 'I think a lot of support is offered to people that should be forced more than anything. Make them get help, make them get back into work, make them do this and that.' (Josh, W3)

Overall, then, individuals directly affected by welfare reform and conditionality could often see the rationale behind the reforms and overall direction of travel. This only reinforces the reach and power of the framing consensus on welfare, illustrating the ways in which those on benefits operate within and recirculate aspects of this consensus.

'Othering' politicians

While individuals were often supportive of the broader welfare reform policy agenda, they were also very angry and resistant to the application of conditionality, compulsion and benefit changes to themselves – an anger that was itself tied to (and often reinforced) their political disengagement (see Chapter Three). Indeed, in demarcating 'them' and 'us' and 'othering', individuals also engaged in an 'othering' of politicians and elites, who were conceptualised as making decisions with little regard for the negative impact they might have on individual lives. The anger individuals felt was particularly apparent in threats of violence towards politicians – empty threats that perhaps illustrated their powerlessness in the face of the reforms:

> 'I think everyone [in government], all of them want shooting in the head.' (Chloe, W3)

> '[Cameron's] another one that needs a machete … [What he says] make me want to go round and put my hands actually round his neck or shake him.' (Isobella, W3)

Cath felt there was a need for politicians with more empathy and direct experience of poverty:

> 'Get some [politicians] who care, people who are more socially minded. They've got to have experience. It's like having a midwife who's never given birth to a child. You can't take her seriously 'cause she doesn't know what she's talking about. Only when you've walked through a big,

long, dark scary forest, do you have a right to speak about
that forest. If you haven't been through it, keep your mouth
shut.' (additional interview in 2015)

Out-of-work benefit claimants regard politicians as a group ready,
all too often, to criticise, censure and stigmatise their behaviours,
but unwilling to engage with the everyday problems and challenges
they face. Benefit claimants are treated as a 'threatening' population
(Fohrbeck et al., 2014) and only rarely as a segment of the electorate
whose views, opinions and – importantly – votes matter. This was
starkly illustrated by Rachel Reeves' (then Labour's Shadow Secretary
for the Department of Work and Pensions) statement before the 2015
General Election: 'We are not the party of people on benefits. We
don't want to be seen, and we're not, the party to represent those who
are out of work. Labour are a party of working people, formed for
and by working people' (Gentleman, 2015). Politicians' simultaneous
stigmatising of, and distancing themselves from, those on benefits
creates multi-tiered processes of exclusion and undermines the scope
for claimants to exercise their political citizenship rights. It is another
facet of the stigmatisation that individuals on out-of-work benefits face;
and one that reduces the scope for them to engage with the political
system in any effort to challenge or question the status quo.

Conclusion

This chapter has illustrated the ways in which the dominant framing
of out-of-work benefit claimants as inactive, passive and responsible
for their own non-work and poverty impacts on how a small group
of out-of-work claimants saw themselves and others. Individuals
commonly saw their own benefits receipt as embarrassing and shameful,
adopting negative colloquial descriptors such as "scrounger", "bum"
and "sponger" to describe their positions. It should be noted that
this stigma is reserved for the receipt of social 'welfare' (working-age
income replacement benefits in particular); occupational and fiscal
welfare attract no such stigma or shame. This is a pertinent example
of the enduring relevance of Titmuss' social division of welfare thesis
(Titmuss, 1958; Sinfield, 1978; Mann, 2009).

The spread of benefits stigma – evident here and confirmed by other
research (Walker, 2014; Baumberg, 2016) – is another example of
the psychological and relational harm caused by poverty and benefits
receipt. Benefits stigma leaves affected individuals feeling marginalised
and excluded from mainstream society (Etherington and Daguerre,

2015). The process of claiming benefits is itself wrapped up in and generative of stigma and shame. As a result, citizens seeking to claim their social welfare entitlement find themselves stigmatised, suggesting that efforts to secure the social rights of citizenship can themselves produce stigma – at least for those at the bottom of the social hierarchy.

Strategies that individuals adopt in their efforts to manage this stigma include 'passing', active attempts to construct more positive moral identities and – most commonly – a deflection of the stigma onto some 'other' judged less deserving. This defensive 'othering' sees claimants seek to shore up their own deservingness by shifting critical attention (and the need for corrective action) onto some 'other'. In so doing, individuals unfortunately give additional authenticity to the dominant portrayal, which is reproduced not only by politicians and the media but also by benefit claimants themselves (Pemberton et al., 2016). This 'othering' operates to divide a potential 'us' into multiple 'others' (Chase and Walker, 2013) and thus undermines the possibility for a more solidaristic and progressive challenge to the status quo.

In their internalisation of stigma and shame around benefits reliance, as well as their active participation in 'othering', individuals could be described as acting as 'conditioned' citizens accepting and appropriating aspects of the dominant narrative (see Chapter Eight). As individuals self-govern their own behaviours in ways that fit with the welfare reform agenda, it is possible that conditionality is superseded by – or at the very least operates alongside – this 'conditioning', which affects how individuals manage their own working and non-working behaviours (Dwyer and Ellison, 2009).

The political class can be characterised as active agents in the production and reproduction of stigmatising narratives around benefit claimants and poverty (Patrick, 2014a; Tyler, 2014c). Combined with the evidence that benefit claimants are internalising this stigma, which directly feeds into their desires and motivations to transition from benefits into employment, the (re)production of stigma can be understood as a deliberate strategy of social control (Tyler, 2014c) – what Tyler tentatively calls the 'stigma doctrine' (2014b). While effective in undermining the 'social rights' of citizenship, this strategy could be counterproductive in terms of assisting the welfare-to-work effort due to the corrosive effects of benefits stigma on affected individuals' self-esteem, self-confidence and mental health.

If the stigma surrounding benefits receipt is to be undone, or at least challenged, there is an urgent need for a more successful and sustained questioning and interrogation of the popular portrayal of 'welfare'. At the same time, though, there is an argument for parallel action to try to undermine the claims stigma associated with benefits receipt. Here, Ruth Lister's (2015) recent emphasis on taking measures to 'shame proof' public services is particularly relevant. So too is the idea that, when we look to service design and institutional delivery, we should prioritise an approach that foregrounds principles of dignity and respect – principles that are currently not much in evidence for those at the sharp end of benefits receipt (Walker, 2014; Baumberg, 2016). The stigma and shame of poverty and benefits delegitimise the lives of those experiencing them (Lister, 2013) and arguably reduces their citizenship status to – at best – second-class citizens.

Note
1. ATOS was the private firm sub-contracted by the government to conduct WCAs at the time of the research.

SEVEN

Diverse trajectories
between 2011 and 2016

Social policy scholars with an interest in welfare reform face a shifting context as each year brings fresh announcements of further measures designed to finally rid Britain of its supposed 'problem' of 'welfare dependency' (cf. Osborne, 2013b; Duncan Smith, 2014d). The year in which this book was written – 2016 – has been a particularly eventful one for the UK. The architect of the post-2010 welfare reforms, Iain Duncan Smith, unexpectedly resigned as Secretary of State for the Department for Work and Pensions in protest at plans announced in the 2016 budget (and then just as quickly withdrawn) to reduce entitlement for the disability benefit, Personal Independence Payments. 2016 has also seen a ratcheting up of efforts to roll out the much-delayed Universal Credit, alongside the introduction of in-work conditionality for those working fewer than the equivalent of 35 hours per week at the National Minimum Wage (see Chapter Two). Most significantly, Cameron and Osborne's tenure as Prime Minister and Chancellor of the Exchequer, respectively, came to an end following the UK's vote to leave the EU in June. With Theresa May newly installed at 10 Downing Street, it will be critical to observe what – if any – changes are made to the Conservatives' approach to and rhetoric on 'welfare' in the coming months and years.

This chapter reports on interviews conducted with nine participants in 2016. These provided a longer view of welfare reform experiences over the five years from 2011 to 2016. What was the cumulative impact of welfare reform for these individuals? How did their relationships with benefits and paid employment evolve over time? Did they manage to achieve the aspirations they had expressed earlier? What triggered or prevented the realisation of positive change in their lives? Through exploring these questions, this chapter highlights key trajectories, discernible patterns and dominant themes emerging from the interviews. A brief summary of the methodological approach is followed by an overview of individuals' relationship with work and benefits over time, examined through individual case studies. Central themes from this fourth wave of interviews are then summarised.

Returning for a fourth time

Nine participants from the longitudinal sample were interviewed for a fourth time in the summer of 2016. Short interviews were also conducted with six of those participating in the 'Dole Animators' project in 2015 and, where relevant, data from these interviews features in the following discussion. I managed to make contact with ten participants, nine of whom agreed to be interviewed (five young jobseekers, two single parents and two disability benefit(s) recipients). One – Cath – initially agreed to be interviewed and then changed her mind, explaining she had lost interest in the project. This is important to record, particularly given that it perhaps illustrates the danger that individuals will disengage from the research process where it makes continued demands of their time without a parallel evident impact. Certainly, Cath – who also took part in the 'Dole Animators' project – had earlier expressed frustrations that neither the film nor the research were reaching a wider audience. She was disappointed that her aspiration for the film to be shown to the Prime Minister (then David Cameron) went unrealised. While I sought to manage these expectations and to detail the ways the research could have some (more modest) impact, there was, perhaps, an irresolvable clash between Cath's politicised aspirations for getting her voice heard and the inherent limitations of this type of research.

Diverse journeys over time

Following individuals for five years showed that, for most of those interviewed, their receipt of out-of-work benefits was temporary; six of the nine interviewed transitioned off (but sometimes back onto) out-of-work benefits between 2011 and 2016. This was closely tied to and driven by individuals' enduring aspirations to move off benefits and into work. In their first interviews back in 2011, eight of the nine detailed aspirations that included entering paid employment (see Chapter Three). The only one not to express work-related hopes for the future was Isobella, a disability benefits recipient whose central aspirations were for her health to not deteriorate further and for her benefits situation to stay the same. Worsening health and continued uncertainty caused by welfare reform meant that these aspirations proved unachievable.

In terms of movements between and experiences of 'welfare' and work, three trajectories were discernible among these individuals. These are described using the shorthand of 'long-term claimants', 'precarious welfare-to-work transitioners' and 'sustained welfare-to-work transitioners'. The distinction made between precarious and sustained transitioners is an important one; it pinpoints the extent to which, for many, movements into paid employment were temporary and not sustained over time. The category of 'sustained transitioners' is reserved for those individuals who remained in paid employment continuously for at least two years in the period preceding the fourth wave of interviews. Table 7.1 outlines the categorisation of the nine individuals by this typology and shows an even split across the three categories.

Table 7.1: Trajectories over time

Sustained welfare-to-work transitioners	Precarious welfare-to-work transitioners	Long-term claimants
Susan	Robert	Adrian
Rosie	Josh	Kane
Sam	James	Isobella

The experiences of Rosie, James and Adrian between 2013 and 2016 are now explored as case studies to better understand these diverse trajectories. Their experiences included upwards and downwards trajectories, constancy and flux – sometimes for the same individual at different points of time. All three expressed clear aspirations to enter paid employment in their first interviews, and at the time of their third interviews, Rosie was in paid employment while James and Adrian were still receiving out-of-work benefits (see Chapter Four).

Rosie: a sustained welfare-to-work transitioner

In 2013, Rosie had secured some paid work with her own housing association. She then moved into a full-time administrative role at another housing association. Rosie described the struggles of this full-time work, highlighting how employment for single parents can have negative dimensions, particularly where it creates additional pressures on family life (Millar and Ridge, 2013):

'While I were working full-time I were really struggling with childcare … in the holidays it were just a nightmare. It were awful. It were just costing me my wage, all the time, even at the end of the month, when it wasn't school holidays. I was still giving so much to the school, it just got me down. I didn't have any money. We [Rosie and her son] were getting ratty with each other, I was dropping him off at … quarter to eight, and picking him up at six. Everything just seemed a rush all the time.'

After unsuccessfully applying for several housing apprenticeship roles, Rosie found a part-time role in the association where she had been working as an administrator, this time as a housing manager with responsibility for a housing scheme of 90 flats. For Rosie, securing part-time work on a better wage was "an absolute godsend" as it made it easier for her to juggle her parenting and working responsibilities. She was also financially better off – despite working 12 fewer hours per week – and her role was quite flexible, enabling her to take time off to attend school events and sports days. Rosie said of her job: "It's brilliant. I love it."

Rosie reflected on the contrast between her current life and her previous experiences on out-of-work benefits:

'I've got a better quality of life … Even going to the Job Centre every other week, and getting the minimum amount of money and then you run out of money and you can apply for a Crisis [Loan] but you feel like you're begging money all the time and I hated that … And it isn't just material things either … it's my own sanity. I feel great getting up and going to work. I don't skip to work, work's work, but I enjoy my job and I enjoy having nice things for myself in life.'

Back in 2011, Rosie expressed resistance to what she saw as the Job Centre's focus on claimants taking *any* job – a manifestation of the work-first approach that dominates the UK's policy agenda (Wright, 2011b):

'If I were shoved [by the Job Centre] in McDonald's I'd have left. I can't say that I wouldn't because I would have done when really I want to do something for myself.'

At the time of her 2011 interview, Rosie had not yet been migrated onto Jobseeker's Allowance (as her son was only four) and so was able to develop her work-based aspirations with additional support from her housing association. As a result of this active work, which included periods of volunteering in order to obtain relevant work experience, she managed to secure paid employment, which, in time, led to her present permanent role. This job includes opportunities for progression and advancement and is flexible, enabling her to effectively combine her parenting and paid work. Her capacity to realise this positive change in her own life was linked to her receipt of Income Support, which meant she was able to undertake almost full-time voluntary work. This might well not have been permitted if she had been in receipt of Jobseeker's Allowance, given its work-related conditions. In the UK, an emphasis on a work-first approach – which prioritises entries into work above progression and securing sustainable, good work (Gregg et al., 2006; Wright, 2009) – may undermine the scope for individuals to develop their capabilities in ways that support transitions such as Rosie's.

James: a precarious welfare-to-work transitioner

James experienced the consequences of Britain's work-first approach first-hand. He felt he had no choice but to abandon his aspirations for 'good work' due to the impossibility of participating in full-time training while on Jobseeker's Allowance and the associated demands created by the welfare-to-work regime. When interviewed in 2013, James was on Jobseeker's Allowance, participating in the Work Programme and actively seeking work without success. He had given up on earlier aspirations to retrain as a support worker and was instead looking for any work he could find. James did not find the Work Programme helpful and worried that the longer he was without employment, the harder it would be to move into work.

Between the third and fourth interviews, James did manage to find a job and spent a year working for a bathrooms showroom until he was made redundant when the business closed down in March 2016:

> 'To say, back end of the job, I didn't like it. I did cry. When I lost my job, I cried. It weren't just the fact of losing my job. It were that routine. And I found myself a week later, I were ironing my clothes to go down to the library and Jeremy Kyle come on the telly and I think "back to this again", and it demoralised me definitely.'

Having been in work for a year, James found the return to unemployment and benefits receipt particularly difficult. He described his feelings about having to return to the Job Centre:

'It were embarrassing. Really embarrassing. You've got your advisers that have seen you from there before, and when I went in the girl that were on the front desk she knew me and recognised me, and went "oh, hi, are you back here again?" and it's like a kick in the teeth, it's like "yeah, I'm back here again". So not nice at all. I hate it. I hate it.'

James immediately struggled with the subsequent loss of income and had to resort to food banks in order to get by. He engaged in informal work, such as cutting people's lawns or painting their living rooms, explaining: "I've got to do it, otherwise I've got no money". He also moved out of his own council property (while retaining the tenancy) and into his mother's home in an attempt to reduce his expenditure. James explained that he simply did not have enough money to cover his bills, buy everyday essentials and support his daughter, who was spending more and more time with him. For James, while this move felt necessary, it was imbued in embarrassment and shame:

'I can't live at my own home. We've got to move into her nana's. It's demoralising. She [daughter] thinks it's great, thinks it's fun; "oh I live with my nana". But when she goes to school and tells her mates, I feel so embarrassed. The parents must think: "why's he moved back?", do you know what I mean? It's embarrassing, really embarrassing ... I've got to do it. Can't do 'owt else about it.'

It is significant that James described his interactions with the Job Centre and feelings about moving back into his mother's home as "embarrassing", especially given that the loss of his most recent job was through no fault of his own. This relates to the stigma and shame so commonly tied up with experiences of poverty and benefits receipt in Britain today (Walker, 2014; Baumberg, 2016), as highlighted in Chapter Six.

During his five months on benefits, James actively sought work. He was really pleased to find out that he had secured a job in a confectionery warehouse:

'I were really excited. I were buzzing. I only found out yesterday properly. I were over the moon, and it's only a picking and packing job, but it's a job, yeah, over the moon ... And I know it's not going to be a fortune, it's minimum wage and that but it's summat.'

The role, which was through an agency, was full-time and temporary but with the suggestion that after 13 weeks it might become permanent. James anticipated that he might not like this new job. He was also wary about how he would manage it alongside his childcare commitments, given the inflexible and anti-social working hours (from 2 pm to 10 pm on weekdays). Nonetheless, he felt he had no choice but to accept it:

'It's a job. Even if I don't like it, I can't refuse it. I've got to go ... It's going to be so hard childcare wise, but I've got to do it. Financially, I can't refuse it.'

Although about to start the job, James had decided not to sign off benefits:

'I haven't signed off yet. I daren't. Well I said to my mam, I'm going to just sign on, do both, 'cause I know you're not meant to, but once I know it's stable [I'll sign off]. I'll give it a month. I might sign on an extra once or twice, and then come off but at first I won't ... I'm scared that if I sign off straight away and then something happens with this job within first week or something, it'll be hard for me to start claiming again, and my rent [arrears] will start building up, so I daren't until I know that I'm safe.'

James risked being convicted of benefits fraud and jeopardising his employment by signing on while working, but he felt this was the best (even only) way of managing in the short-term and providing himself with some protection should the job not prove sustainable. His fear that he might not be "safe" in his new role reflected an awareness of the precariousness of the UK's flexible labour market, as well as his own insecure status as a worker employed on a temporary contract.

The toll that transitioning from work and then back onto benefits had taken on James was considerable; for him, life on Jobseeker's Allowance was financially unsustainable and emotionally difficult. In his mid-30s and with parenting responsibilities, the fact that he felt compelled to move out of his own home – which then sat empty with the Housing Benefit still being paid by the local authority – is perhaps testament to the inadequacy and shortcomings of today's social security 'safety net'.

When asked about any highs and lows during the three years since his last interview, James pinpointed periods in and out of work respectively, indicating the way that his sense of security, self-esteem and identity were all closely related to his experiences of employment and benefits:

'Good points were working, when you feel more normal. When you've got a bit of summat, you've got summat to get up for. Even if you don't like your job, you've got a job, you've got somewhere to go. Your lows are when you're not working, and you've got to, it's like scrimping and saving, begging and borrowing you know. You might get your giro on Friday but on the Monday before you've had to borrow 20 quid to put electric on so ... you're always behind ... When you're working, you were always in front a little bit ... It's always a low point when you're out of work. Always. But there's nowt you can do about it.'

Recent research has highlighted the increasing prevalence of frequent transitions in and out of work, which Shildrick describes as the 'low-pay, no-pay' cycle (Shildrick, 2012). The negative impacts this can have on affected individuals was abundantly clear in the case of James, who experienced repercussions for his mental health, dignity and self-esteem. The welfare conditionality and work-first regime prevented him from taking active steps to try to secure more sustainable forms of employment. Instead, he seemed increasingly resigned to accepting any job he could find. This might be the design and intention of the policy agenda, but it comes at real human and financial costs. These include costs to the exchequer such as the benefits bill for the periods spent between jobs and the costs of providing in-work benefits to top up low pay (Ray et al., 2014).

Adrian: a long-term claimant

While James had spells of employment between 2011 and 2016, Adrian was not able to secure any paid work during this time. Instead, he was subjected to repeat benefit sanctions and frustrations as he tried – and did not always manage – to comply with the demands made of him by Job Centre Plus and the Work Programme. Adrian faced entrenched and significant barriers to employment as a young jobseeker with no previous working experience and a series of convictions for offences carried out as a young adult. While he did not secure paid employment, Adrian consistently engaged in voluntary work at a homeless hostel between 2011 and 2016. In his fourth interview, Adrian reflected on his ongoing unsuccessful work search:

'Five years, nothing has changed jobs and benefits wise. Still volunteering. It's ridiculous innit. A little unnerving.'

Adrian attached some pride to his capacity to cope despite the repeated challenges that he faced:

> 'It's like a cycle innit, it's not nice. It's made me stronger though. I'm quite happy because there's times when you can just snap because [the benefits system] ... keeping throwing at you, throwing at you. It's not nice. They don't seem to see that.'

Repeated sanctions had left Adrian underweight and struggling to find enough food to feed himself. He relied on free meals from the hostel at which he volunteered and support from food banks and community cafes, where the volunteers gave him extra crusts in their efforts – as Adrian put it – to "feed me up". He also made use of emergency food provision intended for the homeless:

> 'There's a curry run on Tuesday nights outside Crown Court so I go there. Well, the problem is that that's meant for the homeless but because I'm sanctioned and I'm starving that's where I have to go.'

Adrian highlighted the limitations with the emergency food provision available from food banks, which today constitutes an increasingly essential and common form of charitable social welfare provision (Garthwaite, 2016; Trussell Trust, 2016):

> 'You can only go three times [to food banks] so I had to ration my food out. The food only lasts three days each time you go, so it's nine days worth of food for a month ... just had half a tin a day.' (2015 interview)

Adrian's repeated experience of sanctions impeded rather than aided his efforts to secure paid employment:

> Sanctions affect my search for work as you find yourself searching more for food than a job. Then when you do find a job interview I have had to travel there and back on an empty stomach. It is a traumatic experience that has caused some mental issues that I never had before sanctions. No nutrition for the brain is like trying to start your car with no petrol inside. It's not going to work. (Written communication, 2016)

In his fourth interview, it was apparent that the cumulative impact of repeated sanctions and continued unsuccessful efforts to secure employment were undermining Adrian's confidence and putting a strain on his (perhaps already fragile) mental health. Recognising the negative impact of sanctions on his employability, Adrian recounted feedback he had received from the Work Programme following the completion of a mock interview:

> 'They said [I had bad] eye contact, which were pretty good 'cause I don't make eye contact after the sanctions and that. I became very unsociable, didn't want to trust … Now it's just lasted, made me unsociable with people and that, made me feel down. It's self-conscious. What people are thinking of me and that. It were since I was starving from the sanctions.'

The experience of repeated benefit sanctions with increasing penalties left Adrian depressed, underfed and unable to trust his fellow citizens. While he sometimes accepted the rationale behind particular benefit sanctions – when he had missed or been late for an appointment – he also pointed to examples where he had been ill and had tried to inform the Job Centre, only to be sanctioned. From Adrian's perspective, the whole benefits system was lopsidedly focused on the threat and instigation of benefit sanctions, with a parallel absence of meaningful and effective job-related support:

> 'The Job Centre's just terrible. There's no advice there. You just walk [in] and they advise you how not to get a sanction. Everything you can get sanctioned for. If you don't have Universal Jobs Match, you get sanctioned. If you're not using Universal Jobs Match you get sanctioned. If you haven't got your signing-on book with you, you get sanctioned. If you're late, you get a sanction. If you don't turn up, you get a sanction. If you haven't got your jobs diary, you get a sanction. There's so many things.' (2015 interview)

For Adrian, the prospect of making a welfare-to-work transition seemed to have become less, rather than more likely over time, despite being repeatedly subject to the harshest components of the welfare conditionality regime. He showed an awareness of the relative bleakness of his situation: 'I feel trapped unless someone gives [me] that opportunity for a job' (written communication, 2016).

Adrian's case study illustrates the dehumanising and punitive edge of today's benefits system and the ways in which it is directly leading to destitution for those who fail to comply with its demands (see also Fitzpatrick et al., 2016). Further, it perhaps suggests the futility of a system focused on 'tough' measures and sanctions, which at the same time neglects to properly consider how to most effectively support and encourage individuals such as Adrian into employment. It adds to a growing body of evidence that questions the appropriateness and effectiveness of the UK's benefit sanctions regime, which certainly seems to do little – if anything – to support welfare-to-work transitions (Batty et al., 2015; Dwyer and Bright, 2016).

What is particularly apparent from exploring the trajectories of Rosie, James and Adrian is the extent to which transitions into employment were seen as critical to enable the realisation of positive change(s) in individual lives. While the political narrative sometimes seems to imply a smooth welfare-to-work transition (cf. Cameron, 2012b; Duncan Smith, 2014b), these findings demonstrate the precariousness of welfare-to-work transitions for so many; cycling between insecure low-paid work and out-of-work benefits receipt is a common experience. What is also apparent is the extent to which, at least for those interviewed, the benefits system seems to be doing little to support and enable these transitions and can actually – as in Adrian's case – *reduce* individuals' employability and work-readiness. Further, James' case study illustrates how, during spells of benefits receipt, the inadequacy of available social security provision can lead to individuals having to make incredibly difficult choices as they contend with getting by on limited resources.

Experiences of welfare-to-work 'support' over time

Several key themes emerged from the 2016 interviews. These included individuals' experiences of welfare-to-work support, the persistence of poverty, dynamic experiences of benefit stigma and the cumulative long-term costs of welfare reform. First, there was evidence of welfare-to-work 'support' being experienced negatively. Further, where support did enable work-based transitions, it was sometimes into a job that was poorly paid and part-time. Of the nine individuals interviewed over five years, only one – Sam – directly attributed her move into paid employment to the support she had received, in this case from the Work Programme:

'Well they [Work Programme provider] sort of had a rapport with [retail store] so any new jobs that came in with them, say a new store opened up, they would be some of the first people to know. So that was how I found out. My adviser … told me, I said "yes, put me forward", and I came in for the interview at [Work Programme provider], found out a few weeks later that I'd got the job.'

Sam explained how the job, which she started in 2014, evolved:

'Starting at [retail shop] was a three-months probationary period. At the end of the period, I got told whether I'd have a permanent job or not. Thankfully I did, but the catch was I had to slash my hours in half. So, at that point, the minimum wage was £6.19, eight hours a week, I was earning less than the average jobseeker.'

Despite being in employment, Sam frequently contemplated using food banks; such was her struggle to get by. She also relied on in-kind support from her boyfriend's mother:

'I didn't have much money so [boyfriend's] mum took it upon herself to give me about half a dozen things to get me through the weekend … and she still gives me a couple of things every time my boyfriend comes over for the weekend.'

While Sam valued the job and compared it favourably to being on benefits, her wage was not sufficient to enable her to escape poverty altogether. Further, she felt compelled to accept a contract of just eight hours a week and then hope for regular over-time on an insecure and ad-hoc basis to boost her earnings. Sam sustained her employment in the retail store for over two years. When interviewed in 2016, she spoke of how her working hours had improved and her duties been extended to include till work rather than just stacking shelves. She was positive about her work, even though it was low-paid:

'I'm earning. Instead of just going to search for jobs, I've actually got one which takes up more of my time. [Now] I'm actually happy about it, I'm earning more, I've got more hours, and it keeps me out of the flat more because if I stay in the flat it drives me nuts. Staring at the same four walls, so I'm glad I've got something to do.'

The Work Programme's support had seen Sam moved off benefits and into what Bailey terms 'exclusionary employment' (2016); that is, work that fails to deliver the inclusionary rewards with which it is commonly associated (see Chapter Four). The longer-term sustainability and appropriateness of a welfare regime that effects welfare-to-work transitions into exclusionary employment demands further attention and hints at the hidden costs of the work-first approach taken.

The others who secured paid employment during the research period had participated in the Work Programme prior to doing so, but did not regard the 'support' they had received as enabling their transitions into work. In 2016, Susan was still working as a Teaching Assistant – a role that she really enjoyed. She felt that, although the Work Programme did not support her in securing this job, they were quick to try to record its details, which she assumed was so they could collect the outcome payment to which they were entitled. This was also highlighted by Josh, who had moved into full-time work at the corner shop where he had been employed in a more ad-hoc manner since 2012 (see Chapter Four). Josh contrasted the lack of support from the Work Programme with their insistent contact now he had been in his job for two years:

'Two years ago, when I was on Jobseeker's they put me onto [Work Programme]. Waste of time. You go there every couple of weeks and didn't really do much. They talk to you, see how you're doing, have a look at your CV. They'd say you could come to a job interview or a job meeting or something. Nothing really come of it. But they do keep harassing me now that I've had a job for the past two years. I keep getting a phone call every four months saying 'we need to prove that you're in work and everything', and they're ringing my boss ... every four months they insist on ringing. It's irritating.'

While Susan and Josh did not see the JCP and WP support as helpful, Adrian, who had been offered work-related support at the time of his fourth interview, was hopeful that it might help in his efforts to finally secure employment:

'[The Job Centre has] put me onto … a maths thing, just learning maths and literacy as well. The maths is [helpful] because I can't count properly, can't even divide or times so that's brilliant. I had a big smile on my face when she said that. That's what I needed, I'll probably get a job straight away. Just blag their head [impress them] with maths [laughs].'

Adrian's enthusiasm for the support provided was reflective of his enduring hope that he might find paid work soon; a hope that he managed to sustain despite repeated setbacks and rejections.

No such support was available to Kane, who was released from prison and then quickly placed in the Support Group of Employment and Support Allowance (ESA). He was disappointed about this:

'I were a bit pissed off really. I'd rather be in the other one [work-related activity group] to try and get me into part-time work or some course or something like that. It feels like they just write you off really.'

This disappointment echoed the earlier frustrations Kane expressed in 2013, following an absence of support being provided to him while in the WRAG (see Chapter Four). While the severity of Kane's mental health problems meant he was perhaps not seen as a priority for welfare-to-work support, the signals that a placement in the Support Group of ESA sends to claimants about their judged work-readiness and future employability requires further consideration. Despite his impairments, Kane did want to enter employment but was left trying to explore options without the provision of any tailored help or support from either Job Centre Plus or a welfare-to-work provider. This speaks to the shortcomings of a conditionality regime; one that is driven by the benefits system's segmentation and demarcation of individuals according to the appropriateness of demanding work-related conditions from the benefit claimant. This is then led by bureaucratic assessments rather than individuals' own views (even expertise) about their readiness to move into employment, which undermines the capacity for such expertise to be recognised.

The persistence of poverty

The 2016 interviews also demonstrated the persistence of poverty for participants, with all nine of those interviewed still living below the poverty line and the four in paid work experiencing in-work poverty. The enduring experience of poverty, even for those moving into paid work, highlights the hollowness of the 'work is the best route out of poverty' policy mantra (Crisp et al., 2009). Those in employment reported their struggle to manage on limited resources and to eke out everyday essentials and occasional luxuries with the money available. Despite securing sustainable employment, Rosie still faced poverty and insecurity, a constant in her life throughout the five years of the research:

> 'I think about [money] all the time and sometimes I do worry about it, especially the week before pay day, that is a horrible week ... I think everything just starts running out the week before pay day. Washing powder you get on pay day when you do your big shop, and then it starts running out and you've got no money.'

For those living in poverty, even small variations in income can make a significant difference (Daly and Kelly, 2015; Lansley and Mack, 2015). For this reason, the April 2016 increase in the National Minimum Wage (which the Government described as the introduction of a National Living Wage) had an evident impact:

> 'It's only 50p but 50p is 50p so ... I mean it was an extra £2 each shift, so I wasn't going to argue. With me, 'cause of my low income every penny counts so even if it's just a penny, or £2, it counts. So I consider it great, if it's gone up, it's brilliant.' (Sam)

By tracking individuals over time, it was possible to observe how cumulative experiences of persistent and enduring poverty impacted negatively on their already difficult lives. Isobella explained how she had exhausted her savings to meet occasional additional expenses:

> 'Because of having to have some work done on the house, I have no safety net now, so if there was anything major, either that I needed to buy or that something happened, I'd be struggling.'

While some academics have questioned whether the struggle to get by over time tests and undermines individuals' capacity for resilience and tenacity (Hickman et al., 2014), what was notable from these interviews was individuals' continued efforts and determination to make do despite their financial hardship. As we saw in James' case study, individuals adapted to their reduced income on benefits, making difficult decisions in their struggle to manage – a struggle that is, for many, not temporary, but long-lasting. Before moving into his mother's house to save money, James described the measures he had taken in his effort to cope with the poverty he faced:

> 'I were saying to my mam, "I'm skint … will you get me a bit of shopping?" … I were getting to the point where I didn't want to put my heating on or I'd only use my washer once a week or summat to save on stuff.'

While individuals displayed this continued resilience, there was no doubt that it was stretched and tested by their ongoing struggles, which were set against a context of welfare reform. Poverty formed a constant backdrop to their lives and often had significant and enduring negative consequences, both for the individuals themselves and their wider families.

The long-term costs of welfare reform

For all of those interviewed in 2016, welfare reform and continual changes to the benefits system had become a recognisable part of the social security landscape. At the time of these interviews, Universal Credit had just been rolled out to single adults in the area in which they all lived and some were anticipating what a move onto the new benefit might mean for them. Anxiety was expressed about the shift to monthly payments and the move to make rent payments directly to the tenant rather than the landlord.

Individuals appeared to have become accustomed to (if not accepting of) regular changes and had partially adjusted to a new status quo of continual flux and uncertainty regarding their future benefit entitlement.

As in 2013, disability benefit(s) claimants such as Isobella were facing repeated – often delayed – reassessments. This impacted negatively on them, given the pervasive and deep-rooted anxiety that the possibility of a reassessment caused:

> 'I'm waiting for the brown envelope and that could tip me over the edge if there was something detrimental or

negative that came back from it ... just feels a bit like there's a Damocles over your head while you're waiting.'

At the time of her interview, Isobella was still in the Support Group of ESA and was receiving Disability Living Allowance but waiting to be migrated onto PIPs. She had anticipated being reassessed for ESA some eight months earlier and was still awaiting news of when the reassessment might take place. Given her previous experiences of being placed in the WRAG, Isobella was understandably worried about the likely outcome of this reassessment, as well as concerned that she might receive less when migrated onto PIPs. Although her benefit eligibility remained in place, the uncertainty over her future entitlement impacted upon her present life:

> 'You talk to people who are being assessed, and you say "when am I?", so it is there on the back of my mind that I'm on borrowed time, waiting till they get round to it, and then of course there's the "will I get it, will I, won't I?" again. So not only are you waiting, you're waiting for the decisions after it, and that does take it its toll. I certainly am less positive than I used to be and I think a lot of that's down to not knowing what's going on, not being kept informed, and of course there's no point in phoning up because they can't tell you anything.'

Isobella reflected on the cumulative, negative impact of this worry and uncertainty:

> 'It's been getting harder to cope ... there's sort of a downward spiral, and I'm less optimistic than I have been over the years with things, and it does feel as though things are more in limbo than they ever have been.'

Like Isobella, Cath reported anxiety about how she would cope if her benefits changed, as well as a gradual weakening of her capacity to continue to fight against and challenge benefit decisions with which she disagreed:

> 'I do know that if my benefits were reduced in any way my quality of life would be even worse, and with the health issues that I do have, life's hardly worth living as it is [crying]. Take away my financial freedoms ... well

I'm not going to live like that. And I'm sick of fighting. I haven't got another fight in me anyway. So, if they take my benefits away from me I'm out of here. I don't want to live in poverty, in isolation, in bad health and I'm not going to.' (2015 interview)

Almost all of the disability benefit claimants interviewed on three occasions between 2011 and 2013 challenged a benefits decision with which they initially disagreed and their successful challenges led to significant material improvements in their circumstances (see Chapter Five). As these individuals faced repeat reassessments, there was evidence of a reduction in their capacity and readiness to continue to make these same challenges. This brings with it a risk that, should such individuals decide not to challenge future benefit decisions with which they disagree, they will not then receive the benefits to which they are entitled.

Aside from the worry and anxiety that welfare reform is causing and the ways in which the cumulative impact of this can be particularly negative, the 2016 interviews powerfully illustrated the negative consequences for those subject to repeat benefit sanctions. We have already seen how Adrian struggled with the welfare conditionality regime – experiences shared by Robert, who was made subject to a three-year sanction in 2014 following a period of depression. While on this sanction, Robert fell into arrears with his rent and so was evicted from his property. Homeless, Robert had to give up the custody of his two dogs – animals to which he had a strong attachment, as he has no family. Robert managed to secure ad-hoc employment labouring and on building sites but was otherwise reliant on the help of friends and food banks, as he was not entitled to hardship payments:

'That sanction, it screwed me over. And I couldn't claim hardship either. I got declined on numerous times. We wrote three letters to them to try and get it but they just wouldn't have none of it. Even a doctor's letter, even that didn't count. [The doctor's letter said] that I need some money to have some food. If I don't get food I'm not going to survive am I, it's one of them things.'

Research has found no evidence of a positive correlation between the increased application of benefit sanctions and job outcomes (Watts et al., 2014, Dwyer and Bright, 2016) – and yet sanctions retain their central place in the UK's benefits system. The hardship they are causing to individuals such as Robert and Adrian illustrates the extent to which they represent a violation of the principle of universal social rights and a retreat from more egalitarian ideals of social citizenship. The costs of welfare reform are keenly felt – not only by those who face a loss of income, but also by those who experience the new status quo of uncertainty, anxiety and worry about their future entitlement and eligibility.

Experiencing and escaping benefits stigma

As well as detailing the material impacts of welfare reform, this book has shown the ways in which benefits receipt is today bound up in stigma and shame (see Chapter Six). It has been posited that this is contributing to a move towards 'conditioning' (Dwyer and Ellison, 2009), whereby individuals self-discipline and self-govern their own behaviours as they seek to move from benefits and into work to rid themselves of the stigma of benefits. The 2016 interviews reinforced this. The individuals who found work during the intervening three years regularly recounted how they saw the move from out-of-work benefits into employment as a way of shedding the stigma of benefits receipt and instead claiming the identity of a 'hard-working, dutiful citizen'. In her earlier interviews, Sam spoke of herself as a "scrounger" and explicitly tied her aspiration to secure work with her wish to correct her negative self-image (see Chapter Six). Having moved into work by 2016, Sam described the difference this had made:

> 'I felt awful having to claim off the government, but now
> not so much, no. The government pay my rent for me due
> to the fact of my low income but that's no fault of my own,
> so I've no need to think about it if that's the case.'

It is notable that Sam implicitly contrasted her position receiving in-work support through "no fault of her own" with her previous receipt of out-of-work benefits, with an underlying suggestion that there was perhaps some fault or blame attached to her former position, even though she was actively seeking work at that time. Sam's account suggests an appropriation of the individualising narrative of 'welfare' and poverty, which places the need for corrective action on individual rather than structural factors (Ferge, 1997; Dwyer and Ellison, 2009). She is then engaged in actively critiquing and self-governing her previous non-working behaviour. Sam could be described here as engaging in 'DIY social policy' (Klein and Millar, 1995). But whereas this has traditionally referred to individuals constructing their own welfare mix, here it is employed to refer to the ways in which individuals such as Sam are seeking to take ownership and responsibility for the behavioural change that both the state and they themselves think they require.

Like Sam, all of the other individuals who were in employment at the time of their fourth interviews received forms of in-work support from the state. They also all differentiated in-work financial support – which was seen as deserved and less stigmatising – from out-of-work benefits receipt:

'It does [feel different getting tax credits] because I am paying the tax out anyway, so I'm only getting it back.' (Josh)

'At least I am entitled to something, and because I've worked I feel comfortable taking what I'm entitled to.' (Rosie)

The contrast drawn suggests an internalisation of dominant narratives and distinctions between deserving and undeserving populations, and an acceptance of in-work financial support as a non-stigmatised form of provision that those in work 'deserve'. With the roll out of Universal Credit and introduction of in-work conditionality, it remains to be seen whether these distinctions will start to collapse as in-work benefits recipients become incorporated into the JCP and work-search regime (Butler, 2016; Wright et al., 2016). As in-work conditionality is implemented and affected individuals mandated to attend JCP in order to demonstrate efforts to secure more hours, such individuals may also become seen as 'welfare dependants' whose not-working-enough behaviours become subject to censure and critique.

Problematising 'poverty porn'

The period between 2013 and 2016 saw a rapid expansion in 'poverty porn'; almost every week seemed to bring a new televised depiction of the 'real lives' of those on 'welfare'. The growth and spread of such programmes inevitably affects how those on out-of-work benefits are seen and arguably further entrenches the framing consensus on 'welfare' (see Chapter Two) (Jensen, 2015). In the 2016 interviews, individuals were asked if they watched these programmes and for their responses and reactions to them. Four of the nine interviewed regularly watched such programmes. Three said they had stopped watching them due to their growing anger about the way in which those on benefits were portrayed (the remaining two had always chosen not to watch them).

Those who did watch such shows often expressed sympathy for those whose lives were placed under scrutiny, while simultaneously being critical of aspects of the behaviour portrayed:

> 'Some people I do really feel for ... Some people, you wish you could help them and some people do deserve [benefits] but then there's some people who stay at home, and they're not interested [in work] but they expect handouts. It's not nice. Why should they be entitled to [benefits] when they've done nothing to earn it?' (Josh)

There was recognition that the behaviour(s) depicted were then generalised to the benefit-claiming population:

> 'They do portray an unintelligent, overweight, beer-guzzling, cigarette-smoking, drug-taking people, and that seems to be all they concentrate on, which obviously gives the impression that everyone's like that, with a big flat TV screen.' (Isobella)

Individuals expressed anger about this portrayal and its likely impact:

> 'I watched *Benefits Street*, I think it were like "poverty porn", that's what you call it isn't it. Basically trying to make them look like dickheads ... I think people definitely thought they're all scrounging bastards after that. I think that's the reason they did it really.' (Kane)

> 'Working class people ... think badly of everyone on benefits now. They think they're scroungers ... It does make me cross, it's the media that's doing that ... they only film what they want to.' (Rosie)

> 'I don't like how [people on benefits] are portrayed. Sometimes I think the government leans on the media to show people in a negative light ... [These shows] feed people's negativity ... [People] like their negativity to be fed because they need something to hate ... it gives the rich and the upper and middle classes ... something to hate.' (Sam)

Sam argues that 'poverty porn' serves a particular function in giving people "something to hate", while there is the suggestion in all three accounts that the media and even politicians are deliberately using such programmes to promote negative attitudes towards 'welfare' – a suggestion also made in recent academic commentaries (Jensen, 2014; Tyler, 2014a).

It was recognised that this distorting of experiences of benefits receipt could negatively impact on how individuals themselves were viewed and treated:

> 'Even the job centre advisers, they watch the shows. That's how they view us, or that's how they get told to view us … [They treat me] like I'm one of them people on one of them shows. "So, what have you been doing? Watching telly?" They act like that's what you do.' (Adrian)

Individuals' responses to 'poverty porn' suggested they were increasingly aware of the ways in which it promotes a negative portrayal of those on benefits and the likelihood of this only worsening the reach and extent of benefits stigma. The decision of three individuals to stop watching such shows reflected a political refusal to participate in a public mass viewing of individual lives on 'welfare', when these lives are being depicted in such a sensationalised and negative light.

Conclusion

Through walking alongside individuals as they experienced welfare reform, out-of-work benefits receipt and transitions between 'welfare' and 'work', this book has documented people's journeys over time and tracked the cumulative impact of successive waves of welfare reform. In concluding the empirical analysis, this chapter has provided an update on nine of the participants, who were interviewed for a fourth time in the summer of 2016. More than anything, what these updates demonstrate is the pivotal role paid employment plays in individual lives – whether as an as-yet unrealised aspiration, a nostalgic element of a previous (now lost) identity or an active component of day-to-day lives. The importance attached to paid employment endures for those participating in 'poor', even exclusionary employment (Bailey, 2016), who often draw a stark contrast between the positive advantages they associate with engaging in the formal labour market and their previous experiences of out-of-work benefits receipt.

The case studies discussed in this chapter – particularly the accounts of Adrian and James – demonstrate the extent to which paid work is valorised as a valued and valuable activity, but also found to be insecure and temporary – where it is available at all. The contemporary labour market features considerable precarity and a preponderance of low-paid, low-status and chronically insecure jobs (Shildrick et al., 2010; Shildrick et al., 2012b; Standing, 2014; Thompson, 2015). Despite this, work continues to be seen as vital for income, social inclusion and a positive sense of self. Frayne (2016) rightly describes the fact that the 'centrality of work persists even while work is in a state of crisis' as 'one of the most troubling contradictions of our times'.

Individuals' valuing of work (even of the insecure, low-paid variety) might be taken to suggest a congruence between recent governments' policy agendas and individual lived experiences. However, this is closely connected to the often severe hardship, demoralisation and perhaps even degradation with which out-of-work benefits receipt is today associated. Whether or not this is an acceptable by-product of a work-first, anti-welfare-dependency policy approach may in part depend on one's political persuasion (cf. Dunn, 2014), but it also illustrates the retreat in recent years from a more redistributive welfare state that upholds at least a basic level of social rights (Lister, 2011b; Bradshaw, 2015).

The whole policy agenda is built upon the assumption that welfare conditionality, benefit sanctions and active labour market policies can together trigger behavioural change and support welfare-to-work transitions (cf. Duncan Smith, 2010b; DWP, 2010a). This is almost entirely unsupported by the evidence emerging from this book – evidence backed up by other, larger-scale qualitative research studies (Watts et al., 2014; Dwyer and Bright, 2016). Admittedly, though, the Work Programme did directly support Sam into work, but work that was poorly paid and guaranteed only eight hours of employment per week.

This chapter has also shown the variability of the trajectories and experiences of the participants over time; some individuals secured sustainable employment while others stayed on benefits throughout the period under study. We have also seen variability within welfare-to-work transitions, clashing with the apparently seamless and unproblematic welfare-to-work journey depicted in the dominant political rhetoric (cf. Osborne, 2013b; Duncan Smith, 2014b). Indeed, a dominant narrative that seems to suggest that all work is inevitably and necessarily transformative is out of step with the uneven and much more complicated experiences of the people in this study (see also Shildrick et al., 2010; Bailey, 2016).

Finally, this chapter and those preceding it have demonstrated the inherent value in foregrounding individual experiences of benefits receipt and welfare reform – experiences better understood when repeat interviews enable a dynamic picture to emerge of individual journeys and changes over time. These individual journeys show the ways in which people are sometimes struggling against the policy agenda. This is despite the overarching objectives of the policy agenda and individual aspirations so often coinciding, with both orientated towards securing transitions from 'welfare' into 'work'. What they also show is the very tangible ways in which the social rights of citizenship have today receded and become increasingly fractured and conditional (Lister, 2011b; Dwyer and Wright, 2014), with benefits receipt further bound up in experiences of stigma, shame and embarrassment (Walker, 2014; Baumberg, 2016). The implications of this for social security policy specifically and social citizenship more broadly are multifaceted and complex. It is now critical to explore some of the political and theoretical ramifications of the contemporary 'welfare' landscape.

Conclusion: social insecurity and 'welfare'

'This government is all about security ... Security is also what drives the social reform that I want this government to undertake in my second term. Individuals and families who are in poverty crave security – for them, it's the most important value of all. ... So for people in Britain who are struggling today, our mission as a government is to look every parent and child in the eye, and say 'Your dreams are our dreams. We'll support you with everything we've got.' (Cameron, 2016)

In his successful 2015 General Election campaign and subsequent keynote speeches, then-Prime Minister David Cameron repeatedly returned to the idea of 'security' as a leitmotif for the reformed society he and his government were seeking to create. He believed – rightly – that the idea of security resonates with the population (Orton, 2015) and speaks to the anxieties of so many that life is all too often insecure and uncertain.

Whether and how far the reforms instigated under Cameron's leadership between 2010 and 2016 increased security is, of course, highly questionable – particularly for those directly affected by successive waves of welfare reform. As the research reported in this book have illustrated, the material impact of reforms have pushed many people further into poverty and undermined physical and mental wellbeing, while a constant backdrop of change has left individuals living with chronic and destabilising insecurity and fears about an uncertain future. Classic liberal citizenship theorist T. H. Marshall argued that the social rights of citizenship should provide at least a 'modicum of economic welfare and *security*' (1950, emphasis added). Now more than ever it is important to interrogate whether this is provided to those at the sharp end of welfare reform.

In this concluding chapter, the key findings from this research are summarised, focusing particular on the disjuncture between citizenship as it is conceptualised from above and citizenship as it is lived and experienced from below. This is particularly evident in competing notions and experiences of (in)security and benefits receipt. The political and theoretical implications of this are then discussed before a brief consideration of areas that would benefit from further research. This chapter asks whether social citizenship retains its emancipatory potential or if – through being co-opted and subverted as a tool of social control and governance – it has instead been rendered ineffective, even redundant, in efforts to generate support for a more solidaristic social security system. First, though, it is important to re-emphasise the central messages to emerge from five years spent researching individuals' lived experiences of benefits receipt and welfare reform.

The disjuncture between citizenship from above and below

It is clear from this book that a stark disjuncture exists between the dominant narrative of citizenship – citizenship from above – and the lived realities of citizenship for those on out-of-work benefits – citizenship from below (Lister, 2011b). The dominant citizenship narrative, propagated by mainstream politicians and echoed in media commentaries, implies static and entrenched divisions between 'hard-working families' busy 'doing the right thing' and 'welfare dependants', depicted in George Osborne's (2012) classic soundbite 'sleeping off a life on benefits'. These divisions between 'strivers' and 'shirkers' represent a contemporary reworking of much older distinctions drawn between the deserving and undeserving 'poor' (Hills, 2015). Strivers are the insiders, already behaving as the government would like, while 'shirkers' are outsiders, requiring intervention and increasingly punitive measures to reform and address their non-working behaviours (Coote and Lyall, 2013).

The dominant narrative implies that those on out-of-work benefits are passive, inactive and all too often irresponsible, displaying none of the characteristics that define the hard-working, responsible lives of those in paid employment. It depicts many of those in receipt of out-of-work benefits as completely detached from the paid labour market, lacking the right 'habit', 'aspirations' and 'work ethic'.

We see the dissemination of this dominant narrative in politicians' speeches, justifications for policy reforms and the reams of newspaper reporting devoted to the 'problem of welfare'. Increasingly, we have also seen it popularised and reanimated as entertainment in the exponential growth of 'poverty porn'. Television shows such as *Benefits Street* claim to provide insight into the 'reality' of 'life on benefits', but in fact provide access to a 'reality' that is heavily edited and sensationalised. It is possible today to speak of a new framing consensus on 'welfare', which sees politicians, the popular media and much of public opinion in agreement around both the 'problem' of 'welfare' and the 'problems' with those who rely on it for all or most of their income (see Chapter Two). This consensus is fundamentally moral in tone. It makes moral judgements about the behaviours and character of others and creates the logic for a 'moral project' to correct and address these perceived shortcomings, with 'active welfare' becoming an 'instrument for forging public morality' (Jones and Novak, 1999, p. 181).

Processes of dichotomous demarcation, judgement and categorisation provide the rhetorical framework for a policy agenda supposedly motivated by efforts to transform the lives of 'welfare dependants' by bringing them into the fold of the 'hard-working majority' (see Chapter One). Drawing on civic republican and liberal ideas of citizenship, frequently in tandem, the dominant citizenship narrative positions paid employment as the primary duty of the responsible citizen. Non-work then becomes associated with a lesser citizenship status. Those not currently engaged in paid employment are characterised as 'irresponsible citizens' who need 'activating' with support from the state to enable their inclusion in both the formal labour market and society as dutiful, contributing citizens. Welfare reforms and measures supposed to support welfare-to-work transitions are then justified on the basis that they will deliver social and citizenship inclusion. The ways in which these policies in fact operate to entrench and cement exclusions between and within different populations are neglected.

Conditionality, which is justified as a mechanism for encouraging people into work, has been steadily intensified and extended in recent years. Today, claimants face the ultimate sanction of three years without benefits if they fail to comply with certain work-related demands three times. As well as advancing the reach of conditionality, Cameron's governments oversaw a range of welfare reforms that effectively lowered the social security 'safety net', reducing both the levels of and eligibility for various forms of out-of-work support (see Chapter Two). Taken together, these reforms constitute a fundamental retrenchment of social welfare, with far-reaching and ongoing implications for those directly affected (Bradshaw, 2015).

By walking alongside a small group of individuals in receipt of out-of-work benefits as they experienced and responded to welfare reform, it has been possible to contrast the conceptualisation of citizenship from above with an understanding of citizenship as it is lived and experienced from below. This powerfully demonstrates the fragility and unworkability of static demarcations between 'workers' and 'non-workers'. Instead, it finds that fluid and repeated movements between low-paid employment and benefits receipt – characterised by the low-pay, no-pay cycle (Shildrick et al., 2012b) – are common. It illustrates the extent to which getting by on benefits requires hard and intensive 'work'; work completely absent from stereotypical portrayals of benefits recipients lazily 'languishing on benefits' (see Chapter Three). Many of those interviewed for this book were also engaged in forms of contribution such as volunteering, care work, parenting and informal support – socially valuable activities that go unrecognised in the persistent equation of responsibility with paid employment.

Several participants moved into paid employment during the initial research period, including examples of exploitation and pay well below the NMW. Paid employment was seen to bring a range of non-pecuniary rewards and participants' perspectives here coincided with politicians' repeated emphasis on the transformative rewards of employment (see Chapter Four). However, while Cameron's governments claimed they were doing all they could to support out-of-work claimants into paid employment, this was not the experience of those interviewed, and many were very critical of the welfare-to-work support they received. Further, welfare reform rarely supported work-related aspirations, and benefit sanctions were found to move people further away from, rather than closer to, the labour market (see Chapter Five).

Most individuals displayed strong, active work aspirations; they spoke of previous experiences in paid employment with pride and as an important aspect of their identity (see Chapter Four). Orientations towards employment endured over time, even when individuals were subject to repeated rejections and setbacks in their efforts to find work. For most of those interviewed, their benefits receipt was unchosen and unwanted – a rebuke to the notion of benefits as a 'lifestyle choice'. Individuals display an awareness of the dominant narrative, which impacts upon their daily lives, most evidently through the stigma and shame they associate with their own benefits receipt (see Chapter Six). This can make efforts to find employment more difficult and has consequences for how affected individuals see themselves, see others and are seen by others. Those interviewed showed an appropriation of the notion of 'welfare' as inherently problematic, particularly in their internalisation of the negative descriptors of benefit claimants and their 'othering' of those who supposedly fit the dominant portrayal.

Chapter Seven summarised the findings from a fourth wave of interviews with nine individuals in 2016. These interviews illustrated the variability in trajectories and transitions over time and it was possible to distinguish between long-term claimants, precarious welfare-to-work transitioners and sustained welfare-to-work transitioners. Of those interviewed, six had moved into work at points during the intervening five years – a pertinent challenge to the idea of static populations of 'workers' and 'welfare dependants'.

Overall, the evidence generated from repeat interviews with individuals as they experienced welfare reform, benefits receipt and work provides a stark, rich, empirically-based counter to the dominant citizenship narrative from above (see Chapter One). This book provides a much-needed longitudinal dimension and complements other research in countering the depiction of benefits recipients by politicians and the media (see, for example, Shildrick et al., 2012b; Dwyer and Bright, 2016). The dominant narrative posits that individual benefits recipients demonstrate flawed decision-making, irresponsibility and a deficit of active agency, which directly lead to their non-employment (Wright, 2016). Welfare reform and activation are then required to alter the behaviour of individual claimants so they can become 'active welfare subjects' as 'workers' (Wright, 2016). But this research indicates that many benefits recipients are already active. This is as evident in their efforts to secure employment and movements in (and out of) employment as it is in the hard work that getting by on benefits demands and in the various ways in which many were contributing. These lived experiences better fit a counter model (Wright, 2016), which recognises that 'welfare subjects' are already active, 'beings' rather than 'becomings', with their agency mediated and sometimes threatened by interactions with bureaucratic systems and processes of welfare reform.

Following people over time provides new evidence to support the argument that the need for a 'responsibilisation of the poor' (Pykett, 2014) is based on a flawed and simplistic characterisation of out-of-work benefit claimants as passive and inactive. Mapping the disjuncture of citizenship from above with citizenship from below is important, particularly given the implications for policy, citizenship and future research priorities. It is to an exploration of those implications that this chapter now turns.

Rethinking the logic for welfare conditionality and sanctions

The centrepiece of recent governments' policy approach to welfare reform in general and welfare-to-work in particular has been a gradual ratcheting up of the application of welfare conditionality and benefit sanctions to promote behavioural change by encouraging entry into employment (and, most recently, increased working hours for those falling within the remit of in-work conditionality). Despite an absence of evidence of a positive association between these policy tools and successful, sustained transitions into employment (Watts et al., 2014), politicians have shown an enduring eagerness to usher in new conditions and sanctions as part of efforts to ensure that all those who can are on a journey from 'welfare' and into 'work'.

Welfare conditionality places the policy focus and corrective lens firmly onto the steps that individuals need to take to become more work-ready and employable. This inevitably entails an 'individualization of the social' (Ferge, 1997), with an associated emphasis on individual supply-side barriers to employment; that is, on what individual out-of-work claimants need to do (and be made to do) to activate them into paid employment. Such an analysis neglects the various demand-side barriers to an individual's employment; barriers that this research found to be significant in preventing out-of-work claimants from moving into secure and sustainable paid employment (see Chapter Four) (Newman, 2011; Patrick, 2014b).

While the policy rhetoric suggests that conditionality encourages people to make the 'right' decisions and supports welfare-to-work transitions, the evidence from both this and other research is that the compulsion it brings to encounters with Job Centre Plus and Work Programme advisers can undermine the scope to develop more productive and supportive relationships (Dwyer and Bright, 2016; Wright, 2016). Further, the very significant material and symbolic hardship that benefit sanctions can cause often operates to create additional barriers to entering the paid labour market. This is most marked when individuals are forced to focus their attention and energies on surviving destitution, which reduces the time available for actively seeking paid employment (Batty et al., 2015; Fitzpatrick et al., 2016). In this way, the conditionality regime can have the perverse consequence of undermining, rather than supporting, transitions into paid work.

An emphasis on conditionality and sanctions might be logical if the starting point were a homogenous group of out-of-work claimants characterised by idleness and an active preference for benefits over paid employment. It becomes rather less logical if out-of-work claimants are recognised to be an already active group, busy with the work of managing on benefits and coping with welfare reforms; individuals who are often strongly motivated to find paid employment, where it is a realistic option (see chapters three to five). This research shows that the rationale for work-related welfare conditionality needs to be reconsidered. Furthermore, much more policy attention is required to consider how far – and whether – the forms of welfare-to-work support provided are actually fit for purpose.

Making work work

While welfare conditionality and sanctions may not be the most effective tools for encouraging welfare-to-work transitions, the congruence between the work-related aspirations of the individuals interviewed for this book and the policy focus on enabling transitions into work was notable. This is to say that individuals shared politicians' characterisation of paid employment as a valuable and valued activity and one they saw as having scope to enable them to live a better life; a life less scarred by poverty, insecurity and experiences of stigma and shame. However, it is not to say that individuals shared the work-first orientation of the policy approach, which so often made their efforts to realise longer-term work-related aspirations harder to achieve.

While individuals saw paid employment as bringing with it a range of pecuniary and non-pecuniary rewards, the transitions they so often made were from the poverty of out-of-work benefits receipt into in-work poverty. There are real ethical issues with a policy approach that supports transitions from 'welfare' and into 'exclusionary employment' (work that fails to deliver the inclusionary reward with which it is so commonly associated; Bailey, 2016). This suggests that more attention needs to be paid to reforming the formal labour market, such that movements into employment can also entail movements out of poverty and into secure and non-exploitative work. This book therefore adds to a growing body of research evidence in calling for more action to improve the nature of available employment opportunities, particularly at the bottom end of the labour market (Shildrick et al., 2012b; Dean, 2014; O'Hara, 2014). The sustained emphasis on engagement in paid employment as the key characteristic of a productive, socially included citizen coexists with ongoing and endemic problems with the way the labour market operates (Frayne, 2016). This creates particular challenges and presents the need for new solutions (Frayne, 2016). Most radically, such solutions might incorporate efforts to build a 'post-work society'; one in which the central place of employment as *the* activity delineating productive from unproductive and responsible from irresponsible behaviour is rethought (Frayne, 2015, 2016).

The burden of welfare reform

This research has also demonstrated the burden of welfare reform, focusing in particular on the costs borne by individuals living with benefit changes and facing increased hardship, worry and chronic insecurity – all of which can impact negatively on individuals' physical and emotional health. The burden of welfare reform also frequently undermines welfare-to-work transitions, particularly when it makes active planning for the future more difficult. In recent years, social security provision has become increasingly fractured and piecemeal in ways that make life harder for those in receipt of out-of-work benefits. Politicians and policy makers should pay more attention to the perhaps unintended consequences of welfare reform's burden and better consider how these consequences rub up against – and even undermine – the central welfare-to-work policy aspiration.

More should also be done to consider how the burden of welfare reform extends not only to those individuals affected but also to the wider social security infrastructure; both national and local government agencies, as well as voluntary sector organisations supporting claimants. Whether it is the work involved in administering (or supporting a claimant with) an ESA appeal or the food banks responding to the impact of benefit delays and sanctions, welfare reform is placing new pressures (with associated costs) on this infrastructure (Dugan, 2014; Garthwaite, 2016). This is not acknowledged within a popular political rhetoric of welfare reform as cost-saving. There is an urgent need to take account of and measure these broader costs of welfare reform and to contrast them with the financial savings judged to arise from the changes. Aside from the financial savings from a (very slightly) reduced social security bill, the advantages of welfare reform have not been identified in this research, which instead shows how a climate of benefit changes and increased benefit sanctions makes it so much harder for individual citizens to get by and realise their own aspirations.

It may be that the 'benefit' of welfare reform is that it does make individuals' lives so much harder (see Garrett, 2015). In a recent report for Civitas on 'Fixing Broken Britain', Frank Field noted that the Coalition government had 'gained success many times over with its policy of making life on benefits that much more difficult' (2016, p. 119). It is possible to argue that, by making life more difficult for those on out-of-work benefits, welfare reform successfully promotes (or even compels) individuals to make welfare-to-work transitions and perhaps discourages others from even applying for social security support. From this political positioning, the stripping back and curtailing of the social rights of citizenship becomes justified, even necessary, to re-embed principles of less eligibility and to ensure that the social security system promotes working behaviours. However, the fairness of this approach can be challenged – particularly if we accept that many receive out-of-work benefits due to impairments or temporary circumstances that make entering paid employment either impossible or undesirable (such as childcare and caring responsibilities). Further, many more may be seeking employment without success. There is, then, a question regarding the fairness of making life on out-of-work benefits increasingly difficult for such individuals.

Citizenship implications

The demise of social rights: (in)equality of status and (in)security

T. H. Marshall described social citizenship as holding the promise of 'equality of status' for all citizens; social rights were seen as offering something of substance to those living in poverty via the provision of a 'modicum of economic welfare and security' (Marshall, 1950; Dwyer, 2010). However, successive changes to social welfare provision mean that social rights have become increasingly residualised and made conditional on compliance with state-defined behaviours. This research has shown that welfare conditionality, while sometimes welcomed, is often experienced as a denial of individual agency and negation of individuals' choice and control over their own lives. This can lead to feelings of powerlessness and anger and can create a climate of fear and insecurity, particularly when people are concerned that they may be targeted with sanctions. The research highlighted examples of welfare conditionality clashing with individuals' desire to prioritise their parenting responsibilities, while the immediacy of work-related demands sometimes interfered with people's longer-term employment aspirations. Such consequences represent an undermining of individuals' citizenship rights. Where these consequences impact negatively on individuals' self-confidence and mental health, they can also – perversely – make individuals' fulfilment of citizenship duty *less* rather than *more* likely.

Today, out-of-work benefits receipt rarely protects people from poverty and hardship, and a lack of financial resources often prevents individuals from being able to participate fully in mainstream society. This inability to participate, although borne out of structural constraints, is often experienced as a source of shame and embarrassment – itself tied to the stigma surrounding poverty and benefits receipt. While social rights still have some value in offering *something* to those living in poverty, they certainly do not enable people to obtain equality of status, nor to achieve even a 'modicum of economic *security*' (Marshall, 1950, emphasis added). Instead, as this book has demonstrated, the lives of those on out-of-work benefits are characterised by uncertainty, insecurity and enduring anxiety over their ability to get by in the future as further welfare reforms are rolled out.

Wacquant (2010) observed the 'normalization of social insecurity' in the US. This is also evident in Britain where endemic insecurity is destabilising and undermining individuals' ontological security and their capacity to look forward and plan for the future (New Economics Foundation, 2012; Hill et al., 2016). Social citizenship rights still help to protect some individuals from the worst extremes of poverty and destitution – particularly, for example, when compared with the US, where many thousands of families are living on less than $2 per household member per day (Edin and Shaefer, 2015). But these rights have been made increasingly precarious and are withheld almost entirely from those subject to multiple benefit sanctions. Taken together, it is thus possible to speak of a process of downgrading and undermining of social citizenship rights, with inevitable consequences not only for those seeking to claim their social rights but for all citizens.

Citizenship as an exclusionary process

Out-of-work benefits recipients' 'welfare dependency' sees them granted a lesser, devalued citizenship status, with their non-work and benefits reliance stigmatised and derided. Government-fuelled demarcations between the 'hard-working majority' and those who rely on benefits operate to 'other' claimants (Lister, 2015) with conditionality and sanctions policy tools that seek to coerce and control them to become 'responsible' citizens. This is often done in the name of inclusion; politicians repeatedly promise that, by promoting and enforcing a work ethic, they will encourage responsible working behaviours on the part of 'the poor' – behaviours that carry with them the potential for integration into society. However, this policy approach only serves to exclude out-of-work claimants, whose behaviours are judged, stigmatised and ultimately found wanting. Those subject to work-related conditionality are also subject to the suggestion that they are failing to fulfil their citizenship duties; meeting welfare conditions is then characterised as not only helping such individuals escape 'welfare dependency' but also enabling them to secure a more certain citizenship status.

Despite the primacy that those interviewed accorded to paid employment, there remains a question of whether such employment should be so exclusively equated with citizenship duty, given the consequences that arise from this for those not currently in paid employment. Both the citizenship conception adopted (with the suggestion that paid employment should be understood as synonymous with fulfilling one's responsibilities as a citizen) and the analysis of the status quo (the association between benefit claiming and passivity and inactivity) are flawed. There are four key shortcomings with the current emphasis on paid employment as the marker of the dutiful citizen. First, it is inevitably exclusionary for those who simply *cannot* enter paid employment, such as many disabled people (Lister, 2003; Roulstone and Prideaux, 2012). Second, it neglects the various other forms of socially valuable contribution in which people are so often engaged, as well as the hard work that being on benefits so often entails (Lister, 2003; Patrick, 2014a) (see Chapter Three). While paid employment is consistently valorised, care work is devalued and all too often rendered invisible. Third, it fails to recognise that paid employment is not a static state, but rather that fluid movements into and out of employment are increasingly common (Shildrick et al., 2012b). Finally, the way in which this analysis has been operationalised by recent governments – with the focus on the individual responsibility of people to enter employment and concurrent neglect of its own responsibilities to enable this transition – is unbalanced and tends to contribute to an individualising of the 'problem' of economic inactivity (Wright, 2016). Ironically, focusing on paid employment as the marker of the dutiful citizen only increases the exclusionary potential of social citizenship, highlighting its 'Janus-faced' nature (Lister, 2003).

Further, the critical lens is firmly focused on those at the bottom end of the income spectrum; those whose wealth enables them to choose not to engage in paid employment are not subject to the same critique or social censure. An authoritarian contractual regime, which ties social welfare rights to state-defined responsibilities, extends only to benefit claimants; the working (and rich) population escapes these conditions and expectations. It could be argued that those not claiming out-of-work benefits due to being in employment are already meeting the terms of the contract and are thus encompassed within a broader contractualist regime. However, the reality is that rich non-workers are able to escape the stigma of unemployment and inactivity. Their wealth obscures their non-participation in the formal labour market. What is more, those with the necessary wealth and resources can *choose* whether or not to engage in paid employment – a choice wholly denied to those who must meet the work-related conditions of benefits receipt.

Harrison and Sanders (2014) developed the idea of a 'social division in social control' to reflect this differential treatment, noting that while those living in poverty are pushed, cajoled and punished for their non-compliance with state-defined expectations, richer populations are treated far more favourably and only subject to occasional encouragement and incentive-led nudges. This relates closely to Wacquant's (2009) idea of a centaur state; 'liberal at the top and paternalistic at the bottom … [the centaur state] presents radically different faces at the two ends of the social hierarchy: a comely and caring visage towards the middle and upper classes, and a fearsome and frowning mug towards the lower class' (Wacquant, 2009, p. 312). Wacquant describes the US as a 'centaur state' but it is a descriptor with evident crossover to the UK. This differential treatment undermines the supposed equality of status of citizens and is yet another driver of the exclusion from the citizenry of those subject to the most heavy-handed and persistent forms of social control through welfare conditionality.

Time, poverty and citizenship

Tracking individuals over time, this book has demonstrated how the experiences of poverty, welfare reform and ongoing benefits receipt have sometimes shortened time horizons, such that individuals feel unable to look beyond the present (see chapters four, five and seven). For many, the future becomes fearful and uncertain rather than a resource or something to which they can look forward. The short-term, immediate demands made of claimants by Job Centre Plus and Work Programme advisers, and the financial uncertainty created by welfare reform, operate together to reduce people's capacity to undertake the future-orientated work necessary to create more positive futures for themselves and their families. Some of those interviewed were living in discontinuous time (Neale, 2015); their preoccupation and blinkered focus on the immediate present – what Chloe described as living "hour by hour" (W3) – set them apart from the dominant flows of time in mainstream society (Bastian, 2014, cited in Neale, 2015). These experiences are best understood as a further form of citizenship exclusion; one that again demonstrates the extent to which social rights currently offer comparatively little to those living in poverty.

Inevitably, living in discontinuous time, day to day, impedes and undermines affected individuals' ability to plan, thus making transitions into paid employment less rather than more likely. This is particularly ironic given that the whole rationale for the government's approach is based on an attempt to 'support' people to make the 'welfare-to-work' journey. To better facilitate this journey, more should be done to create the conditions necessary to ensure that people have the safety, security and space to make plans, here conceptualised as vital preconditions for effective and sustainable transitions into paid employment.

More attention should be paid to relationships between social divisions of welfare and time – to the different abilities of individuals, families, classes and organisations to plan and make arrangements over time (Sinfield, 1978). Citizens should be given sufficient security to enable them to plan and make changes in their lives (Sinfield, 1978). Arguably, a right to a level of ontological security that enables one to plan for the future should be conceptualised as a fundamental citizenship right; one that is certainly not available to out-of-work benefit claimants or those struggling with in-work poverty and insecure employment in contemporary Britain (Shildrick et al., 2012b; Standing, 2014).

From conditional to conditioned citizenship

Seeking to understand the changing shape of social citizenship in the UK, academics have commonly described a social citizenship that has become significantly more conditional; bound up in, and contingent on, fulfilment of state-defined activities and demands (Galston, 2005; Lister, 2011b; Dwyer and Wright, 2014). While this is an important and continuing trend, there is scope to consider how far the conditional nature of citizenship today sits alongside a conditioning that sees individual out-of-work claimants become increasingly accepting of the dominant framing, particularly around the individualisation of responsibility and valorisation of paid employment (Dwyer and Ellison, 2009; Newman, 2011). In this analysis, individuals begin to 'self-govern', engaging in DIY social policy (Klein and Millar, 1995) as they seek to activate themselves to become responsible citizens (see Chapter Six).

The individuals featured in this book certainly showed signs of appropriating the terms of the new framing consensus in ways that could make a descriptor of 'conditioned citizens' appropriate. For example, the equation of paid employment with responsible, independent behaviour was evident across most of those interviewed, and individuals self-critiqued and sometimes questioned their own non-working behaviours (see chapters four and six). Clearly, the association between paid employment and valued, responsible behaviours is longstanding and has much wider roots than recent governments' repeated valorisation of paid work alone. Nonetheless, it is notable how wholeheartedly most of the participants bought into ideas of paid work and out-of-work benefits receipt as positive and negative activities respectively. Throughout, individuals described their benefits receipt as a shameful and negative state; where it was feasible, they were hard at work trying to move from benefits into paid employment. A clear contrast was often drawn between out-of-work benefits receipt and the independence seen to come with earning one's own wage. Individuals also appropriated the ideas of 'undeserving' 'welfare dependants' to describe and 'other' those who were seen not to deserve out-of-work benefits from the state. They therefore became active participants in the processes of demarcating the 'responsible' and 'irresponsible' in ways that ironically only extended their own potential exclusion, given their position on the wrong side of the responsible/irresponsible, work/ non-work divide (Walker, 2014).

It has been posited that the conditionality policy approach is reliant on its stigmatising narrative and that this narrative is actually a tool of governance – what Tyler describes as 'governance through stigma' (2014b). Tyler suggests that stigma may have been designed into policy to nudge people off benefits (2014b). There was certainly evidence in this research of the stigma around benefits forming one of the many motivations for people wishing to move into paid employment. This links closely with Schram et al.'s (2008) argument that 'poverty governance' can include intentional efforts to alter human subjectivities. Efforts are made to change individuals so that they become more likely to self-govern in ways that produce the outcomes desired – in this case, to enter paid employment. Signs of 'poverty governance' and 'governance through stigma' signal an effort not only to make benefit entitlement conditional on state-defined behaviours, but also *to condition* out-of-work benefit claimants so that they self-govern and take action to address those behaviours deemed problematic. The irony of conditionality, however, is that by making clear and unbending demands of its target population – and rarely offering choices or opportunity for the exercise of individual agency – it can actually undermine the potential for individuals to actively 'self-govern' and to take the steps they feel will be most effective in helping them to transition from benefits to paid employment.

Taken together then, it is possible to describe out-of-work benefit recipients as increasingly conditioned citizens, who are faced with a dominant and pervasive stigmatising narrative about their supposed irresponsible and deficit behaviours. As out-of-work citizens become conditioned, there is a risk that anger and a sense of blame for their own situation will turn inwards or be directed at the supposedly undeserving behaviours of 'others'. This further threatens social solidarity, as well as undermining any potential for a more proactive citizenship engagement, which would challenge the current trend for citizenship to operate as a process of exclusion (Walker, 2014).

Citizenship is increasingly reconceptualised as a project and process, which requires the state's involvement and (often punitive) interventions to assist individuals to become 'responsible' via 'processes of responsibilization' (Clarke, 2005). These processes see citizens required to comply with state-defined obligations at the same time as being repositioned as (at least partly) 'empowered citizens' who are expected to self-regulate and self-govern their behaviours (Clarke, 2005). A number of commentators have concluded that citizenship now operates as a mechanism of social control – a subversion of its original emancipatory and inclusive intent (Clarke, 2005; Flint, 2009; Tyler, 2010; Tyler, 2014c). For some time theorists have described social welfare operating as a form of social control (Sinfield, 1978; Becker, 1997; Blakemore, 2003), but the extension of these ideas to social citizenship in particular is notable. Flint (2009) argues that the social rights of social citizenship have been reworked so that they now function to control deviant populations, while Lister (2011b) emphasises how citizenship increasingly operates as a disciplinary tool designed to regulate and sometimes change personal behaviour(s). Similarly, Swyngedouw (2006) describes 'governance innovation', whereby purportedly democratic forms including citizenship are subverted so that they become instruments of government control. This ties in closely with Tyler's (2014c) work on 'social abjection' and her observation that citizenship is operating as a regime of governance that serves to 'abjectify' and exclude specific groups and populations, including those living in poverty. All these writers observe how citizenship has been co-opted by governments as a framework that can be mobilised to justify and defend their programmes of policy reform, which are themselves conceptualised as having profoundly excluding and exclusive outcomes.

Reflecting upon the current state of social citizenship in the UK, where social rights are being increasingly reconceptualised as conditional privileges (Lister, 2013) and citizenship duty narrowly equated with paid employment (Lister, 2013; Patrick, 2014b, Wright, 2016), it is sometimes difficult to see what – if any – egalitarian potential social citizenship still holds (Bode, 2008; Tyler, 2010). Clarke (2005) cautiously posited the 'abandonment of the citizen' under

New Labour – an observation that could equally be made of more recent reforms under Cameron's governments – while Standing (2014) argued that those living in poverty are better thought of as 'denizens' rather than citizens. With citizenship increasingly operating as a tool of government control, there are unanswered questions as to how and whether citizenship ideals can instead be mobilised in calls for greater equality and recognition for all.

Towards a more inclusive social citizenship

It would be, however, a mistake to write off social citizenship entirely. Even in the current context in which it operates as a means of social control, citizenship can still represent an emancipatory concept for marginalised social groups, who can adopt it to make demands on the state (Lister, 2011b). Further, this research has shown how it can also serve as an invaluable benchmark, with Marshall's (1950) 'equality of status' serving as a relatively demanding objective against which to judge how social citizenship is functioning at any given time. Importantly, this underpinning ideal can be used to drive efforts to define the means and ends of a welfare state that most effectively protects and upholds a meaningful citizenship status for all (Duffy, 2016), with the scope to generate greater solidarity and break down unhelpful divisions between 'them' and 'us'.

There is a pressing need to re-emphasise the foundational principle of social citizenship –equality between citizens – and the need therefore to treat one's fellow citizens with dignity and respect (Lister, 2016). This is being undermined daily by a social welfare system and supporting infrastructure that so often treats individual out-of-work benefits recipients in a dehumanising and alienating way, with encounters far too often marked by a complete absence of respectful and dignified treatment. This is only compounded by a political climate in which politicians are far too quick to critique and censure benefits recipients, embedding the pervasive stigma of benefits receipt.

It is vital to return to the first principles of social citizenship and to recognise that the welfare state should be mobilised to defend and uphold the equality of all citizens. In this regard, there is real scope for politicians and policy makers to think much more ambitiously about what a shame-proofed social security system would look like (Walker, 2014; Lister, 2015). Arguably, a social security system that actually reduced (or even removed) the stigma of benefits receipt might be able to support out-of-work benefit claimants more effectively to make sustainable transitions into employment, where this was a realistic option. Social security provision that prioritises dignified and respectful treatment is a cost-free but vital reform (Lister, 2016) – and an essential one, if citizenship's emancipatory potential is to be reclaimed.

In seeking to develop a more inclusive citizenship narrative and practice, it is essential that conceptualisations of citizenship are themselves informed by and grounded in the 'everyday worlds of citizenship' (Desforges et al., 2005, cited in Lister, 2007, p. 58). Breaking down the current disjuncture between citizenship from above and below is a vital precursor to efforts to re-animate and strengthen both the welfare state and social citizenship rights and could further help increase popular support for social security. A first step would be for politicians to seek to 'match the language of public debate with the reality of people's lives' (Baptist Union of Great Britain et al., 2013, p. 29).

Rethinking citizenship responsibility and 'dependency'

There is a long overdue need to challenge the assumed relationships between responsibility, inclusion, independence and participation in the paid labour market. These relationships take a static, unidimensional perspective on the realities of engagement in paid employment and the nature of dependency. More inclusive understandings of citizenship broaden out definitions of 'work' to include other forms of contribution such as care work, volunteering and informal aid and support. When married to an understanding of the dutiful citizen as one undertaking any of these various forms of work, this can then enable many of those not currently in paid employment to fulfil their citizenship responsibilities (Lister, 2003; Dwyer, 2010; Williams, 2012b). This is particularly important for those – such as many disabled people and their carers, as well as single parents with young children – for whom paid employment is not always a realistic option.

It is also time to replace the notion of 'welfare dependency' as a descriptor only applicable to those on out-of-work benefits; most of society is, in fact, dependent on various forms of social welfare. Further, rather than fetishise a mythical independence, *interdependence* needs to be understood as an inevitable and positive feature of the human condition and the basis for all human interaction (Fraser and Gordon, 1994; Dean, 2004; Williams, 2012a; Standing, 2014). Throughout, there should be a focus on individuals' fluid and dynamic citizenship journeys through the life course. Individuals are likely to be variously more or less responsible and more or less dependent at different points in their lives, according to their particular circumstances and complex chains of interdependencies. Critically, taking a more fluid approach across the life course challenges the idea of a narrow group of 'welfare dependants' (Roantree and Shaw, 2014; Hills, 2015). Analysis by the IFS found that almost half (47.8%) of individuals in families received benefits or tax credits (excluding Child Benefit) at some point between 1991 and 2008 (Roantree and Shaw, 2014, p. 10). This illustrates how reliance on social welfare is much more widespread than a snapshot analysis might suggest.

At the same time, there is scope to re-evaluate the policy emphasis on the responsibility to 'work', which could instead be thought of as a right currently denied to many hundreds of thousands of British citizens (Dean, 2014). Dean's emphasis on a 'right to work' fits with the evidence from this research regarding people's strong commitments and aspirations to engage in paid employment. If the 'right to work' is understood as a 'right to decent work' – which could incorporate the right to participate in employment that provides a secure, living wage and enables an individual to escape poverty – this becomes a demanding objective (Dean, 2012). Adopting such an objective would also necessitate greater policy attention on what more governments can do to help those not in paid employment to realise their aspirations to enter the formal labour market. Arguably, reconceptualising engagement in paid employment as a right, as well as – if not instead of – a responsibility, better fits the enduring demand-side barriers to individuals' engagement in the formal labour market. Attention to the much more complex and transient nature of the relationship between paid employment and out-of-work benefits receipt can also have inclusive consequences, given that it typically uncovers a strong and enduring work ethic among those currently out of work, as well as aspirations and orientations to enter paid employment in step with those of 'mainstream' society.

From 'welfare' to 'social security'

Perhaps more ambitiously, there is also great potential in seeking to reframe and reconceptualise the policy problem of 'welfare'. As Bacchi (1999) reminds us, there are competing and alternative representations to every policy problem; it is in constructing the nature and extent of a 'problem' that policy makers so often crowd out alternative narratives and policy approaches. This is abundantly clear in the case of 'welfare', which has been steadily derided and problematised as an inevitably and inherently negative form of public support. This dominant framing can be challenged, with efforts to move away from this negative

Americanisation and instead talk about 'social security' a critical first step (Lister, 2016). Rather than operating from within a framing of the problem of 'welfare', there is scope instead to examine and direct critical attention towards the problem of 'insecurity', which potentially has great purchase and meaning for many of Britain's citizens. Orton (2015) and Standing (2014) have both highlighted how, for the majority of citizens, insecurity characterises daily life. Indeed, (in)security is a key axis between those who are struggling to get by and the relatively small group who enjoy security and comparative certainty about their future. As Orton (2015, p. 47) argues: 'Insecurity provides a lens through which to see and understand that things are not right in contemporary Britain'.

Efforts to challenge insecurity could collapse unhelpful false dichotomies between 'them' and 'us'; between 'welfare dependants' and 'hard-working families'. These dichotomies – overlaid with distinctions between the 'deserving' and 'undeserving', between the 'irresponsible' and the 'responsible' – are based on imagined communities (Anderson, 1983, cited in Flint, 2009). The demarcation and essential differences between these imagined communities blurs and fades away when we move from dominant narratives to lived realities on the ground.

A focus on the problem of 'insecurity' can direct policy attention to the solutions potentially offered by effective 'social security', which should be targeted at seeking to prevent and ameliorate economic and social insecurity (Sinfield, 2012; Lister, 2016). Properly understood, social security should form a preventative function and provide a vital protection when people experience a temporary, or indeed permanent, loss of paid employment. As the International Labour Organisation (ILO) stated in their 1984 report on social security, 'it is the guarantee of security that matters most of all' (ILO, 1984, p. 90).

Richard Titmuss (1968, p. 133) encouraged his readers not to think of 'welfare' as 'benefits or increments of welfare at all: they represent partial compensation for disservices or social costs and social insecurities which are the product of a rapidly changing industrial-urban society'. The notion of social welfare as compensation for social insecurities is an important one and has particular pertinence in a contemporary climate that has seen a significant growth in insecurity in the paid labour market alongside a growing and pernicious problem of in-work poverty (Macinnes et al., 2014a; Inman, 2015; Joseph Rowntree Foundation, 2016). It has particular purchase in helping to make a case for social welfare / security as a mechanism for providing redress to those who live with insecurity and – more ambitiously – even preventing the situations that lead to insecurity arising.

Today, action to deliver security to the population would need to encompass not just a revitalised and improved social security offer, but also measures to improve the operation of the formal labour market and undo some of the harm caused by the rise in insecure and exploitative forms of 'work'. Comparatively generous, unstigmatised social welfare provision could make a decisive difference to people's experiences of insecurity, with reassurance provided by the availability of a genuine safety net in times of need. This is notably absent at present. Emphasis could also be placed on the provision of enforceable social rights, while there are arguments for moving towards a reinvigorated focus on contribution (Harrop, 2016), widely conceptualised to include participation in paid employment, caring, parenting and volunteering. Re-orienting attention away from an assumed problem of 'welfare' and instead towards 'insecurity' and the proposed solution contained within 'social security' could also help build solidaristic support for an ideal of social security as a social good and a fundamental component of the 'good society' (Lister, 2016).

Given the extent of the apparent policy consensus on the welfare 'problem', these suggestions might appear idealistic and out of step with the contemporary climate. Interestingly, however, in recent months there has been some fragmentation of the dominant framing consensus and signs of an alternative approach gaining ground. This has been particularly apparent in Scotland, where the Scottish government is seeking to develop a distinctive approach to social security, making use of the new powers devolved to them under the Scotland Act 2016 (Scottish Government, 2016). As part of this, the Scottish government has drawn on ideas of social investment to make a case for social security available to all. Angela Constance, Scottish Social Security Secretary, has suggested that Scotland may seek to do away with the language of 'welfare' and 'benefits', instead focusing on the ideal of 'social security' (Brooks, 2016). The Scottish government's (2016) consultation document on the forthcoming Social Security Bill proposes enshrining the principle that everyone should be treated with dignity and respect into the legislative framework. An analysis of Scottish government policy documents indicates how it draws on ideas of a social wage and social investment to make the case for more redistributive and comparatively generous social security provision (Wiggan, forthcoming). Alongside the Scottish developments, during the 2016 Labour leadership campaign, leadership contender Owen Smith called for the closure of the Department for Work and Pensions and its replacement by a Ministry for Labour and a dedicated Department for Social Security (Smith, 2016). Significantly, both the

Scottish government's and Smith's interventions constitute an attempt to reframe and re-interpret the representation of both the policy problem of 'welfare' and proposed solution(s) (Wiggan, forthcoming).

Implications for further research

This research has demonstrated the benefits of using qualitative longitudinal methodologies to track individuals over time as they experience and respond to welfare reform. Bringing time into the frame both as a vehicle and object of study (Henwood and Shirani, 2012) has proved invaluable and particularly significant in aiding the generation of new knowledge. The methodological and theoretical tool of time has enabled an exploration of how out-of-work benefits recipients live through the present, anticipate the future and reflect upon the past. Working across and through time starkly demonstrated how the prospect, experience and impact of welfare reform serves as a constant backdrop to the lives of those affected by change(s).

The experience of previous reforms often impinged on the present, particularly where reforms had created hardship or had adverse consequences, such as causing the loss of a home. The everyday realities of dealing with welfare reform required hard work and often entailed changes to daily routines when individuals were required to comply with new forms of welfare conditionality. Living with constant uncertainty and anxiety about future reforms affected individuals' capacities to enjoy the present and undermined their ability to plan for the future. More needs to be done to explore relationships between time, poverty, benefits receipt, welfare reform and citizenship and this represents a rich area for future research.

Furthermore, taking a longitudinal approach has enabled the tracking of both the absence and presence of change in individuals' lives, creating a dynamic and fluid picture of responses to and experiences of welfare reform. The knowledge generated in this study has captured lives in flux as people grapple to comprehend and deal with changes in their benefits, employment status and wider lives. Walking alongside individuals as they responded to and dealt with these various changes provided insight into the nature of the burden of welfare reform. It also illustrated the extent to which an absence of change is (of course) not equivalent to an absence of activity or active effort. For example, despite not making a transition into paid employment during the study, Adrian spent the whole period busy and hard at work seeking employment, as well as volunteering in a homeless hostel (see chapters four and seven).

The evidence generated in this study of activity and hard work, sometimes unaccompanied by measurable change, is particularly pertinent given the enduring dominance of a rhetoric that equates benefits receipt with passivity and inactivity. Such data could not easily be captured by other research methods, again illustrating the potential of qualitative longitudinal enquiry. Reflecting upon her experiences of qualitative longitudinal research after many years as a qualitative researcher conducting one-off interviews, Tess Ridge (2015) describes the shift as moving from seeing the world in black and white to seeing it in Technicolor. This is a very apt description of the vistas and greater depth that researching through time can enable. All those with an interest in social policies, particularly those orientated towards creating behavioural change, would be well served to consider qualitative longitudinal methodologies when developing a new research design.

Just as important is a research approach that recognises the expertise of those directly affected by government policies and positions those experiencing poverty and out-of-work benefits receipt as experts in these fields (Lister, 2004; Walker, 2014). A central objective of this book was to record the experiences of those affected by welfare reform and to consider how these lived experiences mapped onto the dominant narratives. This has shown the extent to which lived experiences and political and media narratives are out of step. Both policy makers and academics need to do much more to put the experiences and perspectives of those with direct experience of poverty and out-of-work benefit receipt at the centre of their policy analysis (Walker, 2014). The need for policy makers to do so is particularly pressing if they are to create a social security system better able to respond to and work with (rather than against) individuals' day-to-day lives and aspirations.

The consequences of welfare reform and their entailing downgrading of social citizenship are still being felt. While impossible to predict, it seems likely that the negative consequences of welfare reform already highlighted may be extended and intensified. It is critical to continue to track lived experiences of welfare reform into the future and it is intended that this study will do so through further interviews, with another wave planned for 2018. In future interviews, it will be particularly important to explore whether individuals' capacities for resistance and resilience are affected by the cumulative and continuing nature of welfare reform, with limited signs of this already noted in both this research and other studies (Hickman et al., 2014; Lister et al., 2014; Roberts and Price, 2014).

Finally, though, a plea must be made for the analytical lens to shift upwards, to incorporate an analysis of the (ir)responsible behaviours of those higher up the income chain (Wright, 2012). Policy makers, academics and politicians are complicit in seeming to focus almost exclusively on the presumed irresponsibility and 'bad agency' of those who are already most marginalised and excluded from society. This research has considered the extent of the mismatch between a presumed irresponsibility and lived experiences; others, such as Dunn (2014), focused on issues of voluntary unemployment and the choosiness of those on out-of-work benefits. What we also need, however, is an examination of these same issues in other areas of society. This is particularly pertinent given the evidence emerging around widespread tax avoidance and evasion among some of our richest citizens and corporations.

At the same time, there is a pressing need to better understand how the agency and practices of politicians and frontline government officials affect the delivery and experience of social security receipt. The growing interest in 'street-level bureaucracy' makes a vital contribution here (see, for example, Lipsky, 2010; Fletcher, 2011; Hupe et al., 2015), but there remains further scope to explore how the agency of policy makers and practitioners interacts with everyday experiences of welfare reform and out-of-work benefits. This is already done by some scholars but deserves greater focus and attention as a central concern for social policy (see Wright, 2002; Shildrick et al., 2012b). This again links back to Bacchi's (1999) ideas regarding problem representations and the construction and representation of policy 'problems'. As academics, we ought to think critically about which behaviours and whose agency we are explicitly and implicitly problematising through our focus on particular cohorts for research – and our parallel neglect of others. A lopsided focus on the most marginalised and excluded in society is problematic and (arguably) short-sighted, preventing the emergence of new knowledge and understanding that could be realised by upstream examinations of behaviours, agency and practices.

Concluding thoughts: social insecurity

David Cameron expressed a desire to create a climate of security for Britain's families, suggesting that his policies and social reforms had the potential to improve security for all and support individuals to realise their dreams. In this book, we have seen how experiences of out-of-work benefits receipt and successive waves of welfare reform have instead created a climate of chronic insecurity in which individuals are fearful about how future changes might further impact upon their lives. We have also seen how transitions into the paid labour market so rarely deliver security or an escape from poverty, but rather are frequently characterised by a continued state of insecurity and struggles to make ends meet. Ironically, what Cameron (2014b) described as his 'moral mission' on welfare reform served to *de*moralise out-of-work claimants, who experienced the surrounding rhetoric and excluding narrative in profoundly damaging ways (Brown and Patrick, 2012).

While Cameron's time in office is now over, there is – as yet – little sign that Theresa May will fundamentally alter the overarching policy direction on welfare reform or disrupt the pervasive rhetoric that problematises and critiques those who rely on benefits for all or most of their income. Upon entering office in July 2016, May (2016) promised to 'make Britain a country that works not for a privileged few, but for every one of us'. She placed particular importance on improving the security and quality of life of those who just-about-managing, who are now known as the JAMs (Sodha, 2016). It appeared that these pledges were directed primarily towards working families – a replication and reiteration of Cameron and Osborne's obsession with supporting the 'hard-working majority'. At the same time, however – in the brief leadership contest that preceded her election as Conservative Party Leader and then Prime Minister, as well as in her early months as Prime Minister – May has promised to scale back Osborne's public sector cuts and the extent of his audacious austerity drive. This could provide opportunities to reconsider the appropriateness and likely effectiveness of some of the welfare reforms timetabled for coming years, which include plans to further extend conditionality and limit eligibility for benefits to just two children in a household claim. The findings from this book suggest that May would be best served by undertaking a complete rethink of the welfare reform policy framing and focus – a rethink that currently, at least, does not appear a likely prospect. Indeed, May's Secretary of State for the Department of Work and Pensions, Damian Green, has said that – while he may adopt a different language on 'welfare' to his predecessors – he is committed to implementing the full programme of welfare reform previously outlined by Cameron's 2015 government (Elgot, 2016). Green has also promised that May's government would not introduce any new cuts or welfare reforms; a promise unlikely to offer much comfort to those bracing themselves for the impact of the introduction of Universal Credit or a disability benefit reassessment.

The title of this book posed a question: who benefits from processes and experiences of welfare reform? The evidence from this study is that those directly affected by the changes, and by the climate of insecurity they create, do not benefit at all and are much more likely to see a deterioration in their circumstances. At the same time, and just as importantly, the pervasive negative rhetoric about 'welfare' that bolsters the logic for continued welfare reform has wide-ranging negative consequences – both for those stereotyped by demeaning characterisations of 'welfare dependants' and for all of us who experience a more fractured and fractious society as a result.

The problematisation of 'welfare' and policy reform direction has created pervasive social insecurity and incurred very real and significant costs for some of Britain's poorest and most disadvantaged citizens. While recent governments have employed a narrative of citizenship inclusion to justify the reform trajectory, this ignores the reality of citizenship exclusion for those on out-of-work benefits and the extent to which the dominant narrative further marginalises and 'others' those judged not to belong to the 'hard-working majority'.

It is only by closely listening to lived experiences that we can better understand the everyday realities of benefits receipt and begin to construct a more solidaristic and egalitarian conceptualisation of social citizenship. It is the task of academics to make sure that the voices of those with direct experiences of social insecurity are recorded, heard and employed in policy debates about the future of social security: a future that matters to us all. It is only fitting that the last word be reserved for one of the participants, James, here talking about how people's security has been undermined by recent governments' welfare reforms:

> 'They're taking people further and further out of [security] aren't they. They're taking more [benefits] away, but I think that's because of the stigma of people saying people on benefits are taking the piss basically, so they're saying we won't let them anymore, but the genuine ones that are needing it, they're getting penalised for it ... They're taking security away, little by little.' (W4)

References

Abrahams, D. 2016. *Debbie Abrahams MP, Shadow Secretary of State for Work and Pensions, speech to Conference* [Online]. London: The Labour Party. Available: http://press.labour.org.uk/post/150965455394/debbie-abrahams-mp-shadow-secretary-of-state-for.

Adam, B. and Groves, G. 2007. *Future Matters: Action, Knowledge, Ethics*, Leiden (The Netherlands), Brill.

AgeUK. 2015. *Care and support* [Online]. AgeUK. Available: www.ageuk.org.uk/professional-resources-home/services-and-practice/care-and-support/experts-by-experience/.

Ahrends, J. 2015. *Sanctions under scrutiny* [Online]. Child Poverty Action Group. Available: www.cpag.org.uk/content/sanctions-under-scrutiny.

Alcock, P. 2006. *Understanding Poverty*, Basingstoke, Palgrave Macmillan.

Aldridge, H. and Hughes, C. 2016. *Informal Carers, Poverty and Work*, London, New Policy Institute.

Archer, L., Dewitt, J. and Wong, B. 2014. Spheres of influence: what shapes young people's aspirations at age 12/13 and what are the implications for education policy? *Journal of Education Policy*, 29, 58–85.

Atkinson, A. B. and Micklewright, J. 1989. Turning the benefits screw: benefits for the unemployed, 1979–1988. *In:* Atkinson, A. B. (ed.) *Poverty and Social Security*, Hemel Hempstead, Harvester Wheatsheaf, pp. 125-157.

Aylott, M., Norman, W., Russell, C. and Sellick, V. 2012. *An insight into the impact of the cuts on some of the most vulnerable in Camden: a Young Foundation report for the London Borough of Camden*, London, The Young Foundation.

Bacchi, C. 1999. *Women, Policy and Politics: The Construction of Policy Problems*, London, SAGE.

Bailey, N. 2016. Exclusionary employment in Britain's broken labour market. *Critical Social Policy*, 36, 82–103.

Bailey, N. and Tomlinson, M. 2012. *Work: conceptual note no. 8*, Poverty and Social Exclusion in the UK, Bristol, University of Bristol.

Baptist Union Of Great Britain, Methodist Church, Church Of Scotland and Church, U. R. 2013. *The lies we tell ourselves: ending comfortable myths about poverty*, London, United Reform Church.

Barnes, C. and Mercer, G. 1997. Breaking the mould? An introduction to doing disability research. *In:* Barnes, C. and Mercer, G. (eds.) *Doing Disability Research*, Leeds, The Disability Press, pp. 1-14.

Barr, B., Taylor-Robinson, D., Stuckler, D., Loopstra, R., Reeves, A. and Whitehead, M. 2015. 'First, do no harm': are disability assessments associated with adverse trends in mental health? A longitudinal ecological study [Online]. *Journal of Epidemiol Community Health*, Online First. Available: http://jech.bmj.com/content/early/2015/10/26/jech-2015-206209.

Batty, E., Beatty, C., Casey, R., Foden, M., Mccarthy, L. and Reeve, K. 2015. *Homeless people's experiences of welfare conditionality and sanctions*, Sheffield, Sheffield Hallam University and Crisis.

Batty, E., Cole, I. and Green, S. 2011. *Low-income neighbourhoods in Britain: the gap between policy ideas and residents' realities*, York, Joseph Rowntree Foundation.

Batty, E. and Flint, J. 2010. *Self-esteem, comparative poverty and neighbourhoods: research paper no. 7*, Centre for Regional Economic and Social Research, Sheffield, Sheffield Hallam University.

Batty, E. and Flint, J. 2013. Talking 'bout poor folks (thinking 'bout my folks): perspectives on comparative poverty in working class households. *International Journal of Housing Policy*, 13, 1–16.

Baumberg, B. 2014. Benefits and the cost of living: pressures on the cost of living and attitudes to benefit claiming. *In:* Park, A., Bryson, C. and Curtice, J. (eds.) *British Social Attitudes 31*, London, National Centre for Social Research.

Baumberg, B. 2016. The stigma of claiming benefits: a quantitative study. *Journal of Social Policy*, 45, 181–99.

Baumberg, B., Bell, K. and Gaffney, D. 2012. *Benefit stigma in Britain*, London, Turn2us and University of Kent.

BBC News. 2010. Welfare 'trapping' people in poverty says Duncan Smith [Online]. *BBC*. Available: http://news.bbc.co.uk/1/hi/uk_politics/8707652.stm.

BBC News. 2015. David Cameron: unemployed young 'should do community work' [Online]. *BBC*. Available: www.bbc.co.uk/news/uk-politics-31500763.

BBC Today. 2011. 'An economy that works for everybody': interview with David Cameron, 4th October [Online]. *BBC*. Available: http://news.bbc.co.uk/today/hi/today/newsid_9606000/9606912.stm.

Beatty, C. and Fothergill, S. 2016. *The uneven impact of welfare reform: the financial losses to places and people*, Centre for Regional Economic and Social Research, Sheffield, Sheffield Hallam University with Oxfam and Joseph Rowntree Foundation.

Beck, U. 1992. *Risk Society: Towards a New Modernity*, London, SAGE.

Becker, S. 1997. *Responding to Poverty: The Politics of Cash and Care*, Harlow, Addison Wesley Longman Limited.

Belfield, C., Cribb, J., Hood, A. and Joyce, R. 2016. *Living standards, poverty and inequality in the UK: 2016*, London, Institute for Fiscal Studies.

Ben-Galim, D. and Lanning, T. 2010. *Strength against shocks: low-income families and debt*, London, IPPR.

Bennett, F. 2012. Universal Credit: overview and gender implications. *In:* Kilkey, M., Ramia, G. and Farnsworth, K. (eds.) *Social Policy Review 24: Analysis and Debate in Social Policy.* Bristol, Policy Press, pp. 15-34.

Bennett, F. and Daly, M. 2014. *Poverty through a Gender Lens: Evidence and Policy Review on Gender and Poverty*, Oxford, University of Oxford with Joseph Rowntree Foundation.

Beresford, P., Green, D., Lister, R. and Woodard, K. 1999. *Poverty first hand: Poor people speak for themselves*, London, CPAG.

Blakemore, K. 2003. *Social Policy: An Introduction*, Buckingham, PA, Open University Press.

Blond, P. 2010. *Red Tory: How the Left and Right have Broken Britain and How We Can Fix It*, London, Faber and Faber.

Bochel, H. 2011. Conservative social policy: from conviction to coalition *In:* Holden, C., Kilkey, M. and Ramia, G. (eds.) *Social Policy Review 23: Analysis and Debate in Social Policy*, Bristol, Policy Press, pp. 7-24.

Bode, I. 2008. Social citizenship in post-liberal Britain and post-corporatist Germany: curtailed, fragmented, streamlined, but still on the agenda. *In:* Clarke, K., Maltby, T. and Kennett, P. (eds.) *Social Policy Review 20: Analysis and Debate in Social Policy*, Bristol, Policy Press, pp. 191-212.

Bottomore, T. 1992. Citizenship and social class, forty years on. *In:* Marshall, T. H. and Bottomore, T. (eds.) *Citizenship and Social Class.* London, Pluto Press, pp. 55-93.

Bradshaw, J. 2015. The erosion of the safety net [Online]. *Discover Society.* Available: www.discoversociety.org/2015/01/03/the-erosion-of-the-uk-safety-net/.

Briant, E., Watson, N. and Philo, G. 2013. Reporting disability in the age of austerity: the changing face of media representation of disability and disabled people in the United Kingdom and the creation of new 'folk devils'. *Disability and Society*, 28, 874–89.

Bright, M. 2014. Unemployed? Don't go to your local jobcentre [Online]. *The Guardian.* Available: www.theguardian.com/society/2014/jul/29/unemployed-jobcentre-failed-young-people.

Brooks, L. 2016. Social security, not benefits: Scotland to ponder words of welfare [Online]. *The Guardian*. Available: www.theguardian. com/society/2016/jul/29/social-security-not-benefits-scotland-to-ponder-words-of-welfare.

Brown, K. and Patrick, R. 2012. Re-moralising or de-moralising: the Coalition government's approach to 'problematic' populations (editorial) [Online]. *People, Place and Policy Online*, 6. Available: http://extra.shu.ac.uk/ppp-online/re-moralising-or-de-moralising/.

Browne, J. and Elming, W. 2015. *The effect of the Coalition's tax and benefit changes on household incomes and work incentives, IFS Briefing Note BN159*, London, Institute for Fiscal Studies.

Butler, P. 2016. Universal Credit: tough love for low-paid workers [Online]. *The Guardian*. Available: www.theguardian.com/society/patrick-butler-cuts-blog/2016/apr/22/universal-credit-tough-love-for-low-paid-workers.

Butler, P. 2017. Thousands of jobs to go in government shakeout of the welfare-to-work sector [Online]. *The Guardian*. Available: www. theguardian.com/politics/2017/jan/13/thousands-of-jobs-to-go-in-government-shakeout-of-welfare-to-work-sector.

Cameron, D. 2006. *Tackling poverty is a social responsibility, Scarman Lecture, 24th November* [Online]. Available: www.conservative-speeches.sayit.mysociety.org/speech/599937.

Cameron, D. 2009a. *Putting Britain back on her feet: Leader speech to Conservative Party Conference, 8th October* [Online]. Conservative Party Speeches. Available: http://conservative-speeches.sayit.mysociety. org/speech/601277.

Cameron, D. 2009b. *The Big Society: Hugo Young Lecture, 10th November* [Online]. Conservative Party Speeches. Available: http:// conservative-speeches.sayit.mysociety.org/speech/601246.

Cameron, D. 2010a. *Our Big Society agenda, 19th July* [Online]. The Conservatives. Available: www.gov.uk/government/speeches/big-society-speech.

Cameron, D. 2010b. Together in the national interest: speech to Conservative Party Conference, 6th October [Online]. *The Guardian*. Available: https://www.theguardian.com/politics/2010/oct/06/david-cameron-speech-tory-conference.

Cameron, D. 2011a. *PM's speech on Big Society, 15th February* [Online]. London, Prime Minister's Office. Available: www.number10.gov. uk/news/speeches-and-transcripts/2011/02/pms-speech-on-big-society-60563.

Cameron, D. 2011b. *PM's speech on the fightback after the riots, 15th August* [Online]. London, Prime Minister's Office. Available: www. number10.gov.uk/news/pms-speech-on-the-fightback-after-the-riots/.

Cameron, D. 2011c. *PM's speech on Welfare Reform Bill, 17 February* [Online]. London, Prime Minister's Office. Available: www. number10.gov.uk/news/speeches-and-transcripts/2011/02/pms-speech-on-welfare-reform-bill-60717.

Cameron, D. 2012a. *Speech to Conservative Party Conference, 10th October* [Online]. The Conservatives. Available: www.cpc12.org.uk/ Speeches/David_Cameron.aspx.

Cameron, D. 2012b. *Welfare Speech, 25th June* [Online]. London, HM Government. Available: www.number10.gov.uk/news/welfare-speech/.

Cameron, D. 2014a. *Prime Minister's Speech to Conservative Party Conference, 1st October* [Online]. The Conservatives. Available: http:// press.conservatives.com/post/98882674910/david-cameron-speech-to-conservative-party.

Cameron, D. 2014b. Why the Archbishop of Westminster is wrong about welfare [Online]. *The Daily Telegraph*, 18th February. Available: www.telegraph.co.uk/news/politics/david-cameron/10646421/ David-Cameron-Why-the-Archbishop-of-Westminster-is-wrong-about-welfare.html.

Cameron, D. 2015a. *Speech by David Cameron to The Centre for Social Justice, 22nd June* [Online]. London, The Centre for Social Justice. Available: www.centreforsocialjustice.org.uk/UserStorage/pdf/ David-Cameron-speech-22.06.15.pdf.

Cameron, D. 2015b. Tory Party Conference 2015: David Cameron's speech in full [Online]. *The Independent*. Available: www.independent. co.uk/news/uk/politics/tory-party-conference-2015-david-camerons-speech-in-full-a6684656.html.

Cameron, D. 2016. *Prime Minister's speech on life chances* [Online]. London, HM Government. Available: www.gov.uk/government/ speeches/prime-ministers-speech-on-life-chances.

Centre For Social Justice 2009. *Dynamic Benefits: Towards Welfare that Works*, London, Centre for Social Justice.

Chase, E. and Walker, R. 2013. The co-construction of shame in the context of poverty: beyond a threat to the social bond. *Sociology*, 47, 739–54.

Citizens Advice Bureau 2010. *Not working: CAB evidence on the ESA work capability assessment*, London, Citizens Advice Bureau.

Clark, T. 2014. *Hard Times: The Divisive Toll of the Economic Slump*, London, Yale University Press.

Clarke, J. 2005. New Labour's citizens: activated, empowered, responsibilized, abandoned? *Critical Social Policy*, 25, 447–63.

Clarke, J., Coll, K., Dagnino, E. and Neveu, C. 2014. *Disputing Citizenship*, Bristol, Policy Press.

Clarke, J. and Newman, J. 2012. The alchemy of austerity. *Critical Social Policy*, 32, 299–319.

Conservatives 2009. *Get Britain working: Conservatives proposals to tackle unemployment and reform welfare*, London, The Conservatives.

Conservatives 2010a. *A new welfare contract*, London, The Conservatives.

Conservatives 2010b. *Invitation to join the Government of Great Britain: the Conservative Manifesto*, London, The Conservatives.

Cook, J., Dwyer, P. and Waite, L. J. 2012. Accession 8 migration and the proactive and defensive engagement of social citizenship. *Journal of Social Policy*, 41, 2, 329–47.

Coote, A. and Lyall, S. 2013. *Mythbusters: 'strivers v. skivers: the workless are worthless'*, London, Tax Justice Network and New Economics Foundation.

Corden, A. and Millar, J. 2007. Qualitative longitudinal research for social policy - introduction to themed section. *Social Policy and Society*, 6, 529–32.

Corlett, A. and Whittaker, M. 2014. *Low pay in Britain 2014*, London, Resolution Foundation.

CPAG (Child Poverty Action Group). 2001. *Poverty, the facts: fourth edition*, London, CPAG.

CPAG. 2013. *Coalition policies to push 600,000 children into absolute poverty by 2015* [Online]. London, CPAG. Available: www.cpag. org.uk/content/coalition-policies-push-600000-children-absolute-poverty-2015.

Crisp, R., Batty, E., Cole, I. and Robinson, D. 2009. *Work and worklessness in deprived neighbourhoods: policy assumptions and personal experiences*, York, Joseph Rowntree Foundation.

Daguerre, A. and Etherington, D. 2014. *Workfare in 21st century Britain: the erosion of rights to social assistance*, London, Middlesex University.

Daly, M. and Kelly, G. 2015. *Families and Poverty: Everyday Life on a Low Income*, Bristol, Policy Press.

Davidson, G. W., Seaton, M. A., and Simpson, J. 1993. *The Wordsworth Concise English Dictionary*, Hertfordshire, Wordsworth Editions Ltd.

DCLG (Department For Communities And Local Government) 2008. *Fair rules for strong communities*, Wetherby: Communities and Local Government Publications.

Deacon, A. 1991. The retreat from state welfare. *In:* Becker, S. (ed.) *Windows of Opportunity: Public Policy and the Poor*, London: CPAG, pp. 9-21.

Deacon, A. 2002. *Perspectives on Welfare: Ideas, Ideologies, and Policy Debates*, Maidenhead, Open University Press.

Deacon, A. and Patrick, R. 2011. A new welfare settlement? The Coalition government and welfare-to-work. *In:* Bochel, H. (ed.) *The Conservative Party and Social Policy*, Bristol, Policy Press, pp. 161-179.

Dean, H. 1999. Citizenship. *In:* Powell, M. (ed.) *New Labour, New Welfare State? The 'Third Way' in British Social Policy*, Bristol, Policy Press, pp. 213-233.

Dean, H. 2004. Reconceptualising dependency, responsibility and rights. *In:* Dean, H. (ed.) *The Ethics of Welfare: Human Rights, Dependency And Responsibility*, Bristol, Policy Press, pp. 193-209.

Dean, H. 2012. The ethical deficit of the United Kingdom's proposed Universal Credit: pimping the precariat? *Political Quarterly*, 83, 353–9.

Dean, H. 2014. 'Life first' welfare and the scope for a 'eudaimonic ethic' of social security. *In:* Keune, M. and Serrano, A. (eds.) *Deconstructing Flexicurity and Developing Alternative Approaches: Towards New Concepts and Approaches for Employment and Social Policy*, New York, Routledge, pp. 152-172.

Dean, H. and Melrose, M. 1999. *Poverty, Riches and Social Citizenship*, Basingstoke, Macmillan.

Dean, H. and Taylor-Gooby, P. 1992. *Dependency Culture: The Explosion of a Myth*, Hemel Hempstead, Harvester Wheatsheaf.

Delanty, G. 2000. *Citizenship in a Global Age: Society, Culture and Politics*, Buckingham, Open University Press.

Digby, A. 1989. *British Welfare Policy: Workhouse to Workfare*, London, Faber and Faber.

Domokos, J. 2011. Jobseekers 'tricked' out of benefits to meet staff targets. *The Guardian*, 2nd April, pp.1-2.

Driver, S. 2009. Work to be done? Welfare reform from Blair to Brown. *Policy Studies*, 30, 69–84.

DSS (Department For Social Security) 1998. *New ambitions for our country: a new contract for welfare* (Green Paper), Cm 3805, London, The Stationery Office.

Duffy, S. 2016. *Citizenship and the welfare state: the need for roots*, Sheffield, Centre for Welfare Reform.

Dugan, E. 2014. Exclusive: claimants lose all their income under disability benefits reform [Online]. *The Independent*. Available: www.independent.co.uk/news/uk/politics/exclusive-claimants-lose-all-their-income-under-disability-benefits-reform-9107586.html.

Duncan, S. and Edwards, R. 1999. *Lone Mothers, Paid Work and Gendered Moral Rationalities*, Basingstoke, Macmillan.

Duncan Smith, I. 2010a. *Our contract with the country for 21st century welfare, speech to Conservative Party Conference, 5th October* [Online]. Conservative Party Speeches. Available: http://conservative-speeches. sayit.mysociety.org/speech/601437.

Duncan Smith, I. 2010b. *Universal Credit: welfare that works – speech by the Secretary of State for Work and Pensions, 11th November* [Online]. London, DWP. Available: www.dwp.gov.uk/newsroom/ministers-speeches/2010/11-11-10.shtml.

Duncan Smith, I. 2011a. *The 2011 Keith Joseph Memorial Lecture, welfare reform: the wider context, 15th March* [Online]. ConservativeHome. Available: http://conservativehome.blogs.com/files/ids-speech.pdf.

Duncan Smith, I. 2011b. We must change our broken benefits system: we owe it to the poorest. *New Statesman*, 13th June, p. 18.

Duncan Smith, I. 2012. *'Reforming welfare, transforming lives': Cambridge Public Policy Lecture, 25th October* [Online]. Cambridge, University of Cambridge. Available: www.csap.cam.ac.uk/events/cambridge-public-policy-lecture-rt-hon-iain-duncan/.

Duncan Smith, I. 2014a. *A welfare state fit for the 21st century: speech to Centre for Social Justice, 28th January* [Online]. London, Department for Work and Pensions. Available: www.gov.uk/government/speeches/a-welfare-state-fit-for-the-21st-century.

Duncan Smith, I. 2014b. *Getting Britain working: speech on 11 August* [Online]. HM Government. Available: www.gov.uk/government/speeches/jobs-and-welfare-reform-getting-britain-working.

Duncan Smith, I. 2014c. Iain Duncan Smith's speech on welfare reform: speech to Centre for Social Justice, 23rd January [Online]. *The Spectator*. Available: http://blogs.spectator.co.uk/the-spectator/2014/01/iain-duncan-smiths-speech-on-welfare-reform-full-text/.

Duncan Smith, I. 2014d. *Social justice: progress towards transforming lives*. Speech on 18th November to GovKnow Social Justice Conference [Online]. London, DWP. Available: www.gov.uk/government/speeches/social-justice-progress-towards-transforming-lives.

Duncan Smith, I. 2015. *Speech on work, health and disability, 24th August* [Online]. Reform. Available: www.reform.uk/publication/rt-hon-iain-duncan-smith-mp-speech-on-work-health-and-disability/.

Dunn, A. 2013. Activation workers' perceptions of their long-term unemployed clients' attitudes towards employment. *Journal of Social Policy*, 42, 799–817.

Dunn, A. 2014. *Rethinking Unemployment and the Work Ethic: Beyond the 'Quasi-Titmuss' Paradigm*, Basingstoke, Palgrave Macmillan.

DWP (Department for Work and Pensions). 2006. *A new deal for welfare: empowering people to work*, Cm 6730, London, DWP.

DWP. 2008a. *Raising expectations and increasing support: reforming welfare for the future*, Cm 7506, London, DWP.

DWP. 2008b. *Transforming Britain's labour market: ten years of the New Deal*, London, DWP.

DWP. 2010a. *21st century welfare* (Green Paper), Cm 7913, London, The Stationery Office.

DWP. 2010b. *Government's response to Professor Malcolm Harrington's independent review of the Work Capability Assessment*, London, The Stationery Office.

DWP. 2010c. *Universal Credit: welfare that works*, Cm 7957, London, The Stationery Office.

DWP. 2011a. *Grayling: community work for the long term unemployed* [Online]. London, DWP. Available: www.dwp.gov.uk/newsroom/press-releases/2011/nov-2011/dwp126-11.shtml.

DWP. 2011b. *The Work Programme*, London, DWP.

DWP. 2012a. *Employment and Support Allowance* [Online]. London, DWP. Available: www.dwp.gov.uk/policy/welfare-reform/employment-and-support/.

DWP. 2012b. *Welfare Reform Act 2012* [Online]. London, DWP. Available: www.dwp.gov.uk/policy/welfare-reform/legislation-and-key-documents/welfare-reform-act-2012/.

DWP. 2013. *Appeals process changes for DWP benefits and child maintenance* [Online]. London, DWP. Available: www.gov.uk/government/publications/appeals-process-changes-for-dwp-benefits-and-child-maintenance.

DWP. 2014. *Simplifying the welfare system and making sure work pays* [Online]. London, DWP. Available: www.gov.uk/government/policies/simplifying-the-welfare-system-and-making-sure-work-pays/supporting-pages/introducing-the-jobseekers-allowance-claimant-commitment.

DWP. 2016. *Welfare Reform and Work Act 2016*, London, DWP. Available: www.legislation.gov.uk/ukpga/2016/7/pdfs/ukpga_2016007_en.pdf.

DWP and DfE (Department for Education). 2011. *A new approach to child poverty: tackling the causes of disadvantage and transforming families' lives*, Cm 8061, London, HM Government.

Dwyer, P. 2010. *Understanding Social Citizenship: Themes and Perspectives for Policy and Practice*, Second Edition, Bristol, Policy Press.

Dwyer, P. and Bright, J. 2016. *Welfare conditionality: sanctions, support and behaviour change. First wave findings: overview, May 2016*, York, University of York.

Dwyer, P. and Ellison, N. 2009. Work and welfare: the rights and responsibilities of unemployment in the UK. *In:* Giugni, M. (ed.) *The Politics of Unemployment in Europe: Policy Responses and Collective Action*, Farnham: Ashgate Publishing, pp. 53-66.

Dwyer, P., Jones, K., McNeill, J., Scullion, L. and Stewart, A. 2016. *Welfare Conditionality: Sanctions, Support and Behaviour Change. First wave findings: disability and conditionality*, York, University of York.

Dwyer, P. and Wright, S. 2014. Universal Credit, ubiquitous conditionality and its implications for social citizenship. *Journal of Poverty and Social Justice*, 22, 27–35.

Edin, K. J. and Shaefer, L. H. 2015. *$2.00 a Day: Living on Almost Nothing in America*, New York, Houghton Mifflin Harcourt Publishing.

Electoral Commission, The. 2005. *Social exclusion and political engagement*, London, The Electoral Commission.

Elgot, J. 2016. No more welfare cuts to come under Theresa May, says minister [Online]. *The Guardian*. Available: www.theguardian. com/politics/2016/sep/18/no-more-welfare-cuts-under-theresa-may-says-minister-damian-green-end-to-austerity.

Elliott, J. 2005. *Using Narrative in Social Research: Qualitative and Quantitative Approaches,* London, SAGE.

Ellison, N. 2000. Proactive and defensive engagement: social citizenship in a changing public sphere [Online]. *Sociological Research Online*, 5. Available: www.socresonline.org.uk/5/3/ellison.html.

Ellison, N. 2011. The Conservative Party and the 'Big Society'. *In:* Holden, C., Kilkey, M. and Ramia, G. (eds.) *Social Policy Review 23: Analysis and Debate in Social Policy, 2011*, Bristol, Policy Press, pp. 45-62.

Esping-Andersen, G. 1990. *The Three Worlds of Welfare Capitalism*, Cambridge, Polity Press.

Etherington, D. and Daguerre, A. 2015. *Welfare reform, work first policies and benefit conditionality: reinforcing poverty and social exclusion?* Centre for Enterprise and Economic Development Research, London, Middlesex University.

Etzioni, A. 1995. *The Spirit of Community: Rights and Responsibilities and the Communitarian Agenda*, London, Harper and Collins.

Ferge, Z. 1997. The changed welfare paradigm: the individualization of the social. *Social Policy and Administration*, 31, 20–44.

Field, F. 2016. *Fixing Broken Britain? An audit of working-age welfare reform since 2010*, London, Civitas.

Financial Services Authority 2006. *Financial capability in the UK: establishing a baseline*, London, FSA.

Finch, D. 2016. *Universal challenge: making a success of Universal Credit*, London, Resolution Foundation.

Finn, D. and Casebourne, J. 2012. *Lone parent sanctions: a review of international evidence: policy paper*, London, Centre for Economic and Social Inclusion.

Finn, D. and Gloster, R. 2010. *Lone parent obligations: a review of recent evidence on the work-related requirements within the benefit systems of different countries*, research report no 633, London, DWP.

Fitzpatrick, S., Bramley, G., Sosenko, F., Blenkinsopp, J., Johnsen, S., Little, M., Netto, G. and Watts, B. 2016. *Destitution in the UK*, York, Joseph Rowntree Foundation.

Fitzpatrick, T. 2004. Time, social justice and UK welfare reform. *Economy and Society*, 33, 335–58.

Fletcher, D. R. 2011. Welfare reform, Job Centre Plus and the street-level bureaucracy: towards inconsistent and discriminatory welfare for severely disadvantaged groups? *Social Policy and Society*, 10, 445–58.

Flinders, M. 2014. *Low voter turnout is clearly a problem, but a much greater worry is the growing inequality of that turnout* [Online]. London, London School of Economics. Available: http://blogs.lse.ac.uk/politicsandpolicy/look-beneath-the-vote/.

Flint, J. 2009. Subversive subjects and conditional, earned and denied citizenship. *In:* Barnes, M. and Prior, D. (eds.) *Subversive Citizens: Power, Agency and Resistance in Public Services*, Bristol, Policy Press, pp. 83-100.

Flint, J. 2010. *Coping strategies? Agencies, budgeting and self esteem amongst low-income households*, research paper no. 5, Centre for Regional Economic and Social Research, Sheffield, Sheffield Hallam University.

Fohrbeck, A., Hiresland, A. and Ramos Lobato, P. 2014. How benefit recipients perceive themselves through the lens of the mass media: some observations from Germany [Online]. *Sociological Research Online*, 19. Available: www.socresonline.org.uk/19/4/9.html.

Fraser, N. 2003. Social justice in the age of identity politics: redistribution, recognition and participation. *In:* Fraser, N. and Honneth, A. (eds.) *Redistribution or Recognition? A Political–Philosophical Exchange*, London, Verso, pp. 7-88.

Fraser, N. 2009. *Scales of Justice: Reimagining Political Space in a Globalizing World*, New York, Columbia University Press.

Fraser, N. and Gordon, L. 1994. 'Dependency' demystified: inscriptions of power in a keyword of the welfare state. *Social Politics*, 1, 4–31.

Frayne, D. 2015. *The Refusal of Work: Rethinking Post-Work Theory and Practice*, London, Zed Books.

Frayne, D. 2016. *Towards a post-work society* [Online]. *ROAR Magazine*. Available: https://roarmag.org/magazine/towards-a-post-work-society/.

Galston, W. A. 2005. Conditional citizenship. *In:* Mead, L. M. and Beem, C. (eds.) *Welfare Reform and Political Theory*, New York, Russell Sage Foundation, pp. 110-126.

Garrett, P. 2015. Words matter: deconstructing 'welfare dependency' in the UK. *Critical and Radical Social Work*, 18, 389–406.

Garthwaite, K. 2014. Fear of the brown envelope: exploring welfare reform with long-term sickness benefits recipients. *Social Policy and Administration*, 48, 782–98.

Garthwaite, K. 2016. *Hunger Pains: Life Inside Foodbank Britain*, Bristol, Policy Press.

Gaventa, J. 2002. Introduction: exploring citizenship, participation and accountability. *IDS Bulletin*, 33.

Gentleman, A. 2012. Judge considers judicial review of Work Capability Assessment [Online]. *The Guardian*. Available: www.theguardian.com/society/2012/jun/29/judicial-review-work-capability-assessment.

Gentleman, A. 2015. Labour vows to reduce reliance on food banks if it comes to power [Online]. *The Guardian*. Available: www.theguardian.com/society/2015/mar/17/labour-vows-to-reduce-reliance-on-food-banks-if-it-comes-to-power.

George, L. K. 2009. Conceptualizing and measuring trajectories. *In:* Elder, G. H. and Giele, J. Z. (eds.) *The Craft of Life Course Research*, New York, The Guilford Press, pp. 163-186.

Gerth, H. and Wright Mills, C. 1953. *Character and Social Structure: The Psychology of Social Institutions*, New York, Harcourt, Brace and Company.

Gingerbread 2010a. *Changing the workplace: the missing piece of the jigsaw*, London, Gingerbread.

Gingerbread. 2010b. *Spending review hits single parents hard* [Online]. London, Gingerbread. Available: www.gingerbread.org.uk/news/80/Spending-review-hits-single-parents-hard.

Gingerbread 2014. *Single parents and benefit sanctions: November 2014*, London, Gingerbread.

Goffman, E. 1990. *Stigma: notes on the management of spoiled identity*, New Edition, London, Penguin.

Golding, P. and Middleton, S. 1982. *Images of Welfare: Press and Public Attitude to Poverty*, Oxford, Blackwell.

Goos, M. and Manning, N. 2007. Lousy and lovely jobs: the rising polarization of work in Britain. *Review of Economics and Statistics*, 89, 118–33.

Graham, H., Lister, B., Egdell, V., Mcquaid, R. and Raeside, R. 2014. *The impact of welfare reform in Scotland. Tracking study: Year 1 report*, Edinburgh, The Scottish Government.

Graham, H. and McQuaid, R. 2014. *Exploring the impacts of the UK government's welfare reforms on lone parents moving into work*, Employment Research Institute, Edinburgh, Edinburgh Napier University.

Green, D. 2016. *From welfare state to welfare system*, Speech by Secretary of State for the Department for Work and Pensions, 16th November [Online]. London, DWP. Available: www.gov.uk/government/speeches/from-welfare-state-to-welfare-system

Gregg, P. 2008. *Realising potential: a vision for personalised conditionality and support*, London, DWP.

Gregg, P., Harkness, S. and Macmillan, L. 2006. *Welfare to work policies and child poverty: a review of issues relating to the labour market and economy*, York, Joseph Rowntree Foundation.

Griggs, J. and Bennett, F. 2009. *Rights and responsibilities in the social security system, Social Security Advisory Committee occasional paper no. 6*, London, Social Security Advisory Committee.

Griggs, J. and Evans, M. 2010. *A review of benefit sanctions: findings*, York, Joseph Rowntree Foundation.

Grover, C. 2012. 'Personalised conditionality': observations on active proletarianisation in late modern Britain. *Capital and Class*, 36, 283–301.

Hale, C. 2014. *Fulfilling potential? ESA and the fate of the Work-Related Activity Group*, London, Mind.

Hall, S. and Perry, C. 2013. *Family matters: understanding families in an age of austerity*, London, Ipsos MORI.

Harkness, S., Gregg, P. and Macmillan, L. 2012. *Poverty: the role of institutions, behaviours and culture*, York, Joseph Rowntree Foundation.

Harrington, M. 2010. *An independent review of the Work Capability Assessment*, London, The Stationery Office.

Harrison, E. 2013. Bouncing back? Recession, resilience and everyday lives. *Criticial Social Policy*, 33, 97–114.

Harrison, M. and Sanders, T. 2014. Introduction. In: Harrison, M. and Sanders, T. (eds.) *Social Policies and Social Control: New Perspectives on the 'Not-So-Big Society'*, Bristol, Policy Press, pp. 3-22.

Harrop, A. 2016. *For us all: redesigning social security for the 2020s*, London, Fabian Society.

Hasluck, C. and Green, A. E. 2007. *What works for whom? A review of evidence and meta-analysis for the Department for Work and Pensions*, research report no. 407, London, DWP.

Hastings, A., Bailey, N., Bramley, G., Gannon, M. and Watkins, D. 2016. *The cost of the cuts: the impact on local government and poorer communities*, York, Joseph Rowntree Foundation.

Haux, T., Salmon, D., Taylor, L., Deave, T., Cohen, S., Dewar, L. and Samzelius, T. 2012. *A longitudinal qualitative study of the journeys of single parents on Jobseeker's Allowance*, Bristol, University of the West of England and The Single Parent Action Network.

Henderson, S., Holland, J. and Thomson, R. 2006. Making the long view: perspectives on context from a qualitative longitudinal (QL) study. *Methodological Innovations Online*, 1. Available: http://oro.open.ac.uk/11701/.

Henwood, K. and Shirani, F. 2012. Researching the temporal. *In:* Cooper, H., Camic, P. M., Long, D. L., Panter, A. T., Rindskopf, D. and Sher, K. J. (eds.) *APA Handbook of Research Methods in Psychology, Vol. 2 – Research Designs: Quantitative, Qualitative, Neuropsychological, and Biological*, Washington, DC: American Psychological Association Publications, pp. 209-223.

Hickman, P., Batty, E., Dayson, C. and Muir, J. 2014. *'Getting-by', coping and resilience in difficult times: initial findings*, Centre for Regional Economic and Social Research, Sheffield, Sheffield Hallam University.

Hill, K., Davis, A., Hirsch, D. and Marshall, L. 2016. *Falling short: the experiences of families living below the Minimum Income Standard*, York, Joseph Rowntree Foundation.

Hills, J. 2015. *Good Times, Bad Times: The Welfare Myth of Them and Us*, Bristol, Policy Press.

HM Government 2012. *Social justice: transforming lives*, Cm 8314, London, DWP.

HM Government 2014. *Child Poverty Strategy 2014–17*, London, The Stationery Office

Holland, J., Thomson, R. and Henderson, S. 2004. *Feasibility study for a possible qualitative longitudinal study: discussion paper*, London, ESRC.

Hood, A., Johnson, P. and Joyce, R. 2013. *The effects of the welfare benefits up-rating bill*, London, Institute for Fiscal Studies.

Hudson, J., Lunt, N., Hamilton, C., Mackinder, S., Meers, J. and Swift, C. 2016. Nostalgia narratives? Pejorative attitudes to welfare in historical perspective: survey evidence from Beveridge to the British Social Attitudes Survey. *Journal of Poverty and Social Justice*, 24, 227-243.

Hupe, P., Hill, M. and Buffat, A. 2015. *Understanding Street Level Bureaucracy*, Bristol, Policy Press.

Hussain, N. and Silver, D. 2014. *Europe's White Working Class Communities: Manchester*, London, Open Society Foundation.

ILO (International Labour Organisation). 1984. *Into the twenty-first century: the development of social security*, Geneva, ILO.

Inman, P. 2015. Almost 700,000 people in UK have zero-hours contract as main job [Online]. *The Guardian*. Available: www.theguardian.com/uk-news/2015/feb/25/zero-hours-contract-rise-staff-figures.

Isin, E. F. 2008. Theorizing acts of citizenship. *In:* Isin, E. F. and Nielson, G. M. (eds) *Acts of Citizenship*, London, Zed Books, pp. 15-43.

Jensen, T. 2014. Welfare commonsense, poverty porn and doxosophy [Online]. *Sociological Research Online*, 19. Available: www.socresonline.org.uk/19/3/3.html.

Jensen, T. 2015. Ignorance in the 'Golden Age of Television' [Online]. *Sociological Imagination*. Available: http://sociologicalimagination.org/archives/16786.

Jones, A. 2012. Welfare reform and labour market activation. *Local Economy*, 27, 431–88.

Jones, C. and Novak, T. 1999. *Poverty, Welfare, and the Disciplinary State*, London, Routledge.

Jones, R. W. 2015. IDS slammed over 'pathetic' response to sanctions probe by sister of man who died after lifeline axed [Online]. *Daily Mirror*. Available: www.mirror.co.uk/news/uk-news/ids-slammed-over-pathetic-response-6684030.

Joseph Rowntree Foundation 2016. *We can solve poverty in the UK: a strategy for government, businesses, communities and citizens*, York, Joseph Rowntree Foundation.

Katungi, D., Neale, E. and Barbour, A. 2012. *People in low-paid, informal work: 'need not greed'*, London, Community Links.

Kempson, E. 1996. *Life on a low income*, York, Joseph Rowntree Foundation.

King, D. and Wickham-Jones, M. 1999. Bridging the Atlantic: the Democratic (Party) origins of welfare-to-work. *In:* Powell, M. (ed.) *New Labour, New Welfare State? The 'third way' in British Social Policy*, Bristol, Policy Press, pp. 257-280.

Klein, R. and Millar, J. 1995. Do-it-yourself social policy: searching for a new paradigm? *Social Policy and Administration*, 29, 303–16.

Kuper, S. 2014. A portrait of Europe's white working class [Online]. *Financial Times*. Available: www.ft.com/cms/s/2/4139381a-f1bb-11e3-a2da-00144feabdc0.html#axzz35SxDrTIQ.

Kymlicka, W. 1995. *Multicultural Citizenship: A Liberal Theory of Minority Rights*, Oxford, Oxford University Press.

Lammy, D. 2014. Jobcentres are no longer fit for purpose and are letting young people down [Online]. *The Guardian*. Available: www.theguardian.com/commentisfree/2014/jul/23/jobcentres-dont-work-employment-letting-young-people-down.

Land, E. and Patrick, R. 2014. SAGE Research Methods Cases: the process of using participatory research methods with film-making to disseminate research: challenges and potential. *SAGE Research Methods Cases*, London: SAGE.

Lansley, S. and Mack, J. 2015. *Breadline Britain: The Rise of Mass Poverty*, London, OneWorld Publications.

Larkin, P. M. 2016. Delineating the gulf between human rights jurisprudence and legislative austerity: the judicial entrenchment of 'less-eligibility'. *Journal of Social Security Law*, 23, 42–60.

Leeds City Council. 2012. *Leeds labour market*. Leeds, Leeds City Council.

Legal Action Group. 2013. *Legal Aid cuts will create a justice gap* [Online]. Legal Action Group. Available: www.lag.org.uk/magazine/2013/04/legal-aid-cuts-will-create-a-justice-gap.aspx.

Leisering, L. and Leibfried, S. 1999. *Time and Poverty in Western Welfare States: United Germany in Perspective*, Cambridge, Cambridge University Press.

Levitas, R. 1998. *The Inclusive Society? Social Exclusion and New Labour*, Basingstoke, Macmillan.

Levitas, R. 2006. The concept and measurement of social exclusion. *In:* Pantazis, C., Gordon, D. and Levitas, R. (eds.) *Poverty and Social Exclusion in Britain*, Bristol, Policy Press, pp. 123-160.

Lewis, G. 1998. Citizenship. *In:* Lewis, G. (ed.) *Imagining Welfare Futures*, London, Routledge and Open University Press, pp. 103-150.

Lipsky, M. 2010. *Street Level Bureaucracy: Dilemmas of the Individual in Public Service*, 30th Anniversary Expanded Edition, New York, Russell Sage Foundation.

Lister, B., Graham, H., Egdell, V., Mcquaid, R. and Raeside, R. 2014. *The impact of welfare reform in Scotland: tracking study, interim report to the Scottish Government on 1st sweep of interviews*, Edinburgh, Scottish Government Social Research.

Lister, R. 1990. *The Exclusive Society: Citizenship and the Poor*, London, CPAG.

Lister, R. 2001a. New Labour: a study in ambiguity from a position of ambivalence. *Critical Social Policy*, 21, 425–47.

Lister, R. 2001b. 'Work for those who can, security for those who cannot': a third way in social security reform or fractured social citizenship? *In:* Edwards, R. and Glover, J. (eds.) *Risk and Citizenship: Key Issues in Welfare*, London, Routledge, pp. 96–109.

Lister, R. 2003. *Citizenship: Feminist Perspectives*, Second Edition, Basingstoke, Palgrave.

Lister, R. 2004. *Poverty*, Cambridge, Polity Press.

Lister, R. 2007. Inclusive citizenship: realizing the potential. *Citizenship Studies*, 11, 49–61.

Lister, R. 2011a. A recovery plan for Labour, Letters, *The Guardian*, 14th May, p. 34.

Lister, R. 2011b. The age of responsibility: social policy and citizenship in the early 21st century. *In:* Holden, C., Kilkey, M. and Ramia, G. (eds.) *Social Policy Review 23: Analysis and Debate in Social Policy*, Bristol, Policy Press, pp. 63-84.

Lister, R. 2013. 'Power, not pity': poverty and human rights. *Ethics and Social Welfare*, 7, 109–23.

Lister, R. 2015. *'To count for nothing': poverty beyond the statistics, British Academy Lecture, 5th February* [Online]. London, British Academy. Available: www.britac.ac.uk/events/2015/To_count_for_nothing. cfm.

Lister, R. 2016. Putting the Security back into Social Security, *In:* Nandy, L., Lucas, C. and Bowers, C. (eds.) *The alternative: towards a new progressive politics*, London, Biteback Publishing.

Lister, R. and Bennett, F. 2010. The new 'champion of progressive ideals'? Cameron's Conservative Party: poverty, family policy and welfare reform. *Renewal*, 18, 84–109.

Living Wage Foundation. 2016. *The Calculation* [Online]. The Living Wage Foundation. Available: www.livingwage.org.uk/calculation.

Loney, M. 1986. *The Politics of Greed: The New Right and the Welfare State*, London, Pluto Press.

Loopstra, R., Reeves, A., Mckee, M. and Stuckler, D. 2015. *Do punitive approaches to unemployment benefit recipients increase welfare exit and employment? A cross-area analysis of UK sanctioning reforms, Sociology Working Papers, paper no. 2015–01, Department of Sociology*, Oxford, University of Oxford.

Lupton, R., Burchardt, T., Fitzgerald, A., Hills, J., Mcknight, A., Obolenskaya, P., Stewart, K., Thomson, S., Tunstall, R. and Vizard, P. 2015. *The Coalition's social policy record: policy, spending and outcomes 2010–2015 – social policy in cold climate, research report no. 4*, CASE, London, London School of Economics and Political Science.

MacDonald, R. and Marsh, J. 2005. *Disconnected Youth? Growing up in Britain's Poor Neighbourhoods*, London, Palgrave.

MacDonald, R. and Shildrick, T. 2014. 'Benefits Street' and the myth of workless communities [Online]. *Sociological Research Online*, 19, Available: www.socresonline.org.uk/19/3/1.html.

MacInnes, T., Aldridge, H., Bushe, S., Tinson, A. and Barry Born, T. 2014a. *Monitoring poverty and social exclusion 2014*, York, Joseph Rowntree Foundation.

MacInnes, T., Tinson, A., Gaffney, D., Horgan, G. and Baumberg, B. 2014b. *Disability, long term conditions and poverty*, York, Joseph Rowntree Foundation.

Macmillan, R. 2003. Getting by. *In:* Alcock, P., Beatty, C., Fothergill, S., Macmillan, R. and Yeandle, S. (eds.) *Work to Welfare: How Men Become Detached from the Labour Market*, Cambridge, Cambridge University Press, pp. 206-227.

Manchester CAB 2013. *Punishing poverty? A review of benefits sanctions and their impacts on clients and claimants*, Manchester, Manchester CAB.

Mann, K. 2009. Remembering and rethinking the social divisions of welfare: 50 years on. *Journal of Social Policy*, 38, 1–18.

Marsh, D. 2015. Welcome to the election. But only if you're a hardworking family [Online]. *The Guardian*. Available: www.theguardian.com/media/mind-your-language/2015/mar/20/welcome-to-the-election-but-only-if-youre-a-hardworking-family.

Marshall, T. H. 1950. *Citizenship and Social Class: And Other Essays*, Cambridge, University Press.

May, T. 2016. *Statement from the new Prime Minister Theresa May* [Online]. HM Government. Available: www.gov.uk/government/speeches/statement-from-the-new-prime-minister-theresa-may.

May, T. 2017. Full text: Theresa May's 'shared society' speech [Online]. *The Spectator*. Available: http://blogs.spectator.co.uk/2017/01/full-text-theresa-mays-shared-society-speech.

McKay, S. and Rowlingson, K. 2011. Social security and welfare reform. *In:* Bochel, H. (ed.) *The Conservative Party and Social Policy*, Bristol: Policy Press, pp. 145-160.

McLeod, J. 2003. Why we interview now: reflexivity and perspective in a longitudinal study. *International Journal of Social Research Methodology*, 6, 201–11.

Mead, L. M. 2010. Can we put poor men to work? *Economic Affairs*, 30, 48–52.

Millar, J. and Bennett, F. 2016. Universal Credit: assumptions, contradictions and virtual reality [Online]. *Social Policy and Society*, first view. Available: http://opus.bath.ac.uk/49374/.

Millar, J. and Ridge, T. 2013. Lone mothers and paid work: the 'family-work project'. *International Review of Sociology*, 23, 564–77.

Ministry of Justice. 2014. *Legal Aid transformation*, London, HM Government.

Miscampbell, G. and Porter, R. 2014. *Joined up welfare: the next steps for personalisation*, London, Policy Exchange.

Moore J. 1988. *Speech to Conservative Party Conference, 12th October*, London, The Conservatives.

Murphy, R. (2016) *What does Corbyn really mean?* [Online]. London: Tax Research UK. Available: http://www.taxresearch.org.uk/Blog/2016/07/27/what-does-corbyn-really-mean/.

Murray, C. 1984. *Losing Ground: American Social Policy, 1950–1980*, New York, Basic Books.

National Audit Office 2014a. *Adult social care in England: overview.* Report by the Comptroller and Auditor General, HC 1102, Session 2013–14, 13 March, London, Department of Health and DCLG.

National Audit Office 2014b. *Department for Work and Pensions, Universal Credit: Progress Update.* Report by the Comptroller and Auditor General, London, National Audit Office.

National Audit Office 2016. *Benefit Sanctions.* Report by the Comptroller and Auditor General, London, National Audit Office.

Neale, B. 2015. Time and the lifecourse: perspectives from qualitative longitudinal research. *In:* Worth, N. and Hardill, I. (eds.) *Researching the Lifecourse: Critical Reflections from the Social Sciences*, Bristol, Policy Press, pp. 1–16.

Neale, B. and Flowerdew, J. 2003. Time, texture and childhood: the contours of longitudinal qualitative research. *International Journal of Social Research Methodology*, 6, 189–99.

Neville, S. and O'Connor, S. 2016. Long-term unemployed funding to be cut [Online]. *Financial Times.* Available: www.ft.com/cms/s/0/d0c75710-c11b-11e5-846f-79b0e3d20eaf.html#axzz489sw2OZD.

New Economics Foundation 2012. *Everyday insecurity: life at the end of the welfare state. November 2012 interim briefing*, London, New Economics Foundation.

Newman, I. 2011. Work as a route out of poverty: a critical evaluation of the UK welfare to work policy. *Policy Studies*, 32, 91–108.

O'Hara, M. 2014. *Austerity bites: a journey to the sharp end of cuts in the UK*, Bristol, Policy Press.

Oakley, M. 2014. *Independent review of the operation of Jobseeker's Allowance sanctions validated by the Jobseekers Act 2013*, London, HM Government.

Oborne, P. 2011. Big Society RIP? [Online] *The Daily Telegraph*. Available: www.telegraph.co.uk/news/politics/david-cameron/8303188/Big-Society-RIP.html.

Organ, J. and Sigafoos, J. Forthcoming. What if there is nowhere to get advice? *In:* Flynn, A. and Hodgson, J. (eds.) *Access to Justice and Legal Aid: Comparative Perspectives on Unmet Legal Need*, Oxford, Hart Publishing.

Orton, M. 2015. *Something's not right: insecurity and an anxious nation*, London, Compass.

Osborne, G. 2010. *Our tough but fair approach to welfare: Chancellor's Speech to The Conservative Party Conference, 4th October* [Online]. Conservative Party Speeches. Available: http://conservative-speeches.sayit.mysociety.org/speech/601446.

Osborne, G. 2012. Speech to Conservative Party Conference, 8th October [Online]. *New Statesman*. Available: www.newstatesman.com/blogs/politics/2012/10/george-osbornes-speech-conservative-conference-full-text.

Osborne, G. 2013a. *Spending Round 2013: Speech, 26th June* [Online]. HM Government. Available: www.gov.uk/government/speeches/spending-round-2013-speech.

Osborne, G. 2013b. *Welfare speech at Morrisons, 2nd April* [Online]. Politics.co.uk. Available: www.politics.co.uk/comment-analysis/2013/04/02/george-osborne-welfare-speech-in-full.

Osborne, G. 2014. *Chancellor of the Exchequer's Speech to Conservative Party Conference, 29th September* [Online]. The Conservatives. Available: http://press.conservatives.com/page/2.

Osborne, G. 2015. *Chancellor George Osborne's Summer Budget 2015 speech* [Online]. London, HM Treasury. Available: www.gov.uk/government/speeches/chancellor-george-osbornes-summer-budget-2015-speech.

Oxfam 2010. *Something for nothing: challenging negative attitudes to people living in poverty*, briefing paper, Oxford, Oxfam.

Page, R. 2001. New Labour and paid work: a break with the past? *Benefits*, 11, 5–10.

Page, R. 2010. Conservative Party, poverty and social justice since 1951: continuity or change? *Journal of Poverty and Social Justice*, 18, 119–22.

Pantazis, C. 2016. Policies and discourses of poverty during a time of recession and austerity. *Critical Social Policy*, 36, 3–20.

Patrick, R. 2011. The wrong prescription: disabled people and welfare conditionality. *Policy and Politics*, 39, 275–91, pp. 55–70.

Patrick, R. 2014a. Welfare reform and the valorisation of work: is work really the best form of welfare? *In:* Harrison, M. and Sanders, T. (eds.) *Social Policies and Social Control: New Perspectives on the 'Not-So-Big Society'*, Bristol, Policy Press, pp. 55-70.

Patrick, R. 2014b. Working on welfare: findings from a qualitative longitudinal study into the lived experiences of welfare reform in the UK. *Journal of Social Policy*, 43, 705–25.

Pemberton, S., Fahmy, E., Sutton, E. and Bell, K. 2016. Navigating the stigmatised identities of poverty in austere times: resisting and responding to narratives of personal failure. *Critical Social Policy*, 36, 21–37.

Pemberton, S., Sutton, E., Fahmy, E. and Bell, K. 2014. *Life on a low income in austere times*, Bristol, Poverty and Social Exclusion in the UK, University of Bristol.

Perry, J., Williams, M., Sefton, T. and Haddad, M. 2014. *Emergency use only: understanding and reducing the use of food banks in the UK*, London, CPAG, Church of England, Oxfam GB and The Trussell Trust.

Peters, M. and Joyce, L. 2006. *A review of the JSA sanctions regime: summary research findings, Research Report No. 313*, London, DWP.

Piggott, L. and Grover, C. 2009. Retrenching Incapacity Benefit: Employment Support Allowance and paid work. *Social Policy and Society*, 8, 159–70.

Plant, R. 1998. So you want to be a citizen? *New Statesman*, 6th February, p. 4371.

Plant, R. 1999. Supply side citizenship? *Journal of Social Security Law*, 6, 124–36.

Plunkett, J. 2015. Benefits Street series two to feature scenes of drug-dealing [Online]. *The Guardian*. Available: www.theguardian.com/media/2015/apr/29/channel-4-benefits-street-drug-dealing-series-two.

Prideaux, S. 2001. New Labour, old functionalism? The underlying contradictions of welfare reform in the UK and the US. *Social Policy and Administration*, 35, 85–115.

Prideaux, S. 2010. The welfare politics of Charles Murray are alive and well in the UK. *International Journal of Social Welfare*, 19, 293–302.

Purnell, J. 2008a. *Independence at the heart of welfare state: speech to the social market foundation, 20th February*, London, Social Market Foundation.

Purnell, J. 2008b. *Speech to employers conference, 28th January* [Online]. UK Politics. Available: www.ukpol.co.uk/2015/12/01/james-purnell-2008-speech-to-employers-conference/.

Puttick, K. 2007. Empowering the incapacitated worker? The Employment and Support Allowance and Pathways to Work. *Industrial Law Journal*, 36, 388–95.

Pykett, J. 2014. Representing attitudes to welfare dependency: relational geographies of welfare [Online]. *Sociological Research Online*, 19. Available: www.socresonline.org.uk/19/3/23.html.

Rawls, J. 1999. *A Theory of Justice*, Oxford, Oxford University Press.

Ray, K., Foley, B. and Hughes, C. 2014. *Rising to the challenge: a policy agenda to tackle low pay*, London, The Work Foundation.

Revi, B. 2014. T. H. Marshall and his critics: reappraising 'social citizenship' in the twenty-first century. *Citizenship Studies*, 18, 452–64.

Riccucci, N. 2002. Implementing welfare reform in Michigan: the role of street-level bureaucrats. *International Journal of Public Administration*, 25, 901–21.

Riddell, P. 1989. *The Thatcher Decade: How Britain Changed during the 1980s*, Oxford, Basil Blackwell.

Ridge, T. 2009. *Living with poverty: a review of the literature on children's and families' experiences of poverty*, Research Report No. 594, London, DWP.

Ridge, T. 2015. *Understanding the 'family-work' project: researching low-income families over time. Conference presentation: Researching Relationships across Generations and through Time*, Leeds, University of Leeds, 9th June.

Roantree, B. and Shaw, J. 2014. *The case for taking a life-cycle perspective: inequality, redistribution, and tax and benefit reforms*, London, Institute for Fiscal Studies.

Roberts, E. and Price, L. 2014. *Tipping the balance? A qualitative study on the cumulative impacts of welfare reform in the London Borough of Newham*, London, Community Links.

Robinson, M. 2016. Judges rule the Bedroom Tax is 'discriminatory' after a domestic abuse victim was docked benefits for a PANIC ROOM built to keep out her rapist ex-partner [Online]. *The Daily Mail*. Available: www.dailymail.co.uk/news/article-3418954/Bedroom-Tax-ruled-discriminatory-judges-domestic-abuse-victim-docked-benefits-PANIC-ROOM-built-rapist-ex-partner.html.

Ronai, C. R. and Cross, R. 1998. Dancing with identity: narrative resistance strategies of male and female stripteasers. *Deviant Behaviour: An Interdisciplinary Journal*, 19, 99–119.

Rose, H. 1981. Rereading Titmuss: the sexual division of welfare. *Journal of Social Policy*, 10, 477–502.

Roulstone, A. and Prideaux, S. 2012. *Understanding Disability Policy*, Bristol, Policy Press.

Sandel, M. 1998. *Liberalism and the Limits of Justice*, Cambridge, Cambridge University Press.

Schmuecker, K. 2013. *The poor are still paying more for basic utilities and financial services* [Online]. Joseph Rowntree Foundation. Available: www.jrf.org.uk/blog/2013/06/poor-paying-more-utilities-financial.

Schram, S. F., Fording, R. C. and Soss, J. 2008. Neo-liberal poverty governance: race, place and the punitive turn in US welfare policy. *Cambridge Journal of Regions, Economy and Society*, 1, 17–36.

Scott, D. and Brien, S. 2007. *Breakthrough Britain: ending the costs of social breakdown. Volume 2: economic dependency and worklessness, policy recommendations to the Conservative Party Social Justice Policy Group*, London, Centre for Social Justice.

Scottish Government. 2016. *New social security powers for Scotland* [Online]. Edinburgh, Scottish Government. Available: www.gov.scot/Publications/2016/06/6390/5.

Selbourne, D. 1994. *The Principle of Duty*, London, Sinclair Stevenson.

Shildrick, T. 2012. Low pay, no pay churning: the hidden story of work and worklessness. *Poverty*, 142, 6–9.

Shildrick, T. and MacDonald, R. 2013. Poverty talk: how people experiencing poverty deny their poverty and why they blame 'the poor'. *The Sociological Review*, 61, 285–303.

Shildrick, T., MacDonald, R., Furlong, A., Roden, J. and Crow, R. 2012a. *Are cultures of worklessness passed down the generations?* York, Joseph Rowntree Foundation.

Shildrick, T., MacDonald, R., Webster, C. and Garthwaite, K. 2012b. *Poverty and Insecurity: Life in Low-Pay, No-Pay Britain*, Bristol, Policy Press.

Shildrick, T., MacDonald, R., Webster, C. and Garthwaite, K. 2010. *The low-pay, no-pay cycle: understanding recurrent poverty*, York, Joseph Rowntree Foundation.

Sinfield, A. 1978. Analyses in the social division of welfare. *Journal of Social Policy*, 7, 129–56.

Sinfield, A. 2012. Strengthening the prevention of social insecurity. *International Social Security Review*, 65, 89–106.

Smith, D. M. 2005. *On the Margins of Inclusion: Changing Labour Markets and Social Exclusion in London*, Bristol, Policy Press.

Smith, N. and Middleton, S. 2007. *Poverty dynamics research in the UK*, York, Joseph Rowntree Foundation.

Smith, O. 2016. 'The kind of revolution I'll deliver': Owen Smith's speech on industry, 27th July [Online]. *LabourList*. Available: http://labourlist.org/2016/07/the-kind-of-revolution-ill-deliver-owen-smiths-speech-on-industry/.

Social Justice Policy Group. 2006. *Breakdown Britain: interim report on the state of the nation*, London, Centre for Social Justice.

Sodha, S. 2016. 'Will Theresa May's "just about managing families" fall for the rhetoric?' [Online]. *The Guardian*. Available: www. theguardian.com/commentisfree/2016/nov/21/theresa-may-jams-just-managing-families-autumn-statement.

Spurr, H. 2016. Increase in Londoners facing bailiffs for council tax arrears [Online]. *Inside Housing*. Available: http://www.insidehousing. co.uk/increase-in-londoners-facing-bailiffs-for-council-tax-arrears/7016638.article.

Standing, G. 2011. End of a Faustian pact: workfare and riots. *Poverty*, 140, 11–14.

Standing, G. 2014. *The Precariat: the new dangerous class*, Revised Edition, London, Bloomsbury Academic.

Stanley, K. 2010. Iain Duncan Smith's welfare reform deserves support [Online]. *The Guardian*. Available: www.theguardian.com/ commentisfree/2010/jul/30/iain-duncan-smith-benefit-reform.

Stanley, K. and Lohde, L. A. 2004. Applying the framework. *In:* Stanley, K., Lohde, L. A. and White, S. (eds.) *Sanctions and Sweeteners: Rights and Responsibilities in the Benefits System,* London: IPPR, pp. 25-82.

Stone, E. and Priestley, M. 1996. Parasites, pawns and partners: disability research and the role of non-disabled researchers. *British Journal of Sociology*, 47, 699–716.

Stone, J. 2016. Universal Credit will increase child poverty, MPs warn [Online]. The *Independent*. Available: www.independent.co.uk/ news/uk/politics/universal-credit-will-increase-child-poverty-mps-warn-a7023061.html.

Swyngedouw, E. 2006. Governance innovation and the citizen: the Janus face of governance-beyond-the-state. *Urban Studies*, 42, 1991–2006.

Tarr, A. and Finn, D. 2012. *Implementing Universal Credit: will the reforms improve the service for users?* York, Joseph Rowntree Foundation.

Taylor, C. 1990. *Sources of the self: the making of modern identity*, Cambridge, MA, Harvard University Press.

Taylor, C. 1994. The politics of recognition. *In:* Heble, A., Pennee, D. P. and Struthers, J. R. T. (eds.) *New Contexts of Canadian Criticism*, Ontario: Broadview Press, pp. 25-73.

Taylor-Gooby, P. 2012. Root and branch restructing to achieve major cuts: the policy programme of the 2010 UK Coalition government. *Social Policy and Administration*, 46, 61–82.

Taylor-Gooby, P. 2015. Bad news for the poor: the British Social Attitudes survey shows a hardening of attitudes towards working age welfare recipients [Online]. *London School of Economics.* Available: http://blogs.lse.ac.uk/politicsandpolicy/bad-news-for-the-poor/?utm_content=bufferff82eandutm_medium=socialandutm_source=twitter.comandutm_campaign=buffer.

Thompson, S. 2015. *The low-pay, no-pay cycle,* York, Joseph Rowntree Foundation.

Timmins, N. 2001. *The Five Giants: A Biography of the Welfare State,* London, Harper Collins.

Tirado, L. 2013. This is why poor people's bad decisions make perfect sense [Online]. *Huffington Post.* Available: www.huffingtonpost.com/linda-tirado/why-poor-peoples-bad-decisions-make-perfect-sense_b_4326233.html.

Titmuss, R. M. 1958. *Essays on 'The Welfare State',* London, Allen and Unwin.

Titmuss, R. 1968. *Committment to Welfare,* London, Allen and Unwin.

Toerien, M., Sainsbury, R., Drew, P. and Irvine, A. 2013. Putting personalisation into practice: work-focused interviews in Job Centre Plus. *Journal of Social Policy,* 42, 309–27.

Townsend, P. 1979. *Poverty in the United Kingdom. A Survey of Household Resources and Standards of Living,* Middlesex, Penguin Books.

Trussell Trust. 2016. *Trussell Trust foodbank use remains at record high with over one million three-day emergency food supplies given to people in crisis in 2015/16* [Online]. The Trussell Trust. Available: www.trusselltrust.org/news-and-blog/latest-stats/.

TUC (Trades Union Congress). 2014. A record number of people are looking for extra hours to top up their wages [Online]. *TUC.* Available: www.tuc.org.uk/economic-issues/labour-market/record-number-people-are-looking-extra-hours-top-their-wages.

Twine, F. 1994. *Citizenship and Social Rights: The Interdependence of Self and Society,* London, SAGE.

Tyler, I. 2010. Designed to fail: a biopolitics of British citizenship. *Citizenship Studies,* 14, 61–74.

Tyler, I. 2013. The riots of the underclass? Stigmatisation, mediation and the government of poverty and disadvantage in neoliberal Britain [Online]. *Sociological Research Online,* 18. Available: www.socresonline.org.uk/18/4/6.html.

Tyler, I. 2014a. *'Being poor is not entertainment': class struggles against poverty porn* [Online]. Manchester, Social Action and Research Foundation. Available: http://mediapovertywelfare.wordpress.com/2014/10/30/being-poor-is-not-entertainment/.

Tyler, I. 2014b. From 'the shock doctrine' to 'the stigma doctrine' [Online]. *Social Abjection.* Available: http://socialabjection.wordpress.com/2014/05/12/from-the-shock-doctrine-to-the-stigma-doctrine-imogen-tyler/.

Tyler, I. 2014c. *Revolting Subjects: Social Abjection and Resistance in Neoliberal Britain,* London, Zed Books.

Verhoeven, I. and Tonkens, E. 2013. Review article: talking active citizenship – framing welfare state reform in England and the Netherlands. *Social Policy and Society,* 12, 415–526.

Vincent, D. 1991. *Poor Citizens: the State and the Poor in Twentieth-Century Britain,* London, Longman.

Wacquant, L. 2009. *Punishing the Poor: The Neoliberal Government of Social Insecurity,* Durham and London, Duke University Press.

Wacquant, L. 2010. Crafting the neoliberal state: workfare, prisonfare, and social insecurity. *Sociological Forum,* 25, 197–220.

Walby, S. 1994. Is citizenship gendered? *Sociology,* 28, 379–95.

Walford, G. 1988. Young people's views about the Youth Training Scheme in Scotland. *British Journal of Sociology in Education,* 9, 437–51.

Walker, R. 2014. *The Shame of Poverty,* Oxford, Oxford University Press.

Walker, R., Kyomuhendo, G. B., Chase, E., Choudry, S., Gubrium, E. K., Nicola, J. Y., Lodemel, I., Mathew, L., Mwiine, A., Pellissery, S. and Ming, Y. 2013. Poverty in global perspective: is shame a common denominator? *Journal of Social Policy,* 42, 215–33.

Walker, R. and Leisering, L. 1998. New tools: towards a dynamic science of modern society. *In:* Walker, R. and Leisering, L. (eds.) *The Dynamics of Modern Society: Poverty, Policy and Welfare,* Bristol, Policy Press, pp. 17-33.

Walker, R. and Wiseman, M. 2003. Making welfare work: UK activation policies under New Labour. *International Social Security Review,* 56, 3–29.

Walters, W. 1997. The 'active society': new designs for social policy. *Policy and Politics,* 25, 221–33.

Walzer, M. 1983. *Spheres of justice: A Defense of Pluralism and Equality,* New York, Basic Books.

Warren, J. 2005. Disabled people, the state and employment: historical lessons and welfare policy. *In:* Roulstone, A. and Barnes, C. (eds.) *Working Futures? Disabled people, Policy and Social Inclusion,* Bristol, Policy Press, pp. 301-313.

Watts, B., Fitzpatrick, S., Bramley, G. and Watkins, D. 2014. *Welfare sanctions and conditionality in the UK,* York, Joseph Rowntree Foundation.

Webster, C., Simpson, D., MacDonald, R., Abbas, A., Cieslik, M., Shildrick, T. and Simpson, M. 2004. *Poor Transitions: Social Exclusion and Young Adults*, Bristol, Policy Press.

Webster, D. 2015. Dr David Webster argues that it's time to abolish benefit sanctions [Online]. *Employment Related Services Association blog*. Available: http://ersa.org.uk/media/blog/dr-david-webster-argues-its-time-abolish-benefit-sanctions.

Welfare Reform Committee, Scottish Parliament. 2014. *Interim report on the new benefit sanctions regime: tough love or tough luck? 4th report (session four)*, Edinburgh, The Scottish Parliament.

White, S. 2003. *The Civic Minimum: On the Rights and Obligations of Economic Citizenship*, Oxford, Oxford University Press.

Whitworth, A. 2013. *Tailor-made? Single parents' experiences of employment support from Jobcentre Plus and the Work Programme*, London, Gingerbread.

Whitworth, A. and Griggs, J. 2013. Lone parents and welfare-to-work conditionality: necessary, just, effective? *Ethics and Social Welfare*, 7, 124–40.

Who Benefits? 2014. *'Second class citizens?' The personal impact of the public debate on benefits*, London, Who Benefits?

Wiggan, J. forthcoming. Contesting the austerity and 'welfare reform' narrative of the UK government: forging a social democratic imaginary in Scotland. *International Journal of Sociology and Social Policy*.

Willetts, D. 2008. *Renewing civic conservatism: the Oakeshott Lecture, 20th February* [Online]. London, London School of Economics and Political Science. Available: www2.lse.ac.uk/publicEvents/pdf/20080220_Willetts.pdf.

Williams, C. 2005. A critical evaluation of hierarchical representations of community involvement. *Community Development Journal*, 40, 1, 30-38.

Williams, F. 1992. Somewhere over the rainbow: universalism and diversity in social policy. *In:* Manning, N. and Page, R. (eds.) *Social Policy Review Four*, London, Social Policy Association, pp. 200-219.

Williams, F. 2012a. Care relations and public policy: social justice claims and social investment frames. *Families, Relationships and Societies*, 1, 101–17.

Williams, F. 2012b. Public lecture: transforming social policy, *International Colloquium in Honour of the Work of Emeritus Professor Fiona Williams OBE, 29th June*, Leeds, University of Leeds.

Williams, F. and Popay, J. 1999. Balancing polarities: developing a new framework for welfare research. *In:* Williams, F., Popay, J. and Oakley, A. (eds.) *Welfare Research: A Critical Review*, London, UCL Press, pp. 156-182.

Women's Budget Group. 2016. *The impact on women of the 2016 budget: women paying for the Chancellor's tax cuts*, London, Women's Budget Group.

Wright, S. 2002. Activating the unemployed: the street-level implementation of UK policy. *In:* Clasen, J. (ed.) *What Future for Social Security? Debates and Reforms in National and Cross-National Perspective*, Bristol: Policy Press, pp. 235-249.

Wright, S. 2009. Welfare to work. *In:* Millar, J. (ed.) *Understanding Social Security: Issues for Policy and Practice*, Second Edition, Bristol, Policy Press, pp. 193-212.

Wright, S. 2011a. Can welfare reform work? *Poverty*, 139, 5–8.

Wright, S. 2011b. Relinquishing rights? The impact of activation on citizenship for lone parents in the UK *In:* Betzelt, S. and Bothfeld, S. (eds.) *Activation and Labour Market Reforms in Europe: Challenges to Social Citizenship*, Basingstoke, Palgrave, pp. 59-78.

Wright, S. 2012. Welfare-to-work, agency and personal responsibility. *Journal of Social Policy*, 41, 309–28.

Wright, S. 2013. On 'activation workers' perceptions: a reply to Dunn (2). *Journal of Social Policy*, 42, 829–37.

Wright, S. 2016. Conceptualising the active welfare subject: welfare reform in discourse, policy and lived experience. *Policy and Politics*, 44, 235–52.

Wright, S., Dwyer, P., McNeill, J. and Stewart, A. B. R. 2016. First wave findings: Universal Credit. *Welfare conditionality: sanctions, support and behaviour change*, York, University of York.

Index

References to tables and figures are shown in *italics*

249